INTERPRETING BIBLICAL TEXTS

THE
GOSPEL
OF
MATTHEW

General Editors

Gene M. Tucker, *Old Testament*

———————————

Charles B. Cousar, *New Testament*

INTERPRETING
I·B·T
BIBLICAL TEXTS

THE

GOSPEL

OF

MATTHEW

Donald Senior

ABINGDON PRESS
Nashville

THE GOSPEL OF MATTHEW

Copyright © 1997 by Abingdon Press

This book is printed on elemental-chlorine-free, acid-free, recycled paper.

Library of Congress Cataloging-in-Publication Data

Senior, Donald.
   The Gospel of Matthew / Donald Senior.
     p.   cm. — (Interpreting Biblical texts)
   Includes bibliographical references and index.
   ISBN 0-687-00848-4 (alk. paper)
     1. Bible. N.T. Matthew—Criticism, interpretation, etc.
   I. Title. II. Series.
   BS2575.2.S45   1997
   226.2 ' 06—dc21

                                        96-53400
                                          CIP

97 98 99 00 01 02 03 04 05 06 — 10 9 8 7 6 5 4 3 2 1

MANUFACTURED IN THE UNITED STATES OF AMERICA

In grateful memory of

Carroll Stuhlmueller, C.P. (1923–1994)
mentor, colleague, and friend

CONTENTS

FOREWORD

Biblical texts create worlds of meaning, and invite readers to enter them. When readers enter such textual worlds, which are often strange and complex, they are confronted with theological claims. With this in mind, the purpose of this series is to help serious readers in their experience of reading and interpreting, to provide guides for their journeys into textual worlds. The controlling perspective is expressed in the operative word of the title—*interpreting*. The primary focus of the series is not so much on the world *behind* the texts or out of which the texts have arisen (though these worlds are not irrelevant) as on the world *created by* the texts in their engagement with readers.

Each volume addresses two questions. First, what are the critical issues of interpretation that have emerged in the recent history of scholarship and to which serious readers of the texts need to be sensitive? Some of the concerns of scholars are interesting and significant, but frankly peripheral to the interpretative task. Others are more central. How they are addressed influences decisions readers make in the process of interpretation. Thus the authors call attention to these basic issues and indicate their significance for interpretation.

Second, in struggling with particular passages or sections of material, how can readers be kept aware of the larger world created by the text as a whole? How can they both see the forest and examine individual trees? How can students encountering the story of David and Bathsheba in 2 Samuel 11 read it in light of its context in the larger story, the Deuteronomistic History that includes the books of Deuteronomy through 2 Kings? How can readers of Galatians fit what they learn into the theological coherence and polarities of the larger perspective drawn from all the letters of Paul? Thus each volume provides an overview of the literature as a whole.

The aim of the series is clearly pedagogical. The authors offer their own understanding of the issues and texts, but are more concerned about guiding the reader than engaging in debates with other scholars. The series is meant to serve as a resource, alongside other resources such as commentaries and specialized studies, to aid students in the exciting and often risky venture of interpreting biblical texts.

Gene M. Tucker
General Editor, *Old Testament*

Charles B. Cousar
General Editor, *New Testament*

PREFACE

Interpreting the Gospel of Matthew is a demanding art. This beautiful Gospel stands at the beginning of the New Testament canon and has been a source of inspiration and teaching for every generation of Christians since the first century. Its commanding sweep of Jesus' life from the turbulent and wondrous events of his infancy to his final commissioning of the disciples on a mountaintop in Galilee, its strong emphasis on Jesus' teachings as in the famed Sermon on the Mount, and its orderly structure quickly made it a capital influence on the church.[1]

For all its appeal, however, Matthew's Gospel can also be strange and baffling to a modern reader. It is, after all, a text originally written in Greek and directed to an audience of a time and culture vastly different from our own. To "interpret" the gospel of Matthew is to help readers or listeners understand the meaning of this ancient text for their lives today. Such interpretation might take place in a traditional setting such as a sermon in church or a lecture in a classroom or on the pages of a commentary. But there are more informal and subtle settings as well: the parish staff designing a Christmas pageant featuring the Magi and Herod; someone reminding a discouraged friend about Jesus' parable on unlimited forgiveness (Matt 18:21-35); the chaplain at the side of a dying patient reading the account of Jesus' prayer in the Garden of Gethsemane (26:36-46); or the interpretation we do for ourselves in a moment of prayer as we might quietly wonder what the Beatitudes (5:3-12) could possibly mean for our lives. Not all interpretations of Matthew are benign—over the centuries many Christians have cited the words of the crowd in Matthew's passion narrative, "His blood be on us and on our children" (27:24-25), as a justification for persecuting Jews. All of these examples involve interpretation of the gospel of Matthew, even when the interpreter may not even be aware of what is going on!

As noted in the editors' foreword, the purpose of this book is to provide an introductory guide to the "textual world" of Matthew's gospel. Our survey of Matthew's textual or narrative world will involve two main sections. In Part 1, we will scan biblical scholarship to discover what have been the chief issues under discussion concerning Matthew's gospel. In line with the intent of this series, our point is not simply to be informed about Matthean scholarship.[2] Rather by becoming aware of the key features of the gospel noted by scholars, we can gain a preview of some of the issues posed for interpretation by this gospel. We might think of this first section as a series of "windows" that enable us to peer into the narrative world of the gospel in order to get the lay of the land and its climate before actually entering that world. Such features as the sources used by the gospel in its composition, its overall structure or "plot," its distinctive portrayal of Jesus and his disciples, its characteristic appeal to the Old Testament, and such concerns peculiar to Matthew as the continuing validity of the Jewish law or the mission to the Gentiles have commanded the attention of scholars not by arbitrary selection but precisely because they are the very features of this gospel that will strike any attentive reader.

There is a certain rationale behind the order of the chapters in Part 1. We begin with some of the gospel's most evident features: its potential use of sources; its structure; its frequent appeal to the Old Testament; its recurring debates about interpretation of the Jewish law; its emphasis on mission; and its somewhat enigmatic references to the Gentiles. From these we move to the more fundamental and encompassing issues of Matthew's christology and his understanding of discipleship. Having scanned all of these characteristic features of the gospel, we are better equipped to consider the kind of introductory questions often posed first in commentaries—namely who wrote this gospel, when and where it was written, and under what circumstances. Since the answers to these questions should come primarily from the evidence in the gospel itself, it is better to tackle these questions at the end rather than at the beginning of our survey of Matthean issues.

In Part 2 we enter into the narrative world of Matthew itself by means of a "reading guide" that takes us through the gospel chapter by chapter and scene by scene. This is not intended to be a commentary on Matthew's gospel, providing detailed information on individual verses of the text.[3] Nor is it an analytical study that extracts from the gospel its apparent message and synthesizes it for the reader in a topical format. The intent, rather, is in the manner of a reliable guide to accompany serious readers as they move through Matthew's story, pointing out the movements of the story, the interconnections in the narrative, its characteristic features, and recurring patterns. By working carefully through the gospel of Matthew with this guide, the serious reader will see the connections between the concerns of biblical scholarship detailed in Part 1 and the actual text of the gospel. Along the way, we will linger over those passages that are key for understanding Matthew's gospel, suggesting possibilities for interpretation and providing leads to further study.

The key to responsible and informed interpretation of Matthew's gospel is attentive reading of the gospel text itself. The point of this introductory guide is to support, not substitute for, the opportunity of exploring firsthand this great Christian treasure.

As I conclude this work I want to thank in a particular way the students in the Gospel of Matthew class at Catholic Theological Union in the Winter Quarter of 1996. They allowed me to "road test" a first draft of this work with them, and their thoughtful comments helped make this a better book.

Donald Senior
Catholic Theological Union
Chicago, Illinois

PART ONE

MODERN BIBLICAL
SCHOLARSHIP
AND THE
INTERPRETATION
OF
MATTHEW'S
GOSPEL

The next seven chapters are an introduction to the principal issues that have dominated studies of Matthew's Gospel in recent scholarship. The purpose is not simply to catalog scholarly opinion, interesting though that might be. The quest of serious scholarship has been to come to a deeper understanding of the nature, context, and content of Matthew's gospel. The main points of debate and discussion in Matthean studies revolve around the most important issues for understanding and interpreting this gospel.

This same spirit guides our review in Part 1 (chaps. 1–7). Just as a thoughtful review of a play or literary piece can prepare a reader to enter more alertly into the narrative world of a text, so being informed about the issues discussed within Matthean scholarship can better equip the reader of the gospel to return to this text with greater intensity and skill. Part 2 (chaps. 8–13), which is a reading guide to the gospel itself, builds on the material in Part 1 and constantly refers back to it.

CHAPTER 1

THE SOURCES AND STRUCTURE OF MATTHEW'S GOSPEL

Tracing the sources for Matthew's Gospel and grasping the overall literary design of his work have been subjects of great interest to modern biblical scholarship. Both questions take us deep into the character of Matthew's gospel and help the attentive reader interpret the gospel more responsibly.

MATTHEW'S SOURCES

One of the first questions considered by the earliest stages of modern biblical scholarship was that of the sources for Matthew's gospel. In the search to find the most historically reliable gospel, scholars as early as the end of the eighteenth century puzzled over the interrelationship of the Synoptic gospels (the so-called

Synoptic problem), attempting to decipher which was the first—and therefore likely to be the most "historical."[1] Traditionally, Matthew had been considered the first gospel written. Augustine of Hippo in the early fifth century stated the common assumption that the canonical order in fact was the chronological order. Thus Matthew was the first, followed by Mark, Luke, and John. In the late–eighteenth century, a variant to this traditional view was offered by J. J. Griesbach, who concluded that Matthew and Luke preceded Mark, whose gospel was in effect a blend and condensation of these two earlier gospels. Griesbach's theory did not triumph in the nineteenth century but has had something of a revival in the past couple of decades.[2]

The traditional view that Matthew was the first gospel was substantially challenged in the nineteenth century, particularly by German scholarship. For a variety of reasons, scholars concluded that Mark, not Matthew, was the first to be written and that Matthew used Mark, along with a collection of sayings of Jesus, as his primary source. Although not without its critics, this hypothesis, called the "two source" theory, has been the dominant working assumption of modern biblical scholarship on the gospel of Matthew and has some significant implications for interpreting the gospel.

The Data

The question of the interrelationship of the Synoptic gospels arises simply by comparing the three gospels.[3] Matthew, for example, absorbs nearly 80 percent of the 661 verses found in Mark's gospel; about 65 percent of Luke's gospel has verses in common with Mark. In some instances the three gospels are virtually identical, with only small variations and most of these easily explainable by the peculiar style and preferences of each evangelist.[4]

Closer comparison of the three gospels as a whole reveals that the order of events in Mark's narrative is the one that sets the pattern for the other two. In other words, when Matthew departs from Mark's order of events, Luke's sequence will preserve the Marcan order. And in those places where Luke's order of events strays from that of Mark, Matthew will be found to retain the Marcan sequence. This does not prove that Mark was necessarily the first to be written, but it does tell us that the three gospels are interrelated and that Mark is pivotal. Put another way, Mark is either the primary source for Matthew and Luke, or else Mark stemmed from some combination of Matthew and Luke.

On the other hand, Matthew and Luke are both much longer than Mark's gospel (Matthew has 1,068 verses compared with Mark's 661; Luke has 1,149). And these two gospels have nearly 220 verses of material in common that are not found in Mark! Most of the Sermon on the Mount (Matthew 5–7), for example, has no parallels in Mark but has much in common with Luke's Sermon on the Plain (Luke 6:17-49). Here, too, in some passages there is often near-literal identity between the two gospels, suggesting some sort of literary relationship.[5]

This proximity between Matthew and Luke in some passages that do not appear in Mark led to the supposition that behind Matthew and Luke stands another literary source, called "Q" (from the German word *Quelle,* which means "source"). No independent examples of Q exist except where Q is incorporated in the gospels. Because the general order of this shared material is practically the same in Matthew and Luke and because of the number of verbal similarities between the two versions, most scholars conclude that Q had a fairly fixed literary form by the time it was used by Matthew and Luke, having been transmitted in the early community orally or, more probably, in writing. The original structure of Q is much debated, but in general it included the opening scenes of Jesus' encounter with John the Baptist, the temptation in the desert, Jesus' ethical teachings, his conflicts with his opponents, and, finally, warnings of eschatological judgment. There is no passion narrative or any emphasis on Jesus' healings and exorcisms.

Parallels to Mark and Q combined, however, do not account for all the material in either Matthew or Luke. A significant number of passages in Matthew, for example, are found neither in Mark nor in Q, such as the peculiar Matthean content of the infancy narrative, certain parables (e.g., 18:21-35; 25:31-46), the story of Judas' death (27:3-10), and the climactic great commission scene (28:16-20)—to name a few. A similar catalog of unique Lucan passages could also be drawn up. For this reason, most scholars assume that Matthew and Luke either drew on other oral or written sources available to them or, what is probable in most cases, composed such materials themselves.

Proposed Solutions

As a result of these considerations, the prevailing hypothesis among most Matthean scholars is that Matthew depended on two main sources for the composition of his gospel: Mark and Q. Several arguments have been put forward for this theory.[6]

1) A strong argument for Mark's priority is the difficulty of explaining why Mark would have omitted so much of the material found in Matthew and Luke, if in fact Mark used them as a source. In Matthew this includes such key gospel material as the infancy narratives, the Sermon on the Mount—including the Lord's Prayer—much of the mission discourse (chap. 10), many of the parables including the ones on forgiveness in chapter 18, Jesus' critique of the religious leaders in chapter 23, much of Jesus' teaching about the endtime in chapters 24 to 25, and all of the resurrection appearances found in chapter 28.

Although scholars can and do assume that Mark "condensed" Matthew and therefore eliminated this material, it is hard to come up with a convincing explanation of why an early Christian writer would do so.

2) Another type of argument for Marcan priority is based on content. In a number of instances, Matthew's gospel seems to enhance the Greek style of Mark. Although it is conceivable, on the supposition that Mark used Matthew, that Mark was an inferior writer of Greek and simply took Matthew's superior style down a peg, it is more convincing to suggest that Matthew improved upon Mark's Greek.

The same holds true for a number of places where Matthew would appear to upgrade Mark's content or to eliminate passages in Mark that were enigmatic or possibly offensive. Matthew, for example, omits Mark 3:21 where Jesus' family believes him to be "beside himself" or out of his mind. Mark's report that Jesus healed "many" (Mark 1:32-34; 3:10) becomes healed "all" in Matthew's version (Matt 8:16; 12:15). These examples can be multiplied many times over.

The Question of Sources and the Character of Matthew's Gospel

If the two-source hypothesis is correct, then Matthew's gospel is composed from two main sources. On the one hand, Matthew depended on the already existing gospel of Mark. We can presume that this gospel already had a place of honor in Matthew's community, perhaps proclaimed in the community's communal prayer and worship and used to instruct community members about Jesus' life and teaching. Mark's gospel was a lean and powerful narrative, focusing on Jesus' public ministry, his dramatic healings and exorcisms, his mission in Galilee, his journey to Jerusalem, and, above all, the taut and compelling drama of his passion and death and the proclamation of Jesus' victory over death in the discovery of the empty tomb. This story would be incorporated almost entirely into Matthew's narrative, and Mark's account of Jesus would be the backbone of Matthew's gospel.

But Matthew also had access to another source of material, a text that presented Jesus as powerful teacher, as one whose words of truth confronted falsehood and hypocrisy, bringing life and threatening judgment. The material in Q has a strong ethical content, spelling out what it meant to follow Jesus. By blending this material into the storyline of Mark, Matthew added a new dimension to his gospel portrayal of Jesus. In the view of some scholars, by fusing Mark's gospel with Q, Matthew in effect prevented the latter from portraying Jesus purely as a teacher of wisdom or as a prophet who punctured certitudes with challenging parables and sayings. This prophet would suffer rejection and persecution, ultimately giving his life as "a ransom for many" (Mark 10:45; Matt 20:28). At the same time, the teaching material in Q gave a discernible ethical dimension to the numinous figure of Jesus in Mark's account. In the composite portrait that Matthew has produced, Jesus is both compassionate healer and ethical teacher, prophetic judge and crucified Messiah.

We know, too, that Matthew was not merely a copyist, blending traditional sources into a new mix. He also reworked these sources, giving them the stamp of his own literary style and theological perspective. At the same time, he added material to his narrative not found in either Mark or Q. This special Matthean material is sometimes referred to as "M." Some of this is extensive, such as the stories that make up the infancy narrative (Matt 1–2) or the stories surrounding the resurrection of Jesus (27:62-66; 28:9-10, 16-20). Other additions are more brief such as the chain of events that explodes at the moment of Jesus' death (27:51-53) or the parable of the unforgiving servant (18:21-35). Some of this material may be traceable to oral traditions handed on in Matthew's community which the evangelist put into written form and incorporated in his gospel. But the profusion of typical Matthean vocabulary and themes in other "M" material strongly suggests that the evangelist has formulated much of this material himself. Consideration of Matthew's potential relationship with his sources can make us more alert to the distinctive shape and character of his narrative. A close comparison between Matthew and Mark—even if we are not fully sure about the literary relationship between these gospels—helps the special features of Matthew stand out.

THE STRUCTURE OF MATTHEW'S GOSPEL

To discover the *sources* for Matthew's gospel means reading the gospel "horizontally," that is, with one eye on potential parallels in the gospel of Mark or in Q (as detected in parallel passages in Luke). Detecting the *structure* or literary design of Matthew's gospel, however, means reading the gospel "vertically," from start to finish (or from top to bottom if one imagines the gospel laid out on the page of a synopsis).

This task also has been a concern of recent Matthean scholarship. Our goal here is not to attempt an in-depth analysis of Matthew's structure, since we will be working our way through the gospel in detail in Part 2 of our study. Instead, we will sample some of the structures for the gospel proposed by Matthean scholars in order to deepen our knowledge of the gospel and alert us to new dimensions of the task of interpretation. Tracing the structure or literary design of the gospel gives insight into the intended message and purpose of the gospel. How the story is put together, in other words, helps determine its impact and meaning for the reader.

Traditional analyses of the structure or literary design of Matthew's gospel have generally fallen into three main categories, each determined by features of the narrative: (1) Structures that take the five discourses as their cue; (2) Structures based on a chiastic pattern; and (3) Structures that follow the story line of the gospel.[7]

Matthew's Five Books

The five great discourses of Jesus are a unique feature of Matthew's gospel.[8] Many commentators on Matthew's gospel have found in these discourses the key to Matthew's literary design. One of the most influential proponents of this approach was the American scholar Benjamin Bacon, who wrote in the early part of this century.[9] He noted the presence in Matthew of a transition statement that occurs five times in the gospel (7:28; 11:1; 13:53; 19:1; 26:1), each marking the end of a main discourse and the beginning of a narrative section. Bacon surmised that these formulae were the results of Matthew's own editorial work and that the five great "books" of narrative and discourse they set off were evidence that the evangelist had patterned his gospel after the five great books of the Pentateuch. This Pentateuchal structure signaled Matthew's ultimate purpose: Jesus was the "new Moses" replacing the authority of the old Law and offering a new law or Torah to the church.

While most scholars agreed that Bacon was correct in giving the five discourses a place of prominence in Matthew's literary design, his theory that Matthew was modeling his entire gospel on the Pentateuch was less successful. Critics pointed out that it tended to leave to the periphery the infancy narrative of chapters 1–2 and the passion and resurrection narratives of 26–28. Bacon had designated these sections "prologue" and "epilogue" respectively, but such a role does not adequately describe these important blocks of material, particularly the passion story which is so dominant in the overall structure of the gospel. In addition, there are other extended blocks of discourse material in Matthew that do not fall within the framework of the fivefold formula, such as the material in 11:7-30 and the critique of the religious leaders in chapter 23. Adhering too rigidly to Bacon's fivefold structure could become a Procrustean bed in which the shape of the gospel is trimmed to meet the assumption of a fivefold division!

While no recent scholarship has tried to rescue Bacon's Pentateuchal model, others have developed his insight about the alternating pattern of narrative and discourse in Matthew's gospel. Dale Allison, for example, believes that such alternation is the key to the gospel.[10] Matthew builds his story of Jesus with successive segments of narrative and discourse, building to the climax of the passion and the resurrection, with its mission instruction:

Chaps. 1–4   Narrative: Introduction of the main character Jesus

5–7   Discourse: Jesus' demands upon Israel

8–9   Narrative: Jesus' deeds within and for Israel

10   Discourse: Extension of ministry through words and deeds of others

11–12   Narrative: Israel's negative response

13   Discourse: Explanation of Israel's negative response

14–17   Narrative: Establishment of the new people of God, the church

18   Discourse: Instruction to the church

19–23   Narrative: Commencement of the passion; beginning of the end

24–25   Discourse: The future—judgment and salvation

26–28   Narrative: The passion and resurrection

Chiastic Patterns

This approach takes its cue from another feature of Matthew's distinctive style. The evangelist has a penchant for ordering material in his gospel: Many of Jesus' sayings and parables are organized into discourses; the miracles are grouped in clusters of three within chapters 8 and 9; words of judgment and eschatological warning are gathered in chapters 23–25; and Matthew seems fascinated with numbers, as many ancient Jewish texts were.[11]

Commentators such as Peter F. Ellis and H. B. Green took this tendency of the evangelist a step farther by proposing that the entire literary design of Matthew's gospel is chiastic in structure.[12] Chiasm is a pattern used in ancient Greek literature in which a text is ordered around a center, with other segments radiating from the center and standing in balance with one another. Put in letter form this would be: a b c b' a'. With c as the center of the literary piece, the other segments [a and a', b and b'] would be in evident thematic parallel with one another. The basic purpose of a chiastic arrangement was to facilitate memorization of material.[13]

Ellis detected the "center" of Matthew's gospel in the parable discourse of chapter 13, where fresh from conflict with his opponents Jesus begins to instruct his disciples about the mystery of the Kingdom. From this centerpiece the other segments of the narrative are suspended and stand in relationship with one another. In the case of the main discourses, for example, the Sermon on the Mount finds its parallel in the judgment discourses of chapters 23–25, and the mission discourse is paralleled by the instructions on life within the community in chapter 18. Ellis also finds a similar set of parallels for the narrative portions of the gospel. The infancy narrative of chapters 1–2, for example, parallels the passion in chapters 26–27. The overall pattern would be as follows:

Sermon	(f) chap. 13 (f')	
Narratives	chaps. 11–12 (e)	(e') chaps. 14–17
Sermons	chap. 10 (d)	(d') chap. 18
Narratives	chaps. 8–9 (c)	(c') chaps. 19–22
Sermons	chaps. 5–7 (b)	(b') chaps. 23–25
Narratives	chaps. 1–4 (a)	(a') chaps. 26–28

H. B. Green, on the other hand, locates the center of Matthew's chiastic pattern in chapter 11. This chapter, Green contends, with its reference to John the Baptist, its summary of the miracles of Jesus, and Jesus' own profound words about his role as Son of God, contains the whole gospel in miniature. From this center all the other segments of the gospel can be placed in parallel:

Chap. 11 as the center

a) Rejection of Proclamation: chap. 10 and chaps. 12–13
b) Miracles performed; miracles rejected: chaps. 8–9 and chaps. 14–18
c) Teaching of the Sermon and its rejection: chaps. 5–7 and chaps. 19–23
d) Manifestation of Christ to Israel and manifestation at the end time: chaps. 3–4 and chaps. 24–25
e) Infancy narrative and passion narrative: chaps. 1–2 and chaps. 26–28.

These proposed structures are not persuasive. As the differing proposals of Ellis and Green illustrate, it is not clear where the "center" of Matthew's gospel is, or if, in fact, there is a center in the sense of a significant middle point that becomes the pivot and summary of the entire gospel. Second, the proposed parallels among the various segments often seem quite weak or arbitrary. Ellis's pattern, for example, leads him to call chapters 11–12 a "narrative," but, in fact, they contain considerable discourse material (see 11:7-30). And is there really a convincing parallel between the miracle chapters 8–9 and the materials in chapters 19–22? Similar problems can be found with Green's proposal. The proposed parallel between the miracle chapters 8–9 and chapters 14–18, based on the theme of "miracles performed and miracles rejected," hardly covers all that is contained in these large segments of the gospel.

Although some formal patterns, including chiasms, can be found in specific passages of Matthew's gospel, it is unlikely that a single, overarching chiastic or other type of pattern provides the key to Matthew's overall literary design.[14]

Structures Relating to the Gospel's Story Line

A number of recent commentators believe that Matthew designed his gospel according to the story line of his continuing narrative. In other words, important features of Matthew's *story* alert the reader to the intent of the gospel's overall literary design.

A Key Matthean Formula—"From that time . . ." Some interpreters of Matthew believe that the linchpins for Matthew's structure can be found in two thematic verses that occur at significant points in his story of Jesus. In Matthew 4:17, as Jesus enters into Galilee and begins his public ministry, the text reads: "*From that time* Jesus began to proclaim, 'Repent, for the kingdom of heaven has come near.'" Again in 16:21, immediately following the crucial encounter between Jesus and his disciples at Caesarea Philippi ("Who do people say that the Son of Man is?"), another key moment arrives as Jesus announces his impending passion and turns the momentum of the story in that direction: "*From that time on,* Jesus began to show his disciples that he must go to Jerusalem and undergo great suffering at the hands of the elders and chief priests and scribes, and be killed, and on the third day be raised."

In each of these texts, Matthew introduces (compared to Mark) the emphatic temporal phrase "From that time" (*apo tote* in the Greek). Jack Dean Kingsbury, building on the work of Edgar Krentz and others, has been a strong advocate for finding in these key verses clues to the fundamental structure of Matthew's gospel.[15] Thus the narrative from 4:17 to 16:20 is concerned with Jesus' proclamation of the reign of God; 16:21–28:20 takes up the suffering, death, and resurrection of Jesus. Kingsbury does not neglect the first part of the gospel. The opening verse of Matthew's gospel, which Kingsbury would translate as "the book of the origin of Jesus Christ, son of David, the son of Abraham" (Matt 1:1), serves as the thematic introduction to the whole section 1:1–4:16. Rather than translate the Greek phrase *"biblos geneseōs"* too literally as the "book or account of the genealogy" and therefore as an introduction only to the first part of the infancy narrative (1:2-18), Kingsbury—with a number of commentators—would see this opening verse as an introduction to the whole origin of Jesus, including the genealogy, the events of the infancy, Jesus' inaugural encounter with John at the Jordan, and his desert test. All of these events are, in a true sense, the introduction to Jesus' public ministry. The result is the following divisions of Matthew's story and their fundamental themes:

1) The Presentation of Jesus (1:1–4:16)
2) The Ministry of Jesus to Israel and Israel's Repudiation of Jesus (4:17–16:20)
3) The Journey of Jesus to Jerusalem and His Suffering, Death, and Resurrection (16:21–28:20)

It is hard to argue with the themes that Kingsbury identifies here, because they are so broad in scope. As one author has observed, this framework basically tells us that Matthew's narrative, like all stories, has a beginning, a middle, and an end![16] Moreover, the key role given to Matthew's phrases in 4:17 and 16:21 may be inflated. Undoubtedly these phrases draw the reader's attention to important milestones in Matthew's story, but are they the structural supports for his entire literary design?

In a recent study, the Belgian scholar Frans Neirynck has given this question close scrutiny.[17] He points out that the verses in which these temporal references appear are not themselves the turning point but are part of a narrative segment which *taken as a whole* is the real turning point. For example, Jesus' public ministry begins not at 4:17 but at 4:12, when Matthew notes that Jesus enters Galilee and then appends an Old Testament quotation to mark this historic moment (4:14-15). The phrase "from that time" catches up this momentous event just narrated and moves the reader forward as Jesus "begins" his proclamation of the reign of God. Thus 4:17 is not a turning point in itself but is an organic part of a narrative unit (4:12-17) that is an important transition in the story. The same holds true for 16:21. Making 16:21 itself a turning point breaks up what is a single narrative unit in Matthew, namely the story of Peter's confession and Jesus' response (16:13-23). Although the event at Caesarea Philippi and the first passion prediction are certainly another important milestone in Matthew's story, it is not a single verse but the entire unit that is key.

In both of these instances, Neirynck suggests, the phrase *apo tote* has both a "retrospective" as well as a "prospective" function; that is, it catches up a significant moment of time just narrated (i.e., Jesus' entry into Galilee; the confession of Peter) and alerts the reader to events to come (i.e., Jesus' public ministry; the passion and resurrection).

Neirynck points out another telling argument against these verses serving as the central structural divisions of the gospel. He notes that 4:17 and 16:21 are not on the same level. The motif about the proclamation of God's reign announced in 4:12-17 carries through the entire gospel, not just until 16:21. The announcement of the journey to Jerusalem and the passion of Jesus do not, in other words, terminate the continuing proclamation of the reign of God. The motif announced in 4:17 has a much broader thematic function in Matthew's narrative than does 16:21 (or for that matter 1:1).

If Kingsbury's focus on these key verses may be overdone, his attention to the story line of the gospel as the key to Matthew's overall literary design remains important. It is unlikely that any single formal structure or a single set of structures (a significant number of discourses; an alternating pattern of narrative and discourse; chiasms; or key verses) will suddenly unlock the master plan of Matthew's gospel. The gospel of Matthew is, after all, a story with a beginning, a middle, and an end. Most good stories are not composed in the same way someone works with a blueprint or mathematically precise plans. The composition of a narrative is more organic, more subtle, and more complex than the kind of literary design one might give to the formulation of a strategic plan or to a closely reasoned philosophical paper. A variety of elements flow into the composition of a good story, as literary critics have reminded us, including: the basic dynamism of the story line (Jesus' origin, ministry, death, and resurrection); the various settings (the desert, Galilee, Jerusalem, the lake, the temple, the mountaintops, etc.); the characters (Jesus, the disciples, the priests, Pharisees, Sadducees, scribes, elders, the Romans, the crowds, and a host of cameo characters)—to name just some of the ingredients in the gospel's plot.

And if one wishes to complicate the picture even more by stepping outside the world of the narrative and take into account the insights of form and source criticism, we will also have to ask what influence Matthew's sources may have had on the literary design of his gospel. The order of events in Mark's gospel certainly seems to have had a strong influence on the way Matthew tells his story of Jesus. And having access to additional material from his other source Q, plus traditions and interpretations from his own community context, probably led Matthew to introduce new features into that basic story including the five great discourses of Jesus, the infancy narrative, and the resurrection appearances.

A Suggested Structure

The structure or literary design of Matthew's gospel absorbs all of these elements and shapes them into a new whole. With that in mind, we suggest the following basic outline of Matthew's structure, leaving to Part 2 a much more detailed elaboration and explanation of Matthew's narrative.

1) *The Origins of Jesus and His Mission (1:1–4:11).* The origin of Jesus is traced in his birth and infancy composed of material special to Matthew, in his inaugural encounter with John in the desert (the point where Matthew joins up with Mark's story), and in his great desert test.

2) *Jesus: Messiah in Word and Deed (4:12–10:42).* The entire scene of 4:12-17 (not just a single verse) is a key transition moment, bridging Jesus' contact with John the Baptist, announcing the start of his public ministry in Galilee, and signaling the motif of the kingdom of heaven that will run throughout the gospel. The pace quickens as Matthew unfolds Jesus' Galilean ministry, ordered around teaching (chaps. 5–7, the first of the great discourses in Matthew) and healing (chaps. 8–9), a ministry

designed to serve as a model for the apostles' own mission (chap. 10, another discourse composed of Marcan and Q material). In this important part of his gospel, Matthew introduces a substantial amount of material not found in Mark's gospel (e.g., the Sermon on the Mount; elements of the mission discourse) and imposes his own order of events (e.g., aligning the miracle stories of chaps. 8 and 9). In the next section, particularly after the parable discourse of chapter 13, Matthew returns to the story line of Mark.

3) *Responding to Jesus: Rejection and Understanding (11:1–16:12)*. A new phase of the story, introduced by John's testimony and Jesus' hymn of thanksgiving to his Father, begins to emerge as Matthew shows varying responses to Jesus, both rejection by Jewish opponents (esp. chaps. 11–12) and the glimmering faith of the disciples (esp. chaps. 14–16, where Matthew links up again with the exact sequence of Mark's story). This section also contains another of the important discourses (chap. 13, the parable discourse).

4) *The Journey to Jerusalem (16:13–20:34)*. Once again the entire story about Peter in 16:13-23 is a "bridge," with the blessing on Peter serving as a culmination of some of the discipleship themes apparent in the preceding section and the orientation to the passion signaled in the passion prediction and Jesus' rebuke to Peter. The drama of the death and resurrection of Jesus looms as Matthew follows Mark's lead and presents Jesus and his disciples on the way to Jerusalem. Instructions to the disciples (e.g., chap. 18), as well as conflicts with the opponents (e.g., 19:3-9), continue throughout the journey, discourse material that Matthew introduces into the sequence of Mark's story.

5) *In the Holy City: Conflict, Death, Resurrection (21:1–28:15)*. The holy city is the center of focus where Jesus has his final days of teaching in the temple area, most of them spent in sharp conflict with his opponents, and when all his teaching is done (26:1), the passion story begins, leading to death and resurrection.

6) *Finale (28:16-20)*. Although it is only a single scene, this vivid finale (found only in Matthew) brings the gospel story full-term, back to Galilee where from the mountaintop Jesus sends his disciples out into the world and promises his abiding presence until the end of the age. The final scene does not simply conclude the preceding section but recapitulates important themes of the entire gospel and directs the reader to the continuing life of the community that is to live out Jesus' commands and example.[18]

CHAPTER 2

MATTHEW'S USE OF THE OLD TESTAMENT

One does not have to read very far into Matthew's Gospel to become aware of his frequent and explicit appeal to the Old Testament as he narrates the story of Jesus. Five times in the first two chapters Matthew explicitly quotes the Old Testament, in four of these instances using a "fulfillment formula" to introduce the text. Thus the miraculous conception of Jesus fulfills the prophecy of Isaiah 7:14 (Matt 1:23); the flight into Egypt fulfills the promise of God in Hosea 11:1 (Matt 2:15); the identity of Bethlehem as the place where the messiah is to be born is confirmed by citing Micah 5:1 (Matt 2:6); the massacre of the infants in Bethlehem is the fulfillment of a lamentation found in Jeremiah 31:15 (Matt 2:18); and in Matthew 2:23 the evangelist cites the fulfillment of the words of the prophets in connection with the displacement of the holy family to Nazareth, although it is uncertain exactly which Old Testament passage he had in mind.[1]

Matthew will place other "fulfillment" quotations at the moment of Jesus' entry into Galilee (4:15-16), to interpret his healings (8:17) and his compassionate and reconciling spirit (12:18-21), his teaching in parables (13:35), his entry into Jerusalem (21:5), his deliverance to the passion (26:56), and to explain the horror of Judas' betrayal and death (27:9-10).

These explicit fulfillment texts hardly exhaust Matthew's use of the Old Testament. There is an abundance of other biblical quotations and allusions in Matthew, some of them very explicit, others detectable barely beneath the surface.[2] Some of this material Matthew absorbs from Mark and Q; in other cases he enriches the text with new layers of biblical reference. In addition to such references to specific Old Testament passages or events, Matthew also uses typology whereby characters within the gospel are clothed in the mantle of significant Old Testament figures. The opening scenes of the gospel are filled with scarcely veiled comparisons to Old Testament figures. The threats to Jesus by a king and his court in the infancy narrative, recalling Pharaoh's threats against the first liberator of Israel, and the majestic portrayal of Jesus as lawgiver on a mountaintop at the beginning of the Sermon on the Mount (5:1-2) are an indication that Matthew portrays Jesus as a new Moses.[3] The Joseph who protects Jesus and Mary, taking them into Egypt as a place of refuge can hardly escape comparison to the Joseph of the Exodus accounts. Conversely, the barbaric genocide of Herod wins him the mantle of Pharaoh.

THE MEANING OF THE FULFILLMENT TEXTS

But within this rich brew of quotations and allusions and typologies, the fulfillment texts remain Matthew's most explicit and characteristic appeal to the authority of the Old Testament and, therefore, have commanded the most attention on the part of biblical scholarship. Several interrelated questions arise about these quotations: Are these quotations Matthew's own translations from the Hebrew or did he use an already existing Greek version such as the Septuagint? Is Matthew alone responsible for gathering these quotations and applying them to Jesus or do they derive from a preexisting collection or mode of interpreting the gospel events? And, finally, what is the precise purpose and meaning of the fulfillment quotations?

One of the first important studies of Matthew's fulfillment quotations was that of Krister Stendahl.[4] He proposed that Matthew's gospel, with its carefully plotted structure and rich use of the Old Testament, derived from an early Christian "school" or tradition of interpretation designed to form Christian leaders and teachers. In this milieu, certain patterns had developed for interpreting the life of Jesus in the light of the Old Testament, not unlike the way the sectarian Jewish group at Qumran read the scriptures from the perspective of its own community's history and theology. The fulfillment quotations are the product of this "school."[5] This, he believed, also explained the form of these quotations. While the Old Testament quotations in passages that Matthew absorbed from Mark are from the Septuagint, the fulfillment quotations seem to be unique in their form. They were apparently composed in Greek but were not identical in wording with any known Hebrew or Greek versions and even show some similarities to the Targums (early Aramaic paraphrases of the Hebrew scriptures used in Jewish preaching). Matthew and his school would have provided their own translation of the fulfillment quotations, often shaping them to fit the particular context in which they would be used in the gospel.

Although Stendahl's suggestion that Matthew's gospel originated in a particular "school" has never gained much support, many of his observations about the form and purpose of the quotations remain valid. Subsequent studies confirm his conclusion that while other quotations in his gospel generally correspond to the Septuagint, Matthew's fulfillment quotations do not follow any single known text form but are a composition of the Evangelist or some immediate source. The novelty of this conclusion has been tempered a bit by the realization that we do not have access to all the Greek versions of the Old Testament that may have been used by the early Christians. Robert Gundry, for example, notes that many Old Testament quotations in the gospels seem to have a mixed form when compared with the versions known to us today. The exception is Mark's gospel, which follows the Septuagint more closely. When Matthew draws on Mark he inevitably draws on Mark's Septuagintal quotations; otherwise Matthew's quotations of the Old Testament coincide with the mixed form found in all the other gospels. Therefore, the special form of Matthew's Greek fulfillment quotations may not be so unusual.[6]

But, at the same time, scholars generally agree that some of the distinctive features found in Matthew's fulfillment quotations are the result of adapting the quotation to the gospel context in which they are used. For example, the plural "they" ("shall name him Immanuel") is not found in any version of the Isaiah 7:14 quotation; Matthew adapts the quotation to fit the context where the people saved from their sins (1:23) will acclaim Jesus as Emmanuel. The phrase "by no means" ("least among . . . Judah") is introduced into the quotation from Micah, completely changing the sense of the original (". . . you, O Bethlehem . . . one of the little clans of Judah . . ."), to fit the context where this city is now the birthplace of Jesus the messiah. In 27:9-10, Matthew blends and adapts quotations from Zechariah and Jeremiah to fit the story of Judas' return of the blood money.[7] Although this may not be evidence of a particular Matthean "school," it does point to a tradition of interpretation already established in the early church that read and interpreted the Old Testament in the light of the gospel events.

Even more significant than the origin or form of the fulfillment quotations is their meaning in the context of Matthew's gospel. The very word "fulfill" (the verb *plēroō* in Greek) expresses the fundamental meaning of these quotations for Matthew. The evangelist views the total reality of Jesus as the "fulfillment" of the history of Israel and its Scriptures. This is stated explicitly in Matthew 5:17 at the beginning of the Sermon on the Mount where Jesus declares that he had not come "to abolish the law or the prophets . . . but to fulfill" them. The very first statement of Jesus in Matthew's gospel declares that he must "fulfill all righteousness" (3:15). Although the precise nuances of the word "fulfill" are debated, its fundamental meaning is clear: For Matthew, Jesus is the flowering of the history of God's people; Jesus and his mission are God's response to the promises of salvation given to Israel. Therefore all the expectations and longings condensed within the Hebrew Scriptures find their outpouring and ultimate resolution in Jesus. Put another way, Jesus "fulfills" the Scriptures by revealing their ultimate intent and meaning. Such a perspective not only enhances Matthew's portrait of Jesus, his christology, but also serves an apologetic purpose. By showing the harmony between the promise of the Scriptures and their fulfillment in Jesus, Matthew equips his community to deal with questions raised about Christian belief in Jesus among Jewish critics.[8]

THE OLD TESTAMENT AND MATTHEW'S STORY OF JESUS

But if the fulfillment quotations are part of this fundamental theology of Matthew, it should be noted that they are not applied evenly to the story of Jesus' life. Most of them occur in the first thirteen chapters of the gospel, and most of these in the opening chapters.[9] This may be partly a result of the rhetorical strategy of Matthew. In the infancy narrative and the events leading up to the public ministry of Jesus, the evangelist introduces the reader to his understanding of Jesus. He connects Jesus to the history of Israel, affirms that the child's conception is an act of God, announces his salvific mission, demonstrates his fidelity and commitment to God's plan, and brings him into the arena of his public ministry. Through the addition of the fulfillment quotations, this majestic overture to the gospel story is welded to the promise of the Scriptures.

It may not be coincidence that the first thirteen chapters, where the majority of the fulfillment texts are to be found, are also that part of the gospel where we discover Matthew's most intense editorial work in relation to his sources Mark and Q.[10] In the latter part of his gospel Matthew simply absorbs the manner and frequency of the Old Testament quotations found in his sources. But in the first half of the gospel, where he exercises more freedom and introduces a lot of his own special material, such as in the infancy narrative of chapters 1–2, he injects his own explicit Old Testament quotations with their strong introductory formula so expressive of Matthew's perspective. Thus rhetorical strategy (orientation for the reader at the beginning of the gospel) and creative intervention regarding his sources (imposing his unique structure in the order of chapters 1–13) both have the same purpose and converge on the same part of the gospel.

Scholars have also noted that the fulfillment quotations are drawn from the prophetic literature and that there is a strong preference for Isaiah, particularly in those texts applied to the ministry of Jesus in chapters 4–13.[11] The Belgian scholar Frans Van Segbroeck has suggested that Matthew favored Isaiah both because this prophet was a messenger of salvation to Israel and because Isaiah had also lamented the failure of his mission to Israel. On both counts, Matthew's gospel would feel kinship with this prophetic message.[12]

37

More recent studies using the methods of literary criticism have tended to reinforce the conclusions reached by redaction critics. Kingsbury, for example, notes that within the narrative world of Matthew's gospel the fulfillment quotations are not the claims of any particular character but are cited by "Matthew" or the implied author-narrator. In this role the narrator becomes "an exponent of God's evaluative point of view in assessing the salvation-historical significance of various events in the life of Jesus."[13] David B. Howell, employing similar methodology, speaks of the fulfillment quotations under the rubric of "generalizations," that is, elements in a narrative which appeal outside the narrative world to a broader authority or perspective. The quotations express God's authoritative point of view as reflected in the Scriptures and thereby confirm the validity and significance of Jesus' life while throwing new light on the Scriptures themselves as now understood from the vantage point of Christian faith.[14]

Matthew's distinctive use of the Old Testament, therefore, is an indicator not only of the complex and creative literary skill of the evangelist but also of this gospel's concern to relate the life of Jesus to its Jewish backdrop.

CHAPTER 3

MATTHEW'S UNDERSTANDING OF THE JEWISH LAW

The way Matthew presents Jesus' teaching on the law is another distinctive feature of this gospel and an important link to its Jewish context. Jesus' statements about the meaning of the law and conflicts over its interpretation are numerous in Matthew's story. A key text is that of 5:17-19, which stands at the beginning of the Sermon on the Mount. Jesus proclaims that he has come not to "abolish" or "destroy" the law and the prophets but to "fulfill" them. The verses that follow seem to strongly reinforce the enduring validity of the law:

For truly I tell you, until heaven and earth pass away, not one letter, not one stroke of a letter, will pass from the law until all is accomplished. Therefore, whoever breaks one of the least of these commandments, and teaches others to do the same, will be

called least in the kingdom of heaven; but whoever does them
and teaches them will be called great in the kingdom of heaven.
(5:18-19)

This text, and its connection with the teaching that follows in
the sermon (particularly 5:20, calling for greater righteousness on
the part of the disciples, and the antitheses of 5:21-48), are obviously central to Matthew's view of the law yet remain some of the
most difficult passages in the gospel to interpret. Similarly conflicts and discussions about the law between Jesus and his opponents occur throughout Matthew's narrative.[1]

SEARCHING FOR A COHERENT VIEWPOINT

Interpreters have had difficulty trying to blend into a unified
and coherent perspective these various statements on the law in
Matthew. On the one hand, the emphatic teaching about the
enduring validity of the law in 5:17-19, even down to "one letter"
or "stroke" (5:18), suggests that Matthew's Jewish Christian community retained its adherence to the Jewish law. This is reinforced by a number of subtle changes introduced by Matthew into
his Marcan source. The references to Hosea 6:6 in the conflict stories of Matthew 9:9-13 and 12:1-8 appear to bolster Jesus' interpretation of the law by an appeal to this prophetic text. In the conflict over washing of hands, when Jesus declares it is not what
goes into a person that defiles, Mark adds a comment "thus he
declared all foods clean" (Mark 7:19); Matthew's version of that
same incident eliminates this blanket declaration (cf. Matt 15:17)!
In his parallel to Mark's apocalyptic discourse where Jesus tells
his disciples to pray that the end may not come "in winter" (Mark
13:18), Matthew poignantly adds "or on a sabbath" (Matt 24:20).
Even in a passage where Matthew's Jesus excoriates the scribes
and Pharisees for their hypocrisy, he still respects their teaching
authority and advises the crowds and his disciples to "do whatever they teach you and follow it" (23:3). And in several passages
unique to Matthew, Jesus warns his disciples about those who are
"lawless" (from the Greek word *anomia;* see 7:23; 13:41; 24:12).

But other aspects of the gospel seem to move in a different
direction. Nowhere does Matthew's gospel mention one of the
most characteristic laws of Judaism, that of circumcision. And in
the Sermon on the Mount Jesus' teaching seems to run contrary

to practices of the law when he forbids the taking of oaths (5:33-37), overturns the law of retaliation (5:38-42), and does not permit divorce (5:31-32; see also 19:3-9). Combined with the conflicts with the scribes and Pharisees over various points of the law and Matthew's emphasis on the love command (5:43-48; 22:34-40), many interpreters conclude that Matthew viewed Jesus as having superseded the law, and therefore the ceremonial and purity laws, in particular, were no longer binding on Matthew's Christian community.

THE KEY ROLE OF MATTHEW 5:17-20

Clearly central to this issue is the meaning of 5:17-20 and the material in the Sermon on the Mount. Fitting this part of the gospel into the overall context of Matthew's narrative must await our discussions in Part 2, but sampling some current scholarship on this text will alert us to the problems at stake.

In many ways, the most problematic text is Matthew 5:18 with its emphasis on the enduring validity of the most insignificant part of the law ("one letter," "one stroke") and its temporal references ("until heaven and earth pass away," "until all is accomplished"). Without this verse, 5:17 about "fulfillment" of the law could easily be taken in a broader and more flexible sense as bringing the law to its completion or intended goal even while superseding some of its specific and more limited injunctions. But how does one reconcile such a broader view with such a narrowly stated text? Three types of responses have been formulated in recent scholarship.

1) *Levels of tradition.* The first type of solution attributes the more traditional sayings about the law's validity to earlier stages of tradition embedded in Matthew's text. For example, the saying urging fidelity even to the smallest part of the law in 5:18 would be assigned to a more conservative Jewish Christian view about the validity of the Jewish law, which Matthew incorporates in his gospel without fully endorsing. These earlier traditions would have been retained either to placate more conservative and traditional wings of the community in a time of transition or as a way of holding in check those in the community whose attitude to the law and its ethical demands was too lax.[2]

2) *Temporal solutions.* Others, agreeing that the verses in 5:17-20 include prior layers of tradition, interpret this text in the light

of Matthew's view of salvation history. John Meier, for example, believes that the double temporal reference in 5:18 is a significant clue.[3] The phrase "until heaven and earth pass away" expresses an apocalyptic viewpoint that on face value would assert that the law remains valid until the end of the world.[4] The second phrase, "until all is accomplished," reminds the reader that it is through Jesus' own mission, particularly his death and resurrection, that all is accomplished. In fact, Matthew interprets the death of Jesus as triggering the kind of cosmic signs expected at the end of the world (see the earthquake and opening of the graves in 27:51-53 as well as the earthquake that accompanies the opening of the tomb in 28:2). The death and resurrection of Jesus are the turning point of salvation history, marking the end of the old age (when the law was valid) and beginning the New Age. A further sign of this is what Meier calls the "proleptic parousia" of 28:16-20 where the triumphant risen Christ, the glorified Son of Man, returns to his community in anticipation of the final coming at the end of time. Thus for Matthew the law was valid until the mission of Jesus comes to its completion ("until all is accomplished") and the new age has begun. The "torah" of Jesus exemplified in the Sermon on the Mount and the other teachings of Jesus as well as his example are now normative for the Christian community. That epic turning point in salvation history explains why it is possible that significant injunctions of the Jewish law can be abrogated or surpassed.

3) *Integrated solutions.* Other authors are convinced that the apparent contradictions in Matthew's attitude to the Law can be woven into an integrated whole. Alexander Sand, for example, emphasizes that in Judaism itself there was considerable discussion about the "weightier" demands of the law; laws dealing with basic concerns of justice and compassion for one's neighbor had an urgency and priority exceeding the ceremonial or cultic laws.[5] Therefore, the conflicts of the Matthean Jesus with his opponents over priorities of the law do not entail a critical stance to the law as such. In fact, Sands maintains, Matthew views the Torah, the "law and the prophets," in a broad sense, encompassing the full span of God's salvific word to Israel as well as the specific commands that spelled out Israel's fidelity to that word. This is the sense of 5:17—Jesus' whole life and teaching stand in radical continuity with the word of God expressed in the Hebrew Scriptures

and reveal its meaning in a fresh and definitive way. As a prophet the Matthean Jesus emphasizes the primacy of the love command within the law (22:33-44; 7:12; 5:43-48) and enacts that command in his own care for the sinner and the "least" (see, e.g., 25:31-46). A text such as 23:23, which condemns the scribes and Pharisees for their inverted priorities, expresses perfectly this view of the law: "Woe to you, scribes and Pharisees, hypocrites! For you tithe mint, dill, and cummin, and have neglected the weightier matters of the law: justice and mercy and faith. It is these you ought to have practiced without neglecting the others."

In his important commentary on Matthew, Ulrich Luz moves in a similar fashion. He believes that Matthew's Christian community was law observant, even if some adaptations had been made for the Gentile mission (e.g., substituting baptism for circumcision). If on the basis of vocabulary or other evidence one assigns some of the strict sayings about the law such as 5:18 to pre-Matthean tradition, the fact is the evangelist has incorporated these perspectives into his gospel and made them his own. For the evangelist there was no inherent contradiction in the way the law was presented in his gospel. The key is Matthew's christology. As Messiah and Son of God, Jesus neither rejects nor even corrects the law; rather through his messianic authority Jesus reveals the ultimate meaning of the law. The programmatic text of 5:17-20 is a necessary preamble to Jesus' radical teaching in the antitheses of 5:21-48, affirming that what Jesus teaches stands in continuity with the Torah. Luz makes an interesting comparison to the fulfillment quotations that we considered earlier. In both instances Matthew appropriates his Jewish heritage to the Christian community. Just as the fulfillment quotations lay claim to the authority of the Scriptures on behalf of the Christian community, so do 5:17-20 and Matthew's subsequent teaching on the law lay claim to this fundamental institution of Judaism.[6]

Even though there are divergent viewpoints on how to explain Matthew's position on the Jewish law, there are some fundamental areas of convergence important for interpreting Matthew's gospel as a whole.

1) As was the case with Matthew's use of the Old Testament, it is clear that in its understanding of the law Matthew's gospel takes seriously the Jewish heritage of Jesus and tries to relate Christian community to it. Whatever may be the subtleties in Matthew's

explanation, the gospel is obviously concerned both to establish continuity with the meaning of the law in the past and its meaning now in the light of Jesus and his teaching.

2) Jesus and his authority stand at the center of Matthew's gospel and ultimately hold the key to its theological perspective. While it may be possible that Matthew's teaching on the law was influenced by and directed to the community's relationship with Judaism contemporary to Matthew, on an even more fundamental level Matthew was concerned with the figure of Jesus and what he meant for the life of the community.

3) The incorporation of so much material about the Jewish law in Matthew's gospel, including its programmatic presentation at the beginning of Jesus' ministry in the Sermon on the Mount, underscores the distinctive ethical concerns of this gospel. Matthew was concerned not simply with apologetic and christology but with Christian practice.

CHAPTER 4

MATTHEW AND THE MISSION TO THE GENTILES

Another issue of interest to current scholarship has been the role of Gentiles and the Gentile mission in Matthew's gospel. Here, too, the evangelist seems to gather differing perspectives under one roof. Scholars approaching the gospel with historical interest have detected here important clues to the original setting of the gospel; those focusing on the gospel's literary dimensions have pondered how to integrate Matthew's apparently divergent viewpoints into a coherent whole.

REFERENCES TO GENTILES IN MATTHEW'S GOSPEL

Scanning the gospel with an eye on Matthew's references to Gentiles immediately alerts the reader to the problem. References to Gentiles fall under three main categories.

1) *Explicit mission references.* On several occasions in texts

unique to this gospel, Jesus directly addresses the issue of the mission to the Gentiles but in seemingly contradictory fashion. In the mission discourse, the Twelve are instructed: "Go nowhere among the Gentiles, and enter no town of the Samaritans, but go rather to the lost sheep of the house of Israel" (10:5-6). And in the remarkable story of the encounter with the Canaanite woman who pleads on behalf of her daughter, Jesus twice seems to rebuff the idea of a Gentile mission: "I was sent only to the lost sheep of the house of Israel" (15:24) and "It is not fair to take the children's food and throw it to the dogs" (15:26).[1]

Yet in the final scene of the gospel, the Matthean Jesus solemnly commissions the disciples for a Gentile mission: "Go therefore and make disciples of all nations, baptizing them in the name of the Father and of the Son and of the Holy Spirit, and teaching them to obey everything that I have commanded you" (28:19-20). Matthew expresses a similar perspective in a verse that he adds to Mark's parable of the vineyard. In this allegory on Israel's rejection of the messiah, the vineyard owners are warned: "Therefore I tell you, the kingdom of God will be taken away from you and given to a people [*ethnei*, the word for "Gentile" in Greek] that produces the fruits of the kingdom" (21:43; see a similar idea in 8:11-12).

Thus explicit strictures on a mission to the Gentiles in the body of the narrative are replaced with instructions to go to the Gentiles at the conclusion of the gospel.

2) *Pejorative references to Gentiles.* In a number of places Gentiles are cast in a negative or unflattering light. They are the outsiders (18:17) who are not expected to lead moral lives (e.g., 6:32; 5:47) or know how to pray (6:7). They are also capable of brutality and will persecute the community (20:25; 10:18; 24:9). Jesus himself will be delivered up to them (20:19).

3) *Positive images of Gentiles.* Along with these portrayals of the Gentiles as the epitome of the outsider and the unbeliever, there are positive generic references as well as some remarkable portrayals of individual Gentiles in the gospel who respond generously to Jesus: for example, the women in the genealogy;[2] the Magi (2:1-12); the centurion at Capernaum (8:5-13); the Canaanite woman (15:28); Pilate's wife (27:19); the centurion and his companions at the cross (27:54). Jesus contrasts favorably the response of Gentiles to that of his fellow Jews (e.g., 11:20-24; 12:41-42), and

in other texts the Gentiles are cited as the object of Jesus' mission (e.g., 4:15; 4:25 [the crowds from the Decapolis]; 12:18-21).

How does the interpreter of Matthew reconcile such seemingly contradictory materials? Some initial sorting can be done. Some of the pejorative statements portray Gentiles in a stereotyped manner as "outsiders" or typical "nonbelievers"; so, for example, they are good to their friends only and don't know how to pray. In these kinds of settings Gentiles are equivalent to "tax collectors" (as in 5:46-47) and contrasted with the followers of Jesus, who have been instructed by him and know better. Conversely, the Gentiles can also be used as a foil to condemn the failures of Israel. Thus Tyre and Sidon, and for that matter Sodom itself, will fare better than Chorazin or Capernaum on the day of judgment (11:20-24). One senses here that the attention falls not on the Gentiles as such but on Jesus' challenging judgment against his fellow Jews.

But in other instances more seems to be at stake and the challenge to reconcile Matthew's viewpoints is more difficult. How does one understand Jesus' prohibition of the Gentile mission in 10:5 and 15:24, especially in the light of the final scene of the gospel when he sends his disciples out to the whole world (28:16-20)? And why does Matthew, at the same time, present characters such as the Magi and the centurion in such a positive light? And how does one make sense of the story of the Canaanite woman where Jesus begins by emphasizing the confinement of his mission to Israel and ends with the healing of her daughter and lavish praise for this Gentile woman's tenacious faith? Two fundamental approaches seem to dominate recent biblical scholarship on this issue, each illustrating different methodologies.

MISSION WITHIN THE CONTEXT OF SALVATION HISTORY

Some interpreters believe that Matthew's comments about the Gentiles become coherent in the light of the gospel's overall understanding of "salvation history." In other words, the evangelist views the history of Israel, Jesus' own ministry, and the continuing experience of his community within the overarching framework of God's plan within history. One of the fundamental purposes of the gospel would be, in fact, to convey this understanding of history to the recipients of Matthew's gospel, a community in the midst of a profound transition.

Although there is general agreement about the central elements that need to be incorporated within Matthew's view of history, there is no fast consensus on the precise delineation of that history. For example, the German scholar Rolf Walker concluded that Matthew has a three-stage view of salvation history:[3] (1) The first period covers the history of Israel or the "pre-messianic" stage that began with Abraham (whom Matthew cites in his genealogy of Jesus [1:1]) and ends with the birth of the Messiah; (2) the second period would incorporate Jesus' ministry to Israel, a period extending not only through the mission of the historical Jesus (which as Matthew notes was restricted to Israel) but into the time of the early church; (3) a new period begins around AD 70 with the destruction of the Jerusalem Temple and the community's decisive turn to the Gentiles. This third stage of salvation history would last until the end of time. It is this stage that is reflected in the finale of the gospel when the risen Christ sends his disciples out into the world. By casting history in this fashion, Matthew provides perspective for his own community, which has experienced the failure of the church's mission to Israel and an accelerating influx of Gentiles into the church.

Other commentators have accepted this basic three-stage schema (Israel, Jesus, the church) but with some variations. Georg Strecker, for instance, believed that the evangelist was presenting Jesus' life in a certain "historicizing" manner; that is, the gospel was trying to situate Jesus' life and ministry in a historical framework.[4] The first stage of sacred history would be the history of Israel prior to Jesus. The life, death, and resurrection formed a stage of history all its own. Now subsequent to the time of Jesus, the community lived in a new epoch of history when the ethical demands of Jesus were to be carried out. During the lifetime of Jesus the mission was restricted to Israel—hence the historicizing texts of 10:5 and 15:24—but now in the final stage of history the Gentiles are included. John Meier also considers salvation history a key concept for interpreting Matthew, and he, too, would accept a threefold division.[5] But, he notes, Matthew does not view the life of Jesus in a generic fashion; the death and resurrection of Jesus form the summit of his messianic mission and consequently mark the turning point of history. Prior to this moment the mission was restricted to Israel, but now the new age has come and the mission is open to the Gentiles, as Matthew indicates in the final resurrection appearance of Jesus to his disciples (28:16-20).

In his analysis, Jack Dean Kingsbury has suggested a different schema. Matthew's view of history has only two, not three, stages: (1) the time of Israel, which in Matthew's narrative framework stretches from Abraham to the time of the Messiah Jesus; (2) the time of Jesus, which incorporates both his pre- and post-Easter existence. Kingsbury notes that in Matthew's perspective the risen Christ never leaves the church but promises to remain with it until the end of time (28:20; as was already promised in the name "Emmanuel," God-with-us, given to Jesus at his birth). Thus the history of Jesus and the history of the church become one and the same. Matthew's portrayal of Jesus' life shows the impact of this transition in that the mission once restricted to Israel is now, through the authority of the risen Jesus, extended to all nations.

Kingsbury believes that the key to understanding Matthew is his christology, not his ecclesiology. Decisive for Matthew's view of history is not the church's mission experience as such but its view of Jesus as the Son of God whose messianic mission ushers in a new age of history and whose authority enables the community to take bold new initiatives.

MISSION WITHIN THE CONTEXT OF MATTHEW'S NARRATIVE WORLD

In assessing these interpretations, some narrative critics have noted that such schema depend on information drawn from outside Matthew's gospel, namely the history of the early church including the relative failure of its mission to Israel, the cataclysmic impact of the destruction of the Temple in AD 70, and the growing dominance of the Gentile church. Interpreters using historical-critical approaches believe that these experiences have left their impact on Matthew's gospel and that the evangelist is probably attempting to put such profound experiences in perspective for his community.

Interpreters who use a strict literary-critical approach have attempted to reconcile Matthew's view of the Gentiles and the Gentile mission within the narrative world of Matthew itself, without immediately assuming a historical reference. David B.

Howell, for example, notes that one of the reasons scholars have interpreted Matthew in terms of "salvation history" is that they want to link the experience of Matthew's readers with the gospel.[6] But ascribing to Matthew the notion of "salvation history" may not be the best way to do this. Among the array of rhetorical devices used by Matthew's narrative, Howell detects what he calls "prolepses" or anticipations, which project the story into the future and thereby include the world of Matthew's readers. Obvious examples of such "prolepses" would be where Matthew declares that false rumors about the empty tomb have circulated "to this day" (28:15) or when Jesus predicts future persecutions that will afflict the community (e.g., 10:16-23; 24:9-14).

Howell concludes there are really two "nows" in Matthew's narrative; one "now" is that of the past story of Jesus and his disciples; the other "now" extends into the world of the reader of the gospel as the life of Jesus has an impact on their experience. These two levels within the narrative help explain the seemingly contradictory viewpoints on the Gentile mission. On one level—that of the past "now"—the mission of Jesus was restricted to Israel, but on another level—the "now" that intrudes into the life of the reader of the gospel—the mission extends to all the nations. These levels cannot be neatly separated. The mission discourse, although spoken by Jesus to the disciples within the confines of Matthew's narrative and thus entwined with a past "now," also has meaning for the reader of the text and so the entire discourse has validity. The same entwined levels of the narrative would hold true, for instance, in considering the disciples within Matthew's story. On one level their interactions with Jesus are part of the "past now" related by the story; but on another level the reader knows that the relationship of Jesus and his disciples extends into the present to mirror the qualities of the reader's relationship to Jesus.

In an interesting study of Matthew's view of history, Amy Jill Levine employs an array of methods to arrive at a somewhat similar conclusion.[7] Starting with the assumptions of narrative criticism, she believes that there should be an internal consistency among the key texts of 10:5, 15:24, and 28:19. Sensitive to the issue of subtle anti-Semitism, Levine is not convinced by solutions that would assign the restrictive sayings of 10:5 and 15:24 to an older and, by implication, more narrow Jewish Christian perspective while assigning the inclusive text of 28:19 to a Gentile perspective. In fact, within the body of Matthew's narrative both Jews (the disciples, Matthew the tax collector, the sick who seek healing, et al.) and Gentiles (the Magi, the centurion, the Canaanite woman, et al.) respond positively to Jesus.

Her own solution is to locate two intersecting "axes" in the gospel, one temporal and one social. The temporal axis encompasses the chronological sequence of events that begins with Jesus' mission first restricted to Israel (10:5; 15:24) and then through his death and resurrection opened to include Gentiles (28:19-20). However, this opening to the Gentiles means not that the mission to the Jews ends but only that it is no longer exclusive to Israel.

At the same time there is a "social axis" in the narrative world of the gospel that runs through the various layers of religious, social, and economic status among the characters of the gospel. From this vantage point, Jesus' mission extends to include those who are at the bottom of the social ladder—Gentiles, women, social outcasts such as tax collectors and sinners, the sick. These respond well to Jesus while those who enjoy positions of power and prestige—the religious leaders, the political rulers such as Herod and Pilate—respond negatively to Jesus.

Taking a cue from feminist hermeneutics, in which texts or features of a narrative sidelined in traditional interpretation often provide the clue to fresh readings, Levine suggests that the temporal and social axes of the gospel intersect precisely in those texts that have seemed incomprehensible to many commentators. At the same time that Jesus states that his mission is restricted on the temporal axis ("Go nowhere among the Gentiles" 10:5) the inclusive nature of his mission is apparent on the social axis ("Go rather to the *lost* sheep of the house of Israel" 10:6, emphasis added). The story of the Canaanite woman (15:21-28) is a perfect example of this convergence: The restrictions of Jesus' mission on the chronological axis fall away as he comes to enact his inclusive mission on the social axis. A woman and a Gentile—thus one from the very bottom of the social ladder—confronts Jesus on behalf of her ill daughter. Through her tenacious faith she leads Jesus to reveal the ultimately inclusive and liberating nature of his mission. Along with other characters in the gospel, including the Magi and the centurion as well as marginal Jewish characters, the story of the Canaanite woman instructs the reader on the nature of the Christian mission and the inclusive nature of the church.

The mission question is one instance in which there is a significant amount of convergence between the parallel methodologies of redaction and literary criticism. While a narrative critic such as Howell is hesitant to draw direct connections between the narrative world of the gospel and the actual historical circumstances of Matthew's community, he concedes that it is likely that the mission experience of Matthew's church has influenced the shape and strategy of Matthew's narrative.[8] In almost every instance, interpreters using a variety of methods, literary and historical, conclude that one of the purposes of Matthew's gospel was to enable the Christian reader to make connections between the Jewish heritage of the Christian movement and its rapidly evolving history. For Matthew's Jewish Christians this meant striving to maintain their Jewish identity at the same time they understood that identity anew in the light of their faith in Jesus. Their Christian commitment brought them into sharp conflict with other Jewish groups who did not accept their view of Jesus as Messiah and authoritative teacher. On the other hand, Matthew's Jewish Christians had also to contend with what may have been for many of them an unsettling future, as Gentile converts with quite different backgrounds, experiences, and concerns began to enter the community in greater numbers and inevitably brought changes to it. Around such issues converges almost every feature of Matthew's gospel scrutinized by modern biblical studies.

CHAPTER 5

MATTHEW'S CHRISTOLOGY

To speak of Matthew's "christology" is to refer to the entire portrayal of Jesus conveyed by this narrative. A gospel's "christology" is the summation of the meaning it assigns to the life, ministry, destiny, and person of Jesus. Unlike systematic theology where a particular "christology" is developed in an orderly and logical fashion, the narrative theology of a gospel creates a christology by means of the distinctive features of its portrayal of Jesus. As such, virtually every aspect of the gospel relates to its christology.

Recent biblical scholarship has concentrated on some aspects of Matthew's christology, which we will review briefly, again for the purpose of alerting us to key issues in Matthean interpretation.

TITLES FOR JESUS

Studies of New Testament christology tend to focus on the titles conferred on Jesus in the Gospels and other New Testament books. Titles such as "Son of God," "Son of Man," "Christ," "Lord," and others are understood in a sense as "code words" that convey the early Christians' confession of Jesus' identity. Many of these titles applied to Jesus were drawn from the Old Testament or Judaism, some were borrowed from Greek culture or at least given new layers of meaning as they moved from a Jewish and biblical into a more Hellenistic context.[1] Tracing the traditional background of such titles and noting their specific use within the context of a particular New Testament author or New Testament book can yield important leads to a particular christology.

One of the leading exponents of this approach to Matthew's christology has been Jack Dean Kingsbury. In his later publications, Kingsbury has moved from a reliance on redaction criticism to turn to literary-critical methodologies, so his work is instructive.[2]

Kingsbury has consistently affirmed that the key title for Matthew's christology is that of *Son of God*. This is not the most frequent title for Jesus in Matthew, but its use and content mark it as the most important title to which all other appellations for Jesus are subordinate. Building on his analysis of the structure of the gospel, Kingsbury notes that reference to this title occurs in all of the principal sections of Matthew.[3] In the opening section of the gospel, the title first appears in Matthew 3:17 when the voice from heaven (= God) declares Jesus is "my Son, the Beloved." But even before this dramatic declaration, Matthew lets the reader know that Jesus is God's Son in the events of the infancy narrative: the virginal conception of Jesus; the naming of Jesus as "Emmanuel" (God-with-us, 1:23); the repeated references to Jesus as the "child" (1:20; 2:2, 8, 9, 11, 13, 14, 20, 21); the quotation of Hosea 11:1 "Out of Egypt I have called my son" (Matt 2:15)—these all affirm Matthew's introduction of Jesus as Son of God.

The confession of Jesus as Son of God begun in the introductory chapters of Matthew's story continues throughout the rest of the gospel. In 11:25-27, Jesus identifies himself as God's unique Son. The disciples confess Jesus as Son of God after the miracle of his walking on the sea (14:33), and Peter solemnly confesses Jesus as Son of God at Caesarea Philippi (16:16). Similar to the Baptism scene, a voice from heaven (a euphemism for God) once again declares Jesus as God's beloved Son on the mountain of transfiguration (17:5). In the important parable of the vineyard and its wicked tenants, the designation of Jesus as "Son" again plays a role (21:33-46), as it does in the following parable of the king who gave a wedding banquet for "his son" (22:1-10). The charge against Jesus in the trial before the Sanhedrin is his claim to be "Son of God" (26:63). The passersby mock Jesus for this (27:40, 43), while the climactic declaration of the centurion and his companion is: "Truly this man was God's Son!" (27:54).

Even though the title is not used in the final scene of the gospel (28:16-20), Kingsbury believes that it underlies the majestic appearance of Jesus on the mountaintop and his declaration that all authority in heaven and on earth has been given to him. In effect, the challenge to Jesus' identity as Son of God in the passion is vindicated through Jesus' resurrection.

Just as in the infancy narrative, Jesus' identity as Son of God is affirmed by more than just explicit use of the title. Matthew's portrayal of Jesus as the great teacher and lawgiver in chapters 5–7 and Jesus' powerful healings in chapters 8–9, along with a host of other indications in the gospel, illustrate Jesus' identity as God's Son. Through this title, Matthew affirms that Jesus has a unique relationship to God and acts with definitive authority in his role as teacher, revealer, and savior.

One of the points emphasized in Kingsbury's analysis is that other titles for Jesus are subordinate to and find their ultimate meaning in Jesus' role as Son of God. He readily concedes that titles such as "Son of David," "Christ," "Servant," "Lord," and others have particular meaning for Matthew, but they serve in effect only to highlight certain features of the unique authority and vocation that Jesus holds as Son of God.

The designation "Son of Man" is a special case for Kingsbury. The Son of God title is used in the gospel where people explicitly confess Jesus' unique messianic identity, either by God in passages such as the Baptism and Transfiguration, or by the disciples as in 14:33, 16:16, or the centurion in 27:54. This confessional title reflected the Christian community's deepest convictions about the mystery of Jesus' identity. By contrast the "Son of Man" is not used in confessional contexts but usually as Jesus' own self-designation when addressing the general public or unbelievers in contrast to those who explicitly recognize Jesus (an excellent example of this is Jesus' response to the high priest in 26:64). As such the title has no particular content of its own. It is used in contexts referring to Jesus' public ministry, his rejection by his opponents and the sufferings of his passion, and his role in the *parousia*.

In his later works where he employs literary-critical methods, Kingsbury notes that the importance of the "Son of God" title in Matthew's narrative rests not simply on its appearance in each section of the gospel or its significant content, but also on the authoritative source of this designation within the narrative world of Matthew's gospel. The declaration of Jesus as God's beloved Son at the moment of his baptism (3:17) and the similar designation in 17:5 are supremely important because this is God speaking within the narrative world of the gospel story. God's "point of view" is the ultimate norm of truth within this world, so there can be no doubt for the reader of the narrative that the designation "Son of God" reveals the deepest truth about Jesus.[4]

On the other hand the designation "Son of Man" is not really a "christological title" intended to reveal the identity of Jesus but a "technical term," that is, "some word or expression that bears, within the story-world of Matthew, a precise meaning."[5] Its function is twofold, in Kingsbury's view, first of all to call attention to the divine authority by which Jesus acts, such as his power to forgive sins (9:6), his authority over the sabbath (12:8), and his mission to associate with sinners (11:19). With this same authority he will return in triumph at the end of time (26:64). By applying the Son of Man term to his sufferings, as in the Passion predictions (e.g., 17:22-23; 20:18-19), Jesus emphasizes that he acts in accord with God's will. The second function of the Son of Man designation is to highlight the opposition Jesus encounters. The term often appears in contexts of conflict and opposition (e.g., 8:19-20; 9:3, 6; 12:24, 32; 13:37-39; 16:13-14; 20:25-28, as well as the passion predictions).

Although few scholars would dispute that the "Son of God" title is extremely important for Matthew's christology, not all accept Kingsbury's contention that other titles are "subordinate" to this key title. And many would take exception to his particular way of describing the function of the Son of Man title in Matthew.

Graham Stanton and others have pointed out the importance of the title "Son of David" in Matthew.[6] This title, he observes, is used nine times in Matthew (compared with only three times in Mark), including the opening line of the gospel (1:1). The title is applied to Jesus particularly in the healing stories (e.g., 9:27; 12:23; 15:22; 20:30, 31) but also in some of the conflicts with Jesus' opponents (see, e.g., 12:42). Stanton believes that this title was important for Matthew because it enabled him to assert the distinctive features of Jesus' messianic identity; Jesus truly was the "Son of David," the Messianic King, but one who was a healer (2:2-6), who was meek (11:29), and humble (21:5), the servant of God (12:17-21).

David Hill has also challenged Kingsbury's view.[7] The other titles given to Jesus in Matthew are not necessarily subordinate to the Son of God title. In fact, he contends, Matthew may intend to add particular nuance to the Son of God designation by the use of other titles. Such an example may be the "Servant" designation, which Matthew applies to Jesus and his mission in the long citation from Isaiah 42:1-4 (see Matt 12:17-21). The humble and compassionate qualities of the Servant of God typify the nature of Jesus' messianic authority as Son of God.

Another Matthean scholar, John Meier, has also contested Kingsbury's views about the function of the "Son of Man" title in Matthew's gospel.[8] It is, he believes, a title with its own particular meaning, one strongly influenced by its use in the apocalyptic theology of Daniel (7:17). Matthew frequently uses this title for Jesus (some thirty times in the gospel), applying it to various facets of his ministry (e.g., 9:6; 11:19; 12:8), his rejection and suffering (17:12, 22; 20:18; 26:2), and Jesus' role as future triumphant judge coming at the end time (10:23; 13:41; 16:27-28; 24:27, 30, 37, 39, 44; 25:31). Meier believes, although the title is not explicitly used in the final scene of the gospel (28:16-20), that Matthew has Jesus' identity as Son of Man in mind. Matthew's portrayal of the risen Christ who holds all authority in heaven and on earth and who returns triumphantly to his community of disciples is, in a sense, a foreshadowing of the end time—a "proleptic parousia" as Meier calls it—when the Son of Man will come in glory. Matthew's portrayal of the triumphant Jesus in this scene recalls the glorified "Son of Man" in the book of Daniel. Thus the Son of Man designation is not subordinate to the Son of God title but used alongside it. Matthew may even have in mind the qualities of this title as well as the Son of God title in those passages when God designates Jesus simply as "my Son" (see 3:17; 17:5).

57

BEYOND TITLES

The difficulty of pinning down the meaning and role of the various titles ascribed to Jesus in Matthew, much less their precise interrelationship, indicates the limits of deciphering Matthew's christology on the basis of titles alone. As the proponents of literary criticism keep reminding us, the gospel is a narrative not a theological treatise. Therefore titles are part of an overall narrative and cannot be isolated from that context. Although titles such as Son of God, Son of David, and Son of Man certainly had meaning prior to and apart from Matthew's story, their role in Matthew's christology is only one part of an organic whole—Matthew's compelling story of Jesus. Thus other features of Matthew's story contribute to his christological portrait as much as titles do.

Typology

Within the Jewish and biblical world, "typology" played an important role in assigning meaning to a person or event. By portraying a character in the hues and tones of a famed predecessor, an author added a new layer of meaning to his portrayal. The device of typology, too, is a significant feature of Matthew's christology.

Dale C. Allison, for example, has traced the way Matthew portrays Jesus as a "new Moses."[9] Within Jewish literature and even early Christian literature, Moses was understood to be an epic character with multiple roles. Building on the Exodus stories, this literature portrayed Moses as lawgiver, leader, liberator, and savior of his people, worker of miracles, revealer, prophet, and one who suffered on behalf of his people. The work of Benjamin Bacon on the structure of Matthew had suggested that a strong connection was to be made between Jesus and the Pentateuch, thus portraying Jesus as a New Moses.[10] Allison, however, scans the content of Matthew's gospel and finds a number of passages where Matthew has clothed the figure of Jesus in the mantle of Moses. Moses typology is surely present in the opening chapters of the gospel where a wicked king slaughters the children of Israel in an attempt to destroy the infant messiah (Matt 1–2; cf. Exod 1:1–2:10) and when Jesus faces a desert test (Matt 4:1-11; cf. Exod 16:1–17:7). The presentation of Jesus as lawgiver (chaps. 5–7), his intimate knowledge of God (11:25-30), the transfiguration on the mountain (where Moses is explicitly named, 17:1-9), and, in Allison's view, the commissioning of his disciples in the final scene of the gospel (Matt 28:16-20; cf. Deut 31:7-9) are some of the most obvious places in Matthew's story where he portrays Jesus as a new Moses.

In doing so, Matthew intended to underscore Jesus' messianic authority: "Just as philosophers wore clothing of a certain kind in order to advertise their office, similarly did Matthew drape the Messiah in the familiar mantle of Moses, by which dress he made Jesus the full bearer of God's authority."[11] Allison also suggests that such typology emphasized the Jewish heritage of Jesus and the Christian community. As the new Moses, Jesus represented not a break with the sacred history of Israel but its fulfillment. This was a useful emphasis as Matthew's community became increasingly Gentile; by emphasizing the Jewish roots of the Christian message, Matthew wanted to prevent "the disassociation of Christianity from Judaism."[12]

Another instance where Matthew may have used Old Testament and Jewish traditions to enhance his portrayal of Jesus is "Wisdom" typology. M. Jack Suggs has suggested that Matthew imported Wisdom motifs through his use of material from the Q source.[13] Poetic descriptions of God's Wisdom such as those in Proverbs, Sirach, and Wisdom, presented Wisdom as a personification of God's self manifestation in creation and in the history of Israel (see, e.g., Prov 8; Sir 51:23-30). "Wisdom" was God's emissary or messenger to humanity and experienced both rejection and acceptance. Suggs finds the influence of Wisdom mythology in Matthew 23:34, where the "prophets and sages and scribes" sent to Israel suffer rejection and even death. Similarly, Suggs believes that Matthew 11:2-30 is strongly influenced by Wisdom motifs. Through the mighty deeds of his ministry Jesus is an emissary of Wisdom (see 11:19). And the intimacy of the Son with the Father and the Son's role as privileged revealer of God affirmed in 11:25-30 also reflect Wisdom typology.[14]

Jesus as Healer

Popular assessments of Matthew's gospel usually single out his emphasis on the role of Jesus as teacher. The prominence of the Sermon on the Mount at the beginning of Jesus' mission, the presence of the four other great discourses throughout the gospel, and even the use of Moses typology connecting Jesus to the memory of the lawgiver par excellence certainly justify that emphasis. Yet reading through Matthew's narrative also brings one face to face with Jesus the healer. In his opening summary of Jesus' ministry in 4:23, Matthew gives great emphasis to Jesus' role as healer: He "cur[ed] every disease and every sickness among the people. So his fame spread throughout all Syria, and they brought to him all the sick, those who were afflicted with various diseases and pains, demoniacs, epileptics, and paralytics, and he cured them." And once the Sermon on the Mount is completed and Jesus returns to the crowds, Matthew begins to narrate a series of healings in chapters 8 and 9.

This feature of Matthew's story has also been a point of interest for recent scholarship and has a role to play in assessing Matthew's christology. A study of the miracle stories that had an important influence on establishing the dominance of redaction criticism as a method was that of Hans Joachim Held.[15] Held analyzed Matthew's collection of miracles in chapters 8 and 9, giving particular attention to his characteristic style and his theology. He noted that these two chapters were part of a broader section of the gospel where Matthew lays out his portrait of Jesus. Bounded by the summaries of 4:23 and 9:35, Matthew presented Jesus as teacher (chaps. 5–7) and healer (chaps. 8–9). Matthew formed the miracle section mainly from his source Mark, but also drew on one healing story (the cure of the centurion's servant, 8:5-13) and some sayings from Q. Matthew's main contribution was to arrange these materials in a particular order and to edit the stories in the direction of his theological perspective.[16]

Held detected a three-part arrangement of the ten miracles in these chapters, with each section having an overall theme. Thus the three miracles in 8:1-17 spotlight Jesus' power to heal, the miracles in 8:18–9:17 focus on the theme of discipleship, and those in 9:18-34 focus on the "praying faith" of the community. Held underscored the way Matthew tended to abbreviate Mark's stories in order to focus on the essential points of the story and to give emphasis to key sayings within the stories. In the first segment on christology (8:1-17), for example, the three miracles of the cleansing of the leper, the healing of the centurion's servant, and the healing of Simon's mother-in-law stress Jesus' authority and power; the three miracles conclude with the fulfillment text from Isaiah: "He took our infirmities and bore our diseases" (Matt 8:17).

Although some have added further nuance to Held's proposed division of the miracle chapters, his analysis has stood up remarkably well.[17] The Scandinavian scholar Birger Gerhardsson has incorporated Held's work in his own study of the miracles in Matthew but moves beyond the scope of Held's work to include the full span of the gospel.[18] He notes that stories of healing—what he calls "therapeutic" stories—occur throughout the gospel of Matthew, from the beginning of Jesus' ministry in Galilee until his final days in Jerusalem. These are joined by other miracles, such as the multiplication of the loaves (14:13-21; 15:32-39), the stilling of the storm (8:23-27), or the walking on the sea (14:22-33), that Gerhardsson calls "non-therapeutic" miracles. All of these miracles are important for Matthew's christology, and in the case of the "non-therapeutic" miracles that christological emphasis is quite emphatic, as in the walking on the water where the story concludes with the disciples worshiping Jesus as "Son of God" (14:33). A key motif of the miracle stories is their focus on Jesus' "incomparable *exousia* [the Greek word for "power" or "authority"] as healer of Israel."[19] While conceding that the title "Son of God" is Matthew's most important title for Jesus, Gerhardsson notes that the term "Servant" is explicitly applied to Jesus in his role as healer in 8:17 and 12:18. By thus portraying Jesus as compassionate healer and gentle servant of God, Matthew helps define the manner in which Jesus is the exalted Son of God.

This brief review of studies on Matthew's christology brings home an important point about the gospel. The evangelist has used an array of means to express his understanding of Jesus' identity: applying to Jesus titles that have a tradition of meaning in Judaism and are given special nuance within the context of the gospel; using allusion to biblical characters and motifs such as the figure of Moses and the poetic metaphor of Wisdom; portraying Jesus as authoritative teacher and compassionate and powerful healer; presenting Jesus and his ministry as the fulfillment of the Old Testament and definitive revealer of God's word.

Only after having experienced the full expanse of Matthew's story can the reader take the measure of this gospel's christology.

It is apparent that Matthew portrays Jesus in profound and exalted terms, as one who brings the divine presence to Israel in an unprecedented way and who inaugurates the definitive age of salvation.[20] Tracking this portrayal throughout the narrative of Matthew will command our attention in Part 2.

CHAPTER 6

DISCIPLESHIP IN MATTHEW'S GOSPEL

Matthew's portrayal of the disciples and the implications of this portrayal for Matthew's understanding of the church and the Christian way of life have also been a focus of biblical scholarship. As was the case for Matthew's christology, these issues are so broad that they could take us to every corner of Matthew's narrative world. For example, the very manner in which Matthew portrays Jesus was surely meant to be exemplary for Christian existence.[1] All of Jesus' teaching was intended to be instructive; those who are great in the kingdom of heaven "teach and do" all of Jesus' commands (5:19). And all of Jesus' actions—his prayer, his compassion, his sense of justice, his response to suffering—were models for authentic discipleship.

However, Matthew's distinctive portrayal of the disciples remains most significant for understanding how the evangelist viewed the demands of Christian life. Redaction criticism assumes that one can detect in Matthew's presentation of the disciples some of the circumstances of his own community context and the evangelist's particular response to this situation. Literary criticism agrees that the reader is expected to identify with the gospel's portrayal of the disciples and to see there a certain mirror image of Christian life. This is also an area of Matthean studies where the assumptions and ecclesial experience the interpreter brings to the text can also have a significant influence.

THE DISCIPLES IN MATTHEW

One of the most exhaustive studies of discipleship in Matthew, which can serve as a good orientation, is that of Jean Zumstein.[2] In Matthew, similar to Mark, the disciples form a distinct group, clearly differentiated from the more neutral "crowds," who are the object of Jesus' ministry and the various opponents who reject him. The disciples are explicitly called by Jesus to follow him and leave behind their previous mode of existence (4:18-22; 9:9). They are Jesus' constant companions, receive special instruction from Jesus (all five principal discourses in Matthew are addressed to the disciples), and are entrusted with his mission (10:1, 5-8; 28:16-20). In Matthew's story, Jesus promises to be with them whenever two or three of his followers gather (18:20) and to remain with them forever as they carry out their mission to the nations (28:20).

Some aspects of Matthew's portrayal contrast with that found in Mark's gospel. Unlike the disciples in Mark who do not understand Jesus, the Matthean disciples *do* "understand" (cf., e.g., Mark 6:52 and Matt 14:33; Mark 8:19 and Matt 16:12). Whereas Mark will point to the disciples' lack of faith, Matthew prefers the term "little faith" (6:30; 8:26; 14:31; 16:8); the disciples may be weak and hesitant (e.g., 14:30-31; 28:17), but ultimately they believe in Jesus. The strong ethical emphasis of Matthew's gospel finds its counterpoint in his emphasis on action, not mere words. True disciples, the authentic brothers and sisters of Jesus, are those who not only hear God's will but do it (7:21-27; 12:50).

The term "disciple" or "learner" (*mathētēs*, in Greek) fits well into Matthew's understanding of Jesus as the definitive teacher of God's word to Israel. The true disciple is one who learns from and is responsive to the one and only teacher, the Messiah (23:10, here Matthew uses the term *kathēgētēs*, a word found only here in the

New Testament, but in Greek literature one that emphasizes the authority of the teacher). At the conclusion of the gospel the disciples are commissioned to "make disciples *(mathēteusate)* of all nations . . . teaching them to obey everything that [Jesus] commanded" (28:19-20).

Another term Matthew seems to favor is that of "scribe," suggesting to some scholars that scribes, learned interpreters of the law, may have had an important role in the Jewish Christian community of Matthew.[3] The faithful scribe trained for the kingdom of Heaven is given responsibility for the household and draws out of his "treasure" interpretations of the tradition that are both "old and new" (13:52). Like his master, the Christian scribe can also expect persecution and even martyrdom in carrying out the mission of the community (23:34).

Zumstein believes that one can detect Matthew's understanding of the church by attention to his overall portrayal of the disciples. The Greek term *ekklêsia,* meaning assembly or "church," is used three times in Matthew (16:18; 18:17 [twice]), the only evangelist to do so. The church is none other than the assembly of the disciples, those who respond in faith and obedience to the invitation of the coming Kingdom (22:1-14; 21:33-46). The community discourse of chapter 18 is an important text for retrieving Matthew's vision of the church. True greatness in the community is characterized by concern for the weak (18:6-14), fraternal discipline (18:15-20), and abundant forgiveness (18:21-35). If Jesus' exhortations in the gospel are any indication of actual circumstances, Matthew's community was not a trouble-free community, however. There is concern about "lawlessness" (7:23; 24:12), hints of scandal (18:5-9), divisions (10:21), and persecutions (10:17-23). Setting up a procedure for handling serious disputes suggests that this was more than a hypothetical case in the community (18:15-18). In the uniquely Matthean parables of the wheat and the tares (13:24-30, 36-43) and the net (13:47-50), Jesus reminds the community that it will remain a mixture of good and bad until the final judgment.

Attempts to pinpoint the exact source of tension in Matthew's community have not led to full consensus. Some believe that there was strain between a charismatic and perhaps radically itinerant group and a more stable and traditional sector of the community that stressed ethical integrity over charismatic gifts.[4]

In Matthew 7:21, for example, Jesus warns the disciples it is not those who exclaim "Lord, Lord" who enter the Kingdom but only those who do the will of God. A group claiming to prophesy in Jesus' name and cast out demons and perform other "deeds of power" are condemned as "lawless" (7:22-23). Similar warnings about false prophets and lawlessness are found in the apocalyptic discourse (see 24:5, 11-12, 24).

Others believe the tensions in Matthew's community may have been over the issue of the mission to the Gentiles. Those who were determined to retain the strongly Jewish character of the community and thus to demand strict observance of the law were in tension with those who were pressing for openness to the Gentiles and adaptation of the tradition on their behalf. A story such as the Canaanite woman in Matthew 15:21-28, where Jesus himself at first rebuffs the Gentile woman's entreaties by stressing his obligations to Israel, may have developed in the context of such a community debate.[5]

FEMINIST PERSPECTIVES ON DISCIPLESHIP

Recent feminist studies of the disciples in Matthew have thrown new light on the gospel's ecclesiology. The Australian biblical scholar Elaine Wainwright has interpreted the entire gospel utilizing a feminist hermeneutic and given particular attention to the role of the disciples.[6] She detects in Matthew two streams of tradition or tendencies held in tension. First, in his portrait of the disciples Matthew retains a strong patriarchal perspective, which he seems to have absorbed from his primary source, Mark. The first disciples called are men, and male characters have the main roles in the narrative and do the speaking. Only men are listed as apostles (Matt 10:2-4), and at the conclusion of the gospel it is the "eleven" male apostles who are entrusted with the mission (28:16).

The second current in Matthew's story is one in which women play a significant role, often in contrast to the weakness and infidelity of the male characters. Matthew has placed four women in the genealogy of Jesus, and in some instances (especially the references to Tamar and Bathsheba) they recall spectacular failures of male characters. Mary, too, plays an obviously crucial role in the infancy narrative, even while Matthew puts the spotlight on Joseph. Women such as Simon's mother-in-law (8:14-15) and the woman with the hemorrhage (9:19-22) are the object of Jesus' ministry in the healing chapters. The Canaanite woman plays a pivotal role in the mission of Jesus (15:21-28). In the passion story, the woman who anoints Jesus (26:6-13), Pilate's wife who defends his innocence (27:19), and the women who remain by the cross (27:55-56) and are present at the burial (27:61) are in clear contrast to the male disciples who betray, desert, and deny Jesus. In Matthew's gospel women are the first to discover the empty tomb (28:1), to see and worship the risen Jesus (28:9), and to be entrusted with the Easter message (28:10).

Wainwright believes these two currents in Matthew's gospel reflect a struggle within the evangelist's community. Traditional patriarchal perspectives were being challenged by a more egalitarian vision (23:8-12). The example of women who are faithful to Jesus in Matthew stands alongside that of other minor characters (e.g., the Magi, the tax collector Matthew, the centurion, many of the sick, et al.) who exemplify authentic discipleship without formally bearing the name "disciple."[7] This, in effect, modified the more conventional patriarchal tradition about discipleship and made it more inclusive. The attempt to present a more inclusive vision of the community, including its opening to the Gentiles, was, in Wainwright's opinion, one of the fundamental purposes of Matthew's gospel.

PETER AS DISCIPLE IN MATTHEW

Within Matthew's overall portrayal of the disciples, the figure of Peter stands out. In addition to the Marcan stories of the call of Simon (Matt 4:18-22; cf. Mark 1:16-20), the confession of Peter at Caesarea Philippi (Matt 16:16; cf. Mark 8:29), and his denial during the passion (Matt 26:58, 69-75; cf. Mark 14:54, 66-72), Matthew adds significant new material: Peter's walking on the water (Matt 14:28-31); his question to Jesus about the "parable" of the blind guide (15:15); the blessing he receives from Jesus at Caesarea Philippi (Matt 16:17-19); the story of the temple tax (17:24-27); and Peter's question about forgiveness (Matt 18:21-22).

The portrait of Peter in Matthew is not entirely positive. He allows fear and hesitation to overcome his faith in Jesus when walking on the water (14:30); his resistance to the passion provokes Jesus to call him "Satan" and a "stumbling block" (16:23); he seems to underestimate the abundance of forgiveness that should characterize life in the community of Jesus (18:21); and he denies Jesus "with an oath" (a detail added to Mark's story; see Matt 26:72).

Trying to understand the role of Peter in Matthew's narrative has been, therefore, a specific focus of Matthean interpreters. Because this Petrine material has played such an important role in later Roman Catholic ecclesiology, this discussion has an added dimension. No matter how "objective" or dispassionate an interpreter tries to be, it is inevitable that the history of how a biblical passage has been understood in different ecclesial traditions, as well as the interpreter's own experience and preferences, has an impact.[8] Traditional Roman Catholic interpretation of Matthew 16:16-19, for example, understood this text as the biblical foundation for the papal office. The recent *Catechism of the Catholic Church* cites Matthew 16:16-19 in precisely this vein: "The Lord made Simon alone, whom he named Peter, the 'rock' of his Church. He gave him the keys of his Church and instituted him shepherd of the whole flock."[9] The Catechism, of course, is confessional in nature and not meant to be a work of critical biblical analysis. Working from a different notion of ecclesiology, Protestant interpreters generally view Peter as a "representative" disciple in Matthew, with the attributes conferred on him in the gospel simply personifying those given to the community as a whole.

Recent biblical scholarship has tried to face these issues head-on. In "The Figure of Peter in Matthew's Gospel as a Theological Problem," the Lutheran scholar Jack Dean Kingsbury notes that Peter is a singularly important character in Matthew's story but he remains "squarely within the circle of the disciples."[10] The power of "binding and loosing" given to Peter in 16:19 is also given to the community in 18:18; the blessing of Peter in 16:17 parallels the blessing of all the disciples in 13:16-17; Peter's unhesitant confession of Jesus as "Son of God" is matched by the same confession on the part of all the disciples in 14:33. Peter, therefore, is not a unique figure nor is he the foundation for some continuing ecclesial office. The church of Matthew is egalitarian (23:8-10). However, the figure of Peter in Matthew does have more than a representational position in one important respect. Peter is the first called (4:18; 10:2) and is the spokesperson for the disciples. Within the unfolding of salvation history, Peter was "first among equals," assuming a position of leadership within the historical framework of the gospel drama but not one that extends beyond that narrative world.[11]

The negative aspects in Matthew's portrayal of Peter are highlighted by another Lutheran interpreter, Arlo Nau.[12] He notes that in most of the stories about Peter, the apostle begins well but ends poorly: He begins to walk on the water, but then sinks (14:28-31); he confesses Jesus as Son of God but then attempts to deflect Jesus from the cross (16:22); he bravely claims he will follow Jesus to death but then denies him with an oath (26:33-35, 74). This, Nau believes, is a deliberate rhetorical device of Matthew, an "encomium of dispraise," meant to discredit the figure of Peter. He suggests that within the community of Matthew there was a struggle going on between those who wanted an egalitarian and charismatic form of community structure (reflected in 23:8-12) and those attempting to impose a more hierarchical, authoritarian form. Nau makes perhaps too direct a connection between his reading of the gospel and more recent church experience. The church needs to purge itself of what he calls the "infectious influence of the Matthew 16:17-19 syndrome" if it hopes to recover the authentic gospel spirit and rid the church of "elitism, chauvinism, patriarchy, and defensive self-interest."[13]

Some recent Roman Catholic studies, on the other hand, have moved in a different direction. Raymond Brown, for example, directly engaged the Matthean portrayal of Peter in an essay entitled, "The Meaning of Modern New Testament Studies for an Ecumenical Understanding of Peter and a Theology of Peter."[14] For this essay he drew on his work as a member of the ecumenical team of scholars who reviewed the New Testament evidence on Peter in the study *Peter in the New Testament.*[15] While in most instances Peter is presented as a "representative disciple" as Kingsbury and others have suggested, there are some powers attributed to Peter that are singular and not given equally to the community as a whole. Peter alone is given the "keys of the kingdom of heaven" (16:19) and named the "rock" on which the church is built (16:18). Among all the disciples, Peter's confession of Jesus as Son of God is singled out and he is blessed because he has received a revelation from God (16:17). Furthermore, the story of the temple tax (17:24-27) suggests that the role of Peter as spokesperson or leader goes beyond the lifetime of Jesus and the first disciples and extends into the life of the post-Easter community.

Brown and his colleagues attempted to put Matthew's portrayal of Peter within the framework of the New Testament as a whole. Matthew's image of Peter is part of a developing "trajectory" stretching from Mark's gospel into that of Matthew, Luke-Acts, John, and the Petrine epistles. This trajectory portrays Peter in an increasingly prominent way as pastor, missionary, confessor, and guardian of the faith, receiver of revelation, martyr—as well as a weak and sinful man. A similar tradition develops around Paul's role in the Gentile churches, as one can detect in the portrayals of Paul in the deutero-Pauline letters.[16] However, the Petrine trajectory seems to be more dominant, and ultimately in the Petrine letters, it is Peter who interprets Paul. Brown concludes that the portrayal of Peter in Matthew and later New Testament texts is expressive of a developing function of pastoral leadership within the early church.

Another Roman Catholic scholar, Pheme Perkins, has revisited the Peter material in *Peter: Apostle for the Whole Church*.[17] She is hesitant to weave the various New Testament portrayals of Peter into a developing "trajectory"; rather, she suggests, these portrayals reflect a plurality of diverse traditions about Peter. In the case of Matthew's gospel, Peter appears to stand in contrast to the "blind guides" Jesus condemns (15:10-17; 23:1-36). Peter ultimately understands Jesus' teaching when the Master explains it to him (15:16-17). Peter plays a role in the very issues that would be points of tension between Jew and Gentile within the community: defilement (15:1-20), the temple tax (17:24-27), forgiveness in dealing with errant members (18:21-35). By so portraying Peter, the evangelist wants to assure his community of the importance—for its leadership as well as for the community as a whole—of faithfully understanding and following Jesus' teaching. Perkins finds a link to later ecclesiology in the role that Peter plays not only in Matthew but in the New Testament as a whole. Peter is a bridge figure, mediating between various factions in the community (as in Gal 1:18-24 and often in Acts). This aspect of the New Testament portrayal provides the basis for a renewed understanding of the Petrine office as a ministry of reconciliation and unity among the diverse Christian churches.

Because Matthew's portrayal of the disciples suggests powerful connections to such issues as church structure, the role of authority, and the meaning of Christian life, it is no wonder that here the interpreter's own experience and assumptions play such a capital and often evident role.

CHAPTER 7

MATTHEW
AND HIS
COMMUNITY

A final task in our review of Matthean scholarship is to consider the historical context of the gospel. Assuming, as redaction criticism does, that the community (or communities) for which this gospel was written had an influence on the shape of the gospel, what can we detect about the circumstances of this early church or churches?[1] And what about the evangelist Matthew, whose apostolic name has been traditionally assigned to this gospel? What can we detect in the gospel itself about the background of this key figure? Although literary criticism in its strictest form considers such questions about the actual author and the original readers of the gospel as secondary, at best, for the interpretation of the gospel as a narrative, modern biblical scholarship as a whole has given these issues considerable attention, believing they are crucial to understanding the viewpoint of Matthew's gospel.

THE SETTING OF MATTHEW'S COMMUNITY AND ITS JEWISH CHARACTER

For many recent interpreters a key issue is the relationship of Matthew's community to the developing context of first-century Judaism. In recent decades biblical scholarship has been in the process of thoroughly revising its portrayal of first-century Judaism, which too often had been constructed on the basis of incomplete and sometimes stereotyped assessments.[2] More attentive readings of early Jewish and Christian texts, including the gospels themselves, access to the Dead Sea scrolls and their portrayal of another dimension of first-century Palestinian Jewish life, and the accumulation of archaeological finds in the Mediterranean world have all contributed to this needed revision. Nor could Christian scholars ignore the fact that centuries of prejudice and stereotyping played their part in the grievous tragedy of the Holocaust.

The Judaism of Jesus' day was not monolithic but diverse in character and perspective. While the gospels remain a principal source for our understanding not only of early Christianity but of first-century Judaism itself, most interpreters stress that the decisively negative portrayal of the religious leadership in the four gospels must be tempered by an awareness of the context in which the gospels were written, of the nature and function of such rhetoric in its first-century Jewish and Hellenistic contexts, and of offsetting views provided by other sources.[3]

Matthew's gospel stands near the center of this current discussion. As much of our foregoing discussion indicates, this gospel strikes the reader as thoroughly Jewish in character. Its extensive use of the Old Testament by explicit citation, subtle allusion, and elaborate typology in order to connect Jesus to the history of Israel and to portray him as the embodiment of Jewish hopes, its stress on Jesus as one who comes not to destroy but to fulfill the Jewish law, its respect for Jesus' historic mission to the Jews, and its conviction that Jesus is the longed for Messiah of Israel would seem to establish Matthew's Jewish credentials.

Yet the gospel also contains plenty of material that seems to be "anti-Jewish." Matthew is unrelenting in his criticism of the Jewish leaders, including the "scribes and the Pharisees" as well as the priests and leaders in Jerusalem. They begin to oppose Jesus from the very beginning when news of Jesus' birth "frightens" Herod and "all Jerusalem," including the "chief priests and scribes," who know the place of the Messiah's birth but, unlike the Magi, do not offer him homage (Matt 2:1-6). And particularly from chapter 12 forward, Jesus and the leaders are presented in sharp opposition.

Although Matthew does not ordinarily speak of the "Jews" in a generic sense (in contrast to John's gospel, for example) and cites specific leadership groups as opposed to Jesus, the general populace does not emerge unscathed from this gospel. The "crowds" seem to be a generally neutral group through most of the gospel story, but ultimately, swayed by the leaders, they demand Jesus' crucifixion and seem to accept responsibility for his death (27:24-25). Matthew refers to "*their* synagogues," seeming to imply a rift between the followers of Jesus and the rest of the Jewish community (see 4:23; 9:35; 10:17; 12:9; 13:54). In the important parable of the vineyard, the landowner punishes the murderous tenants by having "the kingdom of God . . . taken away from you and given to a people that produces the fruits of the kingdom" (21:43), a text unique to Matthew that appears to strip from Israel its special status as the people of God. The Great Commission at the end of the gospel, sending the disciples to "all nations," seems to confirm that historic change (28:16-20). The gospel anticipates that mission would be opposed by the Jewish leaders—Matthew's Jesus warns the disciples "they will hand you over to councils and flog you in their synagogues" (10:17) and they might even have to face death just as the prophets did in the past (23:29-36).

It is this apparently ambivalent stance of the gospel—at once thoroughly Jewish and yet stridently critical of the Jewish leaders—that has complicated the question of Matthew's relationship to first-century Judaism. Put in another way, one could ask whether Matthew's church considered itself part of the Jewish community, albeit in some tension with its leaders? Or had a definitive break with the Jewish community already taken place and Matthew's Christians become conscious of being a distinct religious entity separate from Judaism, with their face now turned toward the Gentile world? Modern scholarship has produced a whole spectrum of answers to this question.

Separate from the Jewish Community

On one side of the spectrum are a number of scholars who believe that Matthew's community had experienced a decisive rift with Pharisaic Judaism. One of the most influential voices in this line is that of the eminent British scholar, W. D. Davies. In his magistral work, *The Setting of the Sermon on the Mount*, Davies concluded that Matthew's gospel was in direct confrontation with Pharisaic Judaism in the critical period following the Jewish revolt of AD 66–70.[4] After the collapse of the revolt and the Roman destruction of Jerusalem and its Temple in AD 70, the Pharisees, under the initial leadership of Rabbi Johanan ben Zakkai, were the group that began to knit Judaism back together. At Jamnia, a Mediterranean town south of Joppa, and later at other sites in the Galilee region, the leaders of Pharisaic Judaism took up the work of consolidation that would ensure Jewish survival after the trauma of the loss of the Temple and the Jerusalem aristocracy that traditionally had provided Jewish leadership. Here began the work that would lead ultimately to the codification of law interpretation and the formalizing of the canon of Scripture. The Jewish scholar Jacob Neusner has described this period as "formative Judaism."[5]

Consolidating post-70 Judaism meant the evolution of a new self-identity, centered on the family, the synagogue, and observance of the law. The Temple with its sacrificial cult and its focus as the center of pilgrimage and orthodoxy no longer existed and eventually would take a symbolic role. The cleansing and dedication experienced through sacrifice was now to be experienced solely through observance of the law. Protecting this emerging sense of Jewish identity also resulted in less tolerance for deviant groups within Judaism. Prior to the destruction of the Temple, Judaism was diverse, often experiencing turbulent interaction among various groups and sects yet understanding that all in some fashion were Jewish. In the period of formative Judaism, however, apocalyptic and other fringe groups were expelled from the synagogue, among whom, in Davies' opinion, were the Christians. The introduction of the twelfth benediction, condemning the Christians and *minim* or "heretics," into the Tiffilah, or eighteen benedictions that were part of the synagogue liturgy, probably occurred in this period and is further evidence of the rift between the Jewish Christians and the larger body of Pharisaic Judaism.

Davies saw Matthew's gospel as a direct response to this situation. The hostile portrayal of the Pharisees and other Jewish leaders in the gospel, therefore, reflects not simply the conflicts between Jesus and his contemporaries but the bitter conflict between Matthew's community and his Jewish contemporaries at the time the gospel was being composed. Matthew's stress on

Jesus as authoritative interpreter of the law in the Sermon on the Mount was meant to assure his Jewish Christians that in following Jesus they were not abandoning their Jewish heritage but being faithful to its ultimate intent.

Davies' fundamental thesis remains influential. As Davies himself concedes, he may have overemphasized the importance of the council of Jamnia in the overall reform of post-70 Judaism; its role was probably idealized in later rabbinic texts to underscore the role of the rabbis in Jewish life.[6] The dating and function of the eighteen benedictions in synagogue prayer are also debated. But his basic conclusion remains firm that Matthew's gospel is responding to the challenge posed for his Jewish Christian community by the break with Pharisaic Judaism and the related concern for the self-identity of Christian community at a period of profound transition.

Some scholars, however, would see the break with Pharisaic Judaism as part of the receding past and no longer an active concern of Matthew's community. In his commentary, Ulrich Luz concludes that Matthew is not involved in a direct dialogue with Pharisaic Judaism. The rift with the synagogue is past history. Rather, Matthew's concern with the leaders' rejection of Jesus has a theological purpose. "Thus it has become clear that the Gospel of Matthew is not a Christian answer to 'Jamnia.' Rather it is a Christian answer to Israel's no to Jesus or the attempt to cope with this no in a fundamental definition of a position."[7] Similarly David Garland and Sjef Van Tilborg, each of whom has studied Matthew's negative portrayal of the Jewish leaders, conclude that Matthew's polemic is not part of an interaction with Pharisaic Judaism but is used rhetorically and symbolically to portray negative and unfaithful responses to the Christian message.[8]

Within the Jewish Community

Other interpreters, reviewing the same evidence, are convinced that Matthew and his community have not yet made a definitive break with Judaism. The German exegete Reinhart Hummel, writing at about the same time as Davies, had come to this conclusion.[9] Although Matthew's community may have been embroiled in a sharp debate with other Jewish groups, this was still an intrafamily conflict. For example, the incident about paying the temple tax in 17:24-27 suggests that Matthew's community did not want to scandalize the Pharisees by failing to pay the tax. And in 23:2-3, the Matthean Jesus exhorts his disciples to respect the authority of the scribes and Pharisees even if their example is not to be followed. Warnings about persecutions in the synagogues (10:17; 23:34) imply that members of Matthew's community still belonged to them.

However, Hummel added another dimension, suggesting that there were also internal conflicts, namely between those in the community—probably Hellenistic Jews and Gentiles—who discounted the validity of the law and those who insisted on the continuing validity of the law as interpreted by Jesus. Matthew's gospel responds to both "fronts," sharply criticizing the Jewish leaders through his portrayal of the opponents of Jesus and also attacking the claims of the "lawless" Christians by affirming Jesus as teacher of the law and by insisting on the importance of good deeds as an authentic sign of discipleship.

Although Hummel's suggestion of an "antinomian" front has not received a lot of support in more recent Matthean scholarship, his thesis that Matthew's community was still part of the overall Jewish community is shared by a number of scholars. J. Andrew Overman, for example, emphasizes that "formative Judaism" from the time of the Hasmonean dynasty on through the first century AD was very diverse.[10] Rival factions each claimed to be faithfully Jewish and often characterized other Jewish groups as "corrupt" or "lawless." Matthew's critique of the Pharisees and other Jewish leaders should be read in this light. Overman believes Matthew was aware that the Pharisaic viewpoint seemed to be gaining the ascendancy and his community was being driven to the fringe. This led to a certain intensity in his effort to discredit the religious leaders and to claim legitimacy for those who followed Jesus' teaching. Although Overman believes that Matthew's community was still thoroughly Jewish and had as yet relatively few Gentile members, the commission at the end of the gospel (28:16-20) signals the evangelist's awareness that the future of the community could lie in that direction.

Other authors have refined this position with the help of categories and models drawn from the social sciences. Graham Stanton, for instance, views Matthew's community as one of several "sectarian" groups in Judaism in the crucial formative period following the destruction of Jerusalem.[11] Matthew wanted to define the Christian community in relationship with and in contrast to other parties. Even though Matthew's Jewish Christians were alienated from other Jewish groups they also were wary of the Gentiles. Stanton takes into account the gospel's derogatory comments about the Gentiles we noted earlier.[12]

In *Matthew's Christian-Jewish Community,* Anthony Saldarini attempts an even more precise sociological mapping of Matthew's relationship to Judaism.[13] Despite the apparent anti-Jewish sentiments of the gospel, Matthew's community should be understood as a "deviant" Jewish group within the dominant context of Pharisaic Judaism. By "deviant" Saldarini means a group which does not conform with the majority norms or viewpoints. But being a deviant group, Saldarini maintains, does not put one outside first-century Palestinian Judaism in the sense of shedding fundamental aspects of Jewish identity, values, and behavior. Throughout Matthew's gospel it is apparent that his viewpoint is steeped in Judaism. Therefore Saldarini prefers to describe Matthew's community as "Christian Jewish" rather than "Jewish Christian." In attacking the viewpoint of the Pharisees in the gospel and in stoutly defending the validity of his own community's self-understanding, Matthew intended to persuade the larger society to adopt his "deviant" or minority viewpoint and so make it normative.

Common Ground

So where can one place Matthew's community—within or outside Judaism? At first blush modern scholarship seems hopelessly divided on this issue, just as Matthew's gospel itself seems strangely ambivalent. But even across the wide spectrum of opinion on this subject there is a good bit of common ground.

First, virtually every interpreter agrees that Matthew's gospel was written for a community in the critical transition period after the fall of Jerusalem when both the Jewish and the early Christian communities were experiencing substantial and often turbulent change. One of the chief purposes of the gospel was to provide Matthew's Christian community with a sense of continuity with the past and a vision for the future.

Second, few readers of Matthew would want to deny that this gospel is thoroughly Jewish in character and outlook. Affirming this does not solve the question to what degree Matthew's community still considered itself part of the Jewish community or already separated from it. But from a cultural, social, and theological viewpoint, the preponderance of Matthew's Christians had strong roots in Judaism and understood themselves in the light of Israel's history and values.

Third, authors who maintain that Matthew's community is an integral, if deviant, part of the Jewish community admit that there was considerable tension and alienation between Matthew's community and other Jewish groups. For example, Saldarini concedes that even as a "deviant" group within Judaism, Matthew's church would have felt "separated" from the majority or dominant group. Both Saldarini and Overman also concede that the definitive break with Judaism was imminent even though it had not yet taken place.[14]

Fourth, those who maintain Matthew had not broken with the Jewish community will agree that the strong christology of the gospel was the ultimate source of tension between the Matthean community and other sects or the dominant party within Judaism. As Saldarini notes, the authority given to Jesus by Matthew's community has no precedent or peer in any other Jewish sect.[15]

Finally, even though there are different assessments of Matthew's attitude to the Gentiles, few if any interpreters would deny that Matthew at least foresees a Gentile mission as the future ministry of the church. Stanton, for example, believes that Matthew's Jewish Christian community is still leery of that mission.[16] But Matthew's positive portrayal of some Gentile characters in the gospel and his presentation of them as a preview of the future, and the important thrust to the Gentiles in 21:43, as well as the unequivocal mission commission of sending the community to the "nations" in 28:16-20, stand as solid evidence that Matthew's church anticipated that mission, a stance that would ultimately further distance the community from its status as an integral part of the Jewish community.

With these important points of consensus in place, the apparent distance among the interpretations we have cited narrows considerably.

LOCATING MATTHEW AND HIS CHURCH IN PLACE AND TIME

One final set of questions requires our attention: Who was the author of the gospel? And where and when was the gospel composed? Such background questions are classically treated in introductions to commentaries on the gospel and in introductions to the New Testament.[17] Our goal here is not to repeat such discussions at length but to weigh these issues for the light they may throw on the task of interpretation.

The Evangelist Matthew

Who wrote the gospel? The gospel itself does not reveal its authorship. Matthew's gospel does change the name of Levi to "Matthew" in its version of Mark's story of the call of the tax collector of Capernaum (cf. Mark 2:14 and Matt 9:9). In concert with that change, the gospel identifies Matthew as "the tax collector" in its version of the list of the apostles (cf. Matt 10:3 and Mark 3:18).

One has to rely on external evidence for explicit assignment of the gospel to the apostle Matthew. The gospel was consistently attributed to Matthew in the early patristic period. The earliest reference is that of Papias, Bishop of Hierapolis, an important Roman city in west central Asia Minor. Papias' comments about the origins of the four gospels are preserved in a quotation by Eusebius (AD 260–340), who himself was Bishop of Caesarea Maritima. Although there is uncertainty about the precise dating for Papias, he probably lived in the earliest part of the second century AD.[18]

The so-called testimony of Papias raises as many questions as it answers. A rough literal translation of Papias' comment is as follows: "Now Matthew therefore arranged the sayings *(ta logia)* according to the Hebrew dialect *(hebraidi dialekto)*, and each one interpreted it as he was able." The Greek text is difficult to translate accurately. At first glance, Papias seems to be saying that Matthew wrote the gospel in "the Hebrew dialect," which might mean an original Hebrew or Aramaic version. The problem is that most modern scholarship agrees that the canonical gospel of Matthew does not appear to be a translation from Hebrew or Aramaic but was composed in Greek. And, as we have noted, it seems that Matthew used a great deal of the gospel of Mark in composing his gospel. This has led many scholars to doubt the accuracy of Papias' information (Eusebius himself complains that Papias was not very intelligent!).

But others have cautioned against dismissing Papias so quickly and have taken a more careful look at his testimony. Some have suggested, for example, that Papias may be referring to an earlier version of the gospel that was composed in Aramaic or Hebrew;

an elaborated Greek edition, one that also borrowed from Mark's gospel, would have evolved later.[19] Others have reexamined the meaning of Papias' words. The German scholar J. Kürzinger, for example, notes that earlier in his comments on Mark, Papias uses the term "logia" to refer not just to the words of Jesus but to the content of the gospel as a whole (i.e., the words and actions of Jesus).[20] In mentioning the origin of Matthew's gospel, Papias was apparently contrasting it with Mark, who, Papias claims, reported Peter's recollections of the words and deeds of Jesus, noting them "accurately" but without any real rhetorical order. Matthew on the other hand presented the words and deeds of Jesus in the Hebrew "manner" or "style"; the term *dialektos* in Greek can mean "dialect," but it was also used in a technical fashion to refer to literary style. Thus Papias' statement means not that Matthew wrote in Hebrew but that, in contrast to Mark, he introduced a certain Jewish manner of order or format into his gospel. This description of Matthew, in fact, harmonizes with the Jewish features of the gospel we have been describing in our survey of Matthew's characteristic style and distinctive theology.

Still others have speculated that Papias may have derived his statement about Matthew from earlier traditions that were referring to the incorporation of Q into the gospel. This collection of the sayings of Jesus may have been associated with the apostle Matthew's name and originally composed in Hebrew or Aramaic.

This discussion has to end on an inconclusive note. The fact that the gospel of Matthew as we now have it was evidently written in Greek, and the evidence that it used Mark as a source and may have been written in the last quarter of the first century, are all strong reasons for doubting that the Palestinian Jew and tax collector Matthew could have been its author.[21] It would be unwise, therefore, to draw conclusions about the meaning of the gospel on the basis of its apostolic authorship alone. At the same time, the ancient tradition attested to by Papias suggests that one should be cautious about dismissing out of hand any historical basis for the association of this apostolic author with the origin of the gospel.

Internal evidence does not lead to any more precise identification of the author of the gospel. The gospel's rich use of Old Testament quotations and typology, its concern with Jewish issues such as interpretation of the law, its overt attempt to connect the history of Jesus with the history of Israel, and even its sharp polemic with the Jewish leaders which has the atmosphere of an internecine struggle—all of these features of the gospel suggest it was written by a Jewish Christian author. The fact that the gospel was composed in Greek and its good Greek style, especially in comparison with that of its important source Mark, which Matthew often improves upon, suggest further that the author was a Hellenistic Jew, that is, one who was at home in the Greco-Roman world. As we noted earlier, Matthew's favorable comments about the "scribe . . . trained for the kingdom of heaven" (13:52) and the thoughtful, ordered nature of his gospel narrative may indicate that the evangelist was himself a Jewish scribe, that is an intelligent, educated Jewish Christian steeped in the traditions of Judaism and concerned with the interpretation of those traditions in the light of his faith in Jesus as the Messiah and the Son of God.[22]

When and Where?

In attempting to answer the questions of the date and place of Matthew, the interpreter must again comb through scanty external evidence and tantalizing but inconclusive internal evidence. We know that Matthew's gospel predates Papias, so its date of composition cannot be later than the earliest part of the second century. There are strong indications that Ignatius of Antioch, who died about AD 107, and the Didache, which was written around the turn of the first century, also were familiar with Matthew's gospel.[23] Therefore the gospel must have been written sometime before AD 100. If the hypothesis of Matthew's dependence on Mark is correct, then some time must have elapsed for Mark's text itself to have taken shape, to have been circulated among the Christian communities, and to have gained enough authority that Matthew would be compelled to absorb it almost in its entirety. Therefore a date sometime after the middle of the first century seems reasonable as a starting point.

Features of Matthew's gospel may help us narrow the time frame between AD 50 and 100. The intensity and content of Matthew's debate with the Jewish leaders, as we have noted, suggest that Matthew was contemporary with the formative period for both Judaism and Jewish Christianity after the destruction of the Temple in AD 70. As the whole discussion of the relationship of Matthew's community to formative Judaism indicates, there is a strong consensus that Matthew's community had already broken with its Jewish connection or was experiencing severe tensions that would soon lead to a break. For many scholars a verse that Matthew adds to the parable of the great supper is a clue that the evangelist was writing *after* the destruction of Jerusalem: "He sent his troops, destroyed those murderers, and burned their city" (Matt 22:7; cf. Luke 14:21). For these reasons, a growing number of Matthean interpreters conclude that the gospel was written sometime during the last quarter of the first century AD, probably between 80 and 90.

The possible location for Matthew's gospel must also be an educated guess, drawing on even a thinner reserve of external and internal evidence. The probable influence of Matthew's gospel on Ignatius of Antioch has made this city a prime candidate for the location of Matthew's community.[24] We know from other sources that circumstances of this prominent Syrian city harmonize with the kind of atmosphere reflected in the gospel itself. Antioch was a large Mediterranean city, with a mixed population of Gentiles and Jews. We know from Acts and from Paul's Letter to the Galatians that it was also the site of a significant Jewish Christian community. Acts 11:19-26 claims that the Christian message first reached Antioch through some of the Greek-speaking Jewish Christians of Jerusalem who were scattered in the wake of Stephen's execution and the ensuing persecution. Later Barnabas would be sent to Antioch to confirm the work of these missionaries. It was in Antioch, Acts 11:26 notes, that the followers of Jesus were first called "Christians." While defending his apostolic credentials to the Galatians, Paul gives us another tantalizing glimpse into the Christian community of Antioch. It was in that city Paul had confronted Peter over the issue of accepting Gentiles in the community. Under pressure from strict Jewish Christians, Peter had apparently refrained from eating with Gentile Christians. This led to Paul's blistering criticism of Peter and also his former missionary partner Barnabas (see Gal 2:11-14). Even though Paul's portrayal of Peter is not very flattering in this instance, he does confirm Peter's active presence in Antioch, a fact that also harmonizes with the prominence that traditions about Peter have in Matthew's gospel.[25]

Some interpreters have pushed farther and suggested that there are hints in Matthew that his community was relatively prosperous and located in an urban environment.[26] The gospel uses the word "city" *(polis)* twenty-six times (compared with Mark, who uses the term "city" only four times, preferring the designation "village"). In Matthew's story, Nazareth and Capernaum are designated as "cities" and in summaries the evangelist describes Jesus as extending his mission throughout the "cities" of Galilee (9:23, 35; 11:1). The evangelist also tends to inflate monetary amounts: Thus Mark's "copper coins" in Mark 6:8 become "gold, or silver, or copper" (Matt 10:9); Luke's parable of the "minas" (Luke 19:11-17) becomes the parables of the "talents" in Matthew (25:14-30), a significantly larger denomination. Overall Matthew refers to "gold" and "silver" some twenty-eight times in his gospel while Luke refers to them only four times and Mark once. Although such evidence cannot be decisive for locating Matthew's church in an urban and relatively prosperous community, it does point in that direction.

A MATTHEAN PROFILE

Given the nature of our evidence, we will never be certain about the exact circumstances of the origin of Matthew's gospel. The interpreter has to be content with saying that there is at least persuasive harmony between what we know of a first century location such as Antioch and the circumstances of Matthew's church that may be deduced from distinctive features of his gospel story. Stepping back from all of our discussion, what can we conclude about Matthew? Here is an attempt at a summary:

1) The gospel was written in Greek, probably between AD 80 and 90.

2) The author was a Jewish Christian, steeped in his Jewish heritage, and skilled in the art of narration and interpretation. Though respectful of Mark's gospel, which apparently was already known in Matthew's church, as well as other important resources of the young Christian movement such as the collection of parables and sayings now designated "Q," Matthew did not hesitate to compose a new life of Jesus that absorbed these important sources but significantly recast them to address the specific concerns of his own community.

3) That community (or ensemble of communities) was probably located in Antioch of Syria, a Greco-Roman urban center with a mixed population of Jews and Gentiles, a city reached by the Christian movement shortly after its inception and one destined to

be an influential center of Christian learning in the early centuries of the church.

4) At the time of the gospel's composition, Matthew's community was immersed in a critical transition moment, suffering a wrenching separation from its roots in Judaism on the one hand and faced with the prospect of growing numbers of Gentile Christians on the other. This transition had provoked bitter conflict with the leadership of the emerging Pharisaic Judaism as well as debate within the community over the impact of the Gentile mission. For Matthew's Christians, both non-Christian Jews and Gentiles were "outsiders" and relationships with both were a difficult challenge.

5) An important purpose of the gospel was to address the questions of identity and purpose faced by Matthew's community. On the one hand, the evangelist reassures his community that in following Jesus the promised Messiah and unique Son of God they were being completely faithful to their Jewish heritage and would find in Jesus' teaching and example the embodiment of all that God had promised Israel. On the other hand, the character of Jesus' own teaching and ministry, the decisive turn in the history of salvation effected through Jesus' death and resurrection, and the community's own experience of rejection by the Jewish religious leadership compelled the community to turn its future vision to the Gentiles. Thus faith in Jesus and a profound understanding of and fidelity to his way stand at the very center of Matthew's perspective.

PART TWO

READING MATTHEW

Reading a thoughtful review of a play or enjoying a food critic's evaluation of a good restaurant ultimately do not substitute for going to the theater or eating a gourmet meal. Having reviewed the issues of interest to Matthean scholarship, it is time to savor the gospel itself. In what follows we will work our way through the gospel, noting the content and significance of individual sections in the light of Matthew's overall story. It is essential to first read the relevant portion of Matthew's text before turning to the comments on that section. Reviewing scholarly discussion of Matthew or providing a reading guide are useful only to the extent that they assist—not substitute for—the interpreter's own careful reading of the gospel text.

In order to compare Matthew's text with that of the other gospels, having a synopsis on hand will also be very useful. The intent here is not to provide a detailed commentary on Matthew's text. Although detail is provided on some key passages, the attention here falls more on the overall meaning of each segment of Matthew's narrative. Part 1 alerted us to some of the characteristic features of Matthew's gospel. Part 2 illustrates how those features emerge within the setting of Matthew's narrative. Thus it serves as a "tour guide" for the attentive reader who wants to move more deeply into the narrative world of this gospel, by pointing out significant features of the narrative, placing each section in the context of the gospel as a whole, highlighting recurring and characteristic motifs of the gospel, and suggesting some leads for interpretation. Follow-up with a good commentary on Matthew's gospel can provide detailed information on specific verses and passages of the gospel.

The division of the gospel into six principal sections takes its lead from the foregoing discussion of the structure of Matthew on pages 31-32:

1. The Origins of Jesus and His Mission (1:1–4:11)
2. Jesus: Messiah in Word and Deed (4:12–10:42)
3. Responding to Jesus: Rejection and Understanding (11:1–16:12)
4. The Journey to Jerusalem (16:13–20:34)
5. In the Holy City: Conflict, Death, Resurrection (21:1–28:15)
6. Finale (28:16-20)

CHAPTER 8

THE ORIGINS OF JESUS AND HIS MISSION (1:1–4:11)

In the opening scenes of the gospel, Matthew begins to identify for the reader who Jesus is, tracing the Messiah's roots back into the history of Israel and, at the same time, offering a prelude or overture to important themes that will rise to the surface in Matthew's account of the public ministry of Jesus. Matthew's presentation of the "origin" of Jesus encompasses not only the events surrounding his birth (chaps. 1–2) but also his encounter with John the Baptist at the Jordan (3:1-17) and his contest with Satan in the desert (4:1-11). This "prologue" or "overture" to the gospel is spread across a number of geographical settings: Bethlehem, Egypt, and Nazareth in the infancy gospel, the Jordan River for the encounter with John, and, finally, the Judean "wilderness" or desert where the spirit-filled Messiah is tested by Satan.

As will be typical in many scenes of his gospel, particularly in the first eleven chapters, Matthew composes these opening scenes from a variety of sources.[1] The genealogy and the stories of Jesus' infancy are special to Matthew and appear to be a blend of traditions familiar to the evangelist in his own community, anticipations of motifs drawn from the main body of the gospel, plus his own artful reflections on the events, characters, and quotations from the Hebrew Scriptures.

THE GENEALOGY (1:1-17)

With extraordinary subtlety, Matthew signals the fundamental perspective of his gospel in its opening line: Jesus the Messiah is both "Son of David" and "Son of Abraham" (1:1). As will be the case with many features of the prologue, the implications of these signals become clear only as the rest of the story unfolds. Without hesitation Matthew proclaims Jesus as the Messiah of Israel; thus, Jesus deserves the title "Son of David," a title that will have considerable importance in Matthew's account, particularly in the context of Jesus' healings.[2] But Jesus is also acclaimed "Son of Abraham," the patriarch whom the Scriptures identify as "father of many nations" (Gen 17:5; 22:17-18). Overwhelmed at Capernaum by the Gentile centurion's faith, Matthew's Jesus will envision many "coming from east and west" to sit at Abraham's table (8:11). In the first line of his story, therefore, Matthew hints at the movement from Israel to the nations that will be a fundamental motif of his gospel.

Matthew's dual perspective—a Jesus embedded in the history and hopes of Israel and yet inaugurating a breakthrough to the nations—remains a deep current throughout the prologue and into the body of the gospel. The gospel affirms both continuity with the sacred past of Israel and yet discontinuity as the events of sacred history triggered by Jesus' own mission break beyond the horizons of Israel. All of this, the gospel proclaims, is God's provident intent.

The genealogy, whose contents are drawn mainly from 1 Chronicles 2–3 and Ruth 4:18-22, serves this same purpose. On the one hand it traces Jesus' messianic ancestry from Abraham to David, then through the travail of the Exile and return to final fulfillment in the birth of the messiah (Matthew alerts the reader to this division in 1:17). Thus the theme of continuity is reinforced. But, at the same time, Matthew introduces elements of discontinuity. His organization of the genealogy calls attention to the Babylonian exile, a time of rupture in Israel's history (see 1:11, 17). And his introduction of four women into the family tree of Jesus also underscores moments of "discontinuity." In each case—Tamar, Rahab, Ruth, Bathsheba (whom Matthew identifies significantly as the "wife of Uriah" the Hittite)—the women included in the genealogy were "outsiders" who break into the messianic line only through extraordinary and in some instances disconcerting circumstances.[3] Matthew reminds his readers that even within the pages of Israel's own history there is precedent for moments of surprising discontinuity when God has carried forward the promise of salvation through outsiders.

BIRTH AND NAMING (1:18-25)

The mood of paradox continues in this key passage, which amplifies the reference to Jesus' birth in the genealogy (v. 16). The literary form changes as Matthew now moves into enticing stories about the circumstances of Jesus' birth and childhood. We also encounter the first of many examples where Matthew both uses explicit citations from the Hebrew Scriptures and deftly plays on Old Testament typologies.

In Matthew's account, the narrative focuses on the character of Joseph whom Matthew identifies as a "righteous" *(dikaios)* man (1:19), a quality of great importance to this gospel. The reader learns through Joseph the startling nature of the child Jesus. When he discovers that Mary is pregnant, Joseph first assumes that she has been unfaithful. Because he is "just" and compassionate, he resolves to divorce her quietly but then is given a divine revelation in the first of several dreams that the origin of Mary's child is from the Holy Spirit. Thus right from the start the mysterious, divine origin of Jesus is affirmed by Matthew. And so, too, is a way of interpreting the law that gives emphasis to compassion.[4]

Joseph is also instructed on the name to be given this wondrous child. He is to be called "Jesus," the Greek form of a Jewish name "Yeshua" or "Yeshu" that literally means "God helps." Thus for Matthew's gospel the name "Jesus" points to the intent of his messianic mission to save God's people from their sins (1:21), a mission to be carried out in Jesus' teaching, healing, and, above all, in his death and resurrection.

89

To emphasize that this startling event was intended by God and fulfilled the hopes of Israel, Matthew introduces the first of his "fulfillment" or "formula" quotations, a quotation from Isaiah 7:14.[5] The quotation also gives the child Messiah another name; he is to be called "Emmanuel," that is, "God is with us" (1:23). Once again the extraordinary depth of Matthew's christology is apparent. The divine presence embodied in the person and mission of Jesus will be illustrated in Jesus' words and actions in the rest of the gospel. At the very end of the gospel the risen Christ assures the community that he will be with them until the end of time (28:20). In the community discourse of 18:20, Jesus promises to be present wherever two or three of the disciples gather. And in the judgment parable of 25:31-46, the disciples are reminded of Jesus' presence with the "least" members of the community (see also 10:40-42).

This scene closes with Joseph awaking from his dream and without hesitation obeying the divine command given him by the angel. Matthew's portrayal of Joseph as someone who receives instructions from God through a dream, who is a just man, and one whose mission will be to protect the family of the Messiah and take them into Egypt cannot help recalling the Joseph of the Hebrew Scriptures (Gen 37–50). Here is another example where Matthew employs biblical typology to envelop Jesus in the mantle of Old Testament fulfillment.

HEROD AND THE MAGI (2:1-18)

The prologue's function of signaling to the reader events that will unfold later in the gospel is apparent in this gripping episode. The response of the Magi "from the East" stands in sharp contrast with Herod and the Jewish leaders. Guided by a star (and thus recalling the story of Balaam and Balak in Numbers 22–24 where the threat of the wicked king against Moses and the Israelites fails because of God's intervention), these outsiders come searching for the place of the Messiah's birth in order to pay homage to the "king of the Jews." Yet Herod and his court who have the benefit of the Scriptures and therefore know that Bethlehem is to be the place of the Messiah's birth, respond with dismay and hostility. Herod's treachery becomes apparent in the sequel to the story (2:16-18). The Magi go to Bethlehem and offer homage to the child Messiah. But Herod plots a massacre of all the children of Bethlehem in order to destroy Jesus.

Once again divine intervention in the form of dreams protects Jesus. The Magi are warned in a dream not to report back to Herod (2:12), and in another dream, Joseph is warned by an angel to gather his family and flee to Egypt for refuge.

The evangelist encases this scene in a marvelous Old Testament tapestry. The scenario of a wicked king seeking the death of the Messiah, the killing of the firstborn to ensure his murderous intent, and the saving of the child through miraculous intervention places on Jesus' shoulders the mantle of Moses, who was also destined by God to save his people. Much of this scenario recalls the events concerning Moses' birth as recorded in Exodus and amplified in popular traditions such as those found in Josephus, Philo, and other Jewish writers.[6] To this tapestry of allusion and typology, Matthew adds explicit fulfillment quotations. The citation of Hosea 11:1 ("Out of Egypt I called my son") in Matthew 2:15 links the history of Jesus with Israel's own exile and the exodus event. At the same time, Matthew reaffirms the profound identity of Jesus as God's son. The citation of Jeremiah 31:15 (see Matt 2:18) links the tragedy of the killing of the children with another terrible chapter of Israel's history when the people were deported into exile by Assyria. Thus the infant Jesus seems to recapitulate the whole span of Israel's experience.

At the same time, the threats to Jesus in the infancy narrative also direct the reader's attention forward in the gospel to the story of the passion that looms as the climax of Matthew's narrative (chaps. 26–27). Once again the leaders in Jerusalem will conspire against Jesus, but then, too, despite death God will rescue the beloved Son.

THE WAY TO NAZARETH (2:19-23)

This scene concludes the saga of events surrounding the birth of Jesus and projects the reader toward the opening of Jesus' mission in Galilee. Divine intervention continues to guide the story. Joseph is informed in a dream that Herod is dead and the time for the child Jesus to return to Israel is at hand. The words of the angel continue the link between Jesus and Moses; Moses, too, is informed by God that those who sought his life are dead (cf. Matt

2:20 and Exod 4:19). Matthew continues the mood of threat against Jesus and his family. Archelaus, the son of Herod, is a despot in the manner of his father, and so Joseph is warned in yet another dream not to return to their Davidic home in Bethlehem but to seek refuge in Nazareth of Galilee.

The entrance of Jesus into Galilee is important for Matthew. He adds a fulfillment quotation to signal the moment in 2:23 and will do so again in 4:15-16, as Jesus leaves Nazareth to take up his mission in Capernaum. The text in 2:23—"he will be called a Nazorean"—is enigmatic and reflects no specific Old Testament scripture. Matthew may be playing on the word "sprig" *(neser),* an image applied to the Messiah, the son of Jesse in the beautiful passage of Isaiah 11:1, or to the term "nazirite," dedicated to God as in the case of Samson (Judg 13:5, 7). In any case, the immediate purpose is to assure the reader that Jesus' origin in Nazareth, a tradition Matthew had already received from Mark's gospel, was not an arbitrary historical fact. The circuitous and danger-filled route from Bethlehem to Egypt to Nazareth of Galilee had been guided by God's provident hand.

Matthew's infancy narrative has a sober quality quite unlike that of Luke. This is a Jesus whose life is threatened by a tyrant, who narrowly escapes genocide, whose family must go into exile and cannot return home. Jesus comes to Nazareth and the eventual arena of his ministry as a displaced person. In so portraying the opening scenes of Jesus' life, Matthew not only ties Jesus to the hopes and sufferings of Israel's history but prepares the reader for what is to come. The Messiah Jesus will endure rejection from his own people and their leaders and will face again the threat of death.

AT THE JORDAN (3:1-17)

A new setting, the Jordan River and the Judean wilderness, and a new character in the story, John the Baptist, usher in the next scene of Matthew's prologue, the baptism of Jesus. For the first time Matthew links up with his main source, the gospel of Mark, from whom most of this story comes. Matthew, however, enriches the narrative with judgment sayings from Q (Matt 3:7-10, cf. Luke 3:7-9; Matt 3:12, cf. Luke 3:17).

Powerful themes crowd this scene. First of all, the baptismal story continues Matthew's focus on the identity of Jesus. His coming is announced by the great prophet John, whose bearing and ministry evoke that of Elijah (the camel's hair and belt identify the prophet Elijah the Tishbite in 2 Kgs 1:8). John's message is that the final age of salvation is at hand and that Jesus, who is far greater than John, will usher in this decisive moment. John baptizes with water as a sign of repentance; Jesus will baptize with the Holy Spirit, the mark of the end time.

Even more compelling than the testimony of the prophet John is the voice from heaven that accompanies the moment of baptism. As Jesus emerges from the waters of baptism, the heavens break open, the Spirit of God descends on Jesus, and a voice from heaven declares: "This is my Son, the Beloved, with whom I am well pleased" (3:17). The words, drawn substantially from Mark's account (Mark 1:11), evoke the enthronement Psalm 2:7 and Isaiah 42:1. This emphatic description of Jesus as God's Son at the moment of baptism continues what was already declared in the infancy narrative: Jesus' origin is from God and he has a profound bond of kinship with God.[7]

To this christological focus, Matthew adds other characteristic interests in the baptismal story. John calls for repentance in view of the advent of God's reign; Jesus himself will do the same at the beginning of his own mission (see 4:17). Matthew reinforces this message by two contrasting examples, a trend that will continue throughout the gospel. The negative example is that of the Jewish leaders. Where Luke's account speaks of the "multitudes" who come out for baptism, Matthew refers to the "Pharisees and Sadducees" (cf. Luke 3:7 and Matt 3:7). The ritual they undertake does not reflect the reality of their lives and John excoriates them: "You brood of vipers! . . . Bear fruit worthy of repentance." The insistence on good deeds, rather than words or ritual action, as the sign of authentic discipleship is a hallmark of Matthew's theology and will be taught by Jesus throughout the gospel. Claims to be Abraham's children are meaningless without good deeds. Here, too, is a similar characteristic note. The centurion whose faith is greater than any Jesus found in Israel (8:10), the second son who goes into the field to work despite having said "no" to his father (21:28-32), those who carry out the love command even without recognizing Jesus in the midst of the least (25:31-46)— these are all examples of a consistent ethical touchstone in

Matthew's gospel. As Jesus will declare at the end of the Sermon on the Mount, it is not those who say "Lord, Lord" who will enter the kingdom of heaven, "but only the one who does the will of my Father in heaven" (7:21).

If the Jewish leaders become the stereotype example of false repentance (see especially the woes of chapter 23), Jesus himself is the model of authentic righteousness. Even though he is God's beloved Son, Jesus submits to John's ritual of repentance. The first words of Jesus in Matthew's gospel have strong significance in the gospel: "It is proper for us . . . to fulfill all righteousness" (3:15). The term "righteousness" or "justice" (the literal meaning of the Greek word *dikaiosune*) can refer either to the "justice" or salvation that God steadfastly lavishes on Israel or to the proper and faithful response human beings return to God. It is the latter sense that the word seems to have here and in other occurrences in Matthew's gospel (see, particularly, 5:20). The entire purpose of Jesus' mission is to "fulfill" (the verb *plēroō*, the same used in the fulfillment quotations) or faithfully carry out all that his Father asks. In Matthew's perspective Jesus is God's Son not only because of his mysterious origin from God but also because of his faithful and loving obedience. This commitment to doing God's will is a powerful ethical motif of Matthew's gospel, one demonstrated finally in Jesus' obedient death.[8]

A corollary to Matthew's emphasis on faithful and obedient action as the hallmark of authentic discipleship is his emphasis on judgment. Throughout the gospel, but particularly in the eschatological discourse of chapters 24–25, Matthew describes the result of infidelity. Those who live without integrity will experience God's judgment. So John warns the leaders at the baptism that the ax is at the root of the tree and the Messiah brandishes the winnowing fan (3:7-10).

THE DESERT TEST (4:1-11)

The final scene of the prologue plunges farther into the desert. Here, too, another character is introduced, the ominous figure of the devil. Struggles with demonic powers will continue in Matthew's story, but no longer will Satan play a direct role, being blended instead into the arena of human suffering as Jesus carries out his messianic work of healings and exorcisms. Mark's account of the desert test is brief and cryptic (Mark 1:12-13); both Matthew and Luke (cf. Luke 4:1-13) use material from Q to greatly expand this scene.

The content of the scene is a weave of biblical citations, drawn particularly from Deuteronomy.[9] Thereby, Matthew once again relates the life of Jesus to the fulfillment of the Scriptures. Just as Jesus recapitulated Israel's epic experiences of exodus and exile in the infancy narrative, so here Jesus relives the wilderness test of Israel. If Israel's obedience wavered during those forty years, Jesus is steadfastly faithful. The demon's enticements are rebuffed by appeals to God's word. The mocking tone used by the demon—"If you are the Son of God . . ."—has its chilling echo in the mockeries that will be hurled at the dying Messiah on the cross (see 27:39-43). From beginning to end of the gospel story, the Matthean Jesus remains the faithful Son of God.

The order of the temptations in Matthew is significant. In Luke's version, the climactic encounter takes place in Jerusalem on the pinnacle of the Temple (Luke 4:9), coinciding with Luke's great interest in Jerusalem as the end point of Jesus' mission and the starting point of the community. Matthew will end his story on a mountaintop in Galilee (28:16-20), and at several key points in his story mountains serve as places of revelation.[10] The great discourse of chapters 5–7 will take place on a mountain (5:1), Jesus will heal on a mountaintop (15:29-30); and the transfiguration is on a mountain (17:1-2). As the prologue draws to a close Matthew leaves the reader with a tableau of mythic proportions. On a mountaintop from which all the kingdoms of the world and their glory are visible and in words that recall Deuteronomy 6:13, the Messiah Jesus refuses the lure of evil by proclaiming the abiding commitment of his life and mission: "Worship the Lord your God, and serve only him" (Matt 4:10).

Serving as a prologue or overture to the entire gospel, the first few chapters of Matthew's story have drawn the reader deep into the mystery of Jesus' person and signaled many of the great motifs that will course through the rest of the narrative.

CHAPTER 9

JESUS:
MESSIAH IN
WORD AND DEED
(4:12–10:42)

The heart of Matthew's portrayal of Jesus and his vision of the community's mission is found in this section of his gospel. There is a decisive change of scene; after his baptism at the Jordan and his desert test, Jesus reenters Galilee and begins his messianic mission of teaching and healing. That same redemptive mission will be entrusted to the disciples. Four main segments make up this section:

1) 4:12-25—An introductory or transitional segment that brings Jesus into Galilee, describes the call of the first disciples, and summarizes Jesus' ministry.
2) 5:1–7:28—The Sermon on the Mount, the first great discourse of the gospel.

3) 8:1–9:35—The first account of Jesus' healing ministry.
4) 9:36–10:42—The mission discourse.

Most of the narrative sections come from Mark, but Matthew freely rearranges his source as he builds his overall portrayal of Jesus. The evangelist sketches the content and scope of Jesus' ministry in epic terms—he teaches and heals throughout Galilee ("in *their* synagogues" Matthew pointedly notes), proclaiming the good news of the kingdom. His fame spreads throughout all Syria, and the sick and tormented are brought to Jesus for healing from virtually the whole compass of Israel: Galilee, the Decapolis, Jerusalem, Judea, and from beyond the Jordan. Even before any single incident is described, Matthew has provided the reader with a vivid picture of the impact of Jesus' messianic mission. The promise embodied in the child born in Bethlehem and predicted by John at the Jordan now breaks into fulfillment.

The summary of 4:23, with its emphasis on Jesus' teaching and healing, will be repeated in 9:35, thereby bracketing the intervening chapters, with chapters 5–7 presenting Jesus as teacher, defining the fundamental character of Jesus' message, and chapters 8–9 presenting Jesus as *healer*, a dimension equally crucial to Matthew's portrayal of Jesus as Messiah and savior.

Jesus as Teacher	*Jesus as Healer*	*The Mission of the*
4:23	9:35	*Community*
(chaps. 5-7)	(chaps. 8-9)	(chap. 10)

Most of the material in the Sermon comes from Q or material special to Matthew and has virtually no parallels in Mark. The mission discourse that follows in chapter 10 is also an integral part of this first great section of the gospel. Here Matthew blends material drawn from Mark (particularly the call of the apostles in Mark 3:13-19 and 6:7-13 and the travails of the mission predicted in Mark 13:9-13) and Q (see, e.g., Matt 10:26-33; cf. Luke 12:2-9).

The "crowds" of the sick and those in need form a backdrop for all of these chapters. For the Sermon on the Mount Jesus leaves the crowds and goes up the mountain and addresses his disciples; the sermon is addressed directly to the disciples (5:1-2), but the crowds are never lost to view.[1] They marvel at Jesus' words at the conclusion of the sermon (7:28-29) and are present as Jesus begins his ministry of healing (8:1). The concluding summary of 9:35 repeats that of 4:23 and brings the reader back to the epic scene that began the sermon (4:23-25). Jesus sees the crowds once more and is moved with compassion for them (9:36). And once more he summons his disciples and instructs them on the urgency of their mission (9:37 and following). The mission discourse, therefore, is triggered by the same situation that prompted Jesus' teaching and healing: the urgency of God's coming reign and desperate need on the part of God's people. Now that mission would be formally given to the disciples themselves.

We will consider each segment of Matthew's portrayal in turn, not attempting a detailed commentary but noting features and characteristic motifs critical for interpreting the meaning of the text.

DAWN IN GALILEE (4:12-25)

This passage is a transition from the events of the prologue into the body of Matthew's narrative. John is arrested, thus signaling the close of his ministry that was destined to prepare for the Messiah.[2] And, Matthew notes, Jesus "withdrew" into Galilee, returning to the region where he and his family had sought refuge at the end of the infancy narrative (see 2:23; 3:13). Now the mission of Jesus can begin, so he leaves Nazareth and makes his home in Capernaum by the sea (note the comment in 9:1, "his own town"), the region where Matthew (following Mark's lead) will place most of Jesus' ministry. In effect, the evangelist uses this section to set the stage for the mission of Jesus.

Matthew underscores the significance of Jesus' first footfall in the arena of his mission. The Old Testament fulfillment quotation in 4:15-16 is freely adapted from Isaiah 9:1-3 to express Matthew's vision of the scope and meaning of what Jesus is about to do. Capernaum is in the "territory of Zebulun and Naphtali," two of the Jewish tribes deported by Assyria, once again recalling the anguish and loss experienced by God's people. Galilee was in the heart of Israel; thereby, this setting for Jesus' mission keeps faith with Matthew's understanding that Jesus' mission was first to Israel (see 10:5; 15:24). But it was also "Galilee of the Gentiles," signaling the eventual breakthrough of that mission to the nations

99

(28:16-20) and the incidents in the gospel where Jesus will encounter Gentiles (see 8:5-13; 15:21-28). For both Jew and Gentile the dawn of Jesus' mission would bring light into darkness and dispel the shadow of death.

Matthew's interest in the "geography" of Jesus' ministry is noteworthy. Jesus will teach and heal "throughout Galilee" (4:23). His fame spreads "throughout all Syria" (4:24). And the crowds stream to him from virtually all points of the compass: Galilee (in Matthew's mind extending at least from Nazareth to Capernaum and the surrounding regions); the Decapolis (the league of Gentile cities on the eastern and southern shores of the Sea of Galilee); Jerusalem and Judea (the whole southern region); and the Transjordan (by which Matthew presumably means the east bank of the Jordan). Missing from this picture is the region of Samaria, considered out of bounds from a Jewish perspective, and the far northwestern regions such as Tyre and Sidon (which are included in Mark's summary in 3:8). Jesus will go to the borders of Tyre and Sidon in 15:21. Matthew's "bias" toward the heart of Israel (Judea, Galilee, and the Transjordan) and the north and eastern regions (Syria and the Decapolis) may offer some hint to the evangelist's own location. At the time the gospel was probably written, the Roman province of Syria extended into most of the region mentioned by Matthew in this passage.[3] More important for Matthew, the geographical spread of Jesus' fame illustrates the power of Jesus' words and deeds and points the

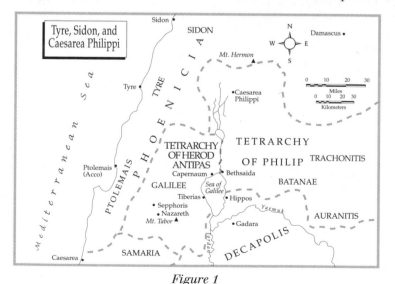

Figure 1

reader to the far horizon of the Christian mission, which will move beyond Israel to the nations.

Other aspects of this rich passage are also important. In 4:17, Matthew introduces the keynote of Jesus' preaching: "Repent, for the kingdom of heaven has come near" (cf. Mark 1:14-15). This repeats the message already announced by John (3:1-2). John's message and ritual of repentance were anticipatory; through Jesus' teaching and healing the reign of God would actually be experienced (see Matt 12:28). Matthew notes the decisive moment—"from that time"; Jesus' proclamation of God's reign begins now with his healing and teaching and will continue through the gospel story.[4]

Still following Mark's sequence, Matthew introduces the first disciples of Jesus (4:18-22; cf. Mark 1:16-20). They are called to follow Jesus and to share in his mission of fishing for people (an image that will be repeated in the Matthean parable of the net, 13:47-50). By introducing the call of the disciples here, prior to his epic description of Jesus' ministry in chapters 5 through 9, the evangelist signals the strong ecclesial interest of this gospel. The disciples will be present for the Sermon on the Mount (5:1-2) and Jesus' healings, thereby being prepared for the mission instruction of chapter 10 (see 9:37-38).

One other feature of this transition passage should be noted. Matthew gives strong emphasis to Jesus' work of healing. Although the summary passage of 4:23 also cites his preaching and teaching, the crowds come to Jesus from all over Israel to be healed (4:24-25). Matthew will not present miracle stories until chapter 8, but the reader encounters Jesus as healer prior to the discourse material of chapters 5–7. This emphasis is echoed in the mission instruction to the Twelve, which gives strong prominence to healing and exorcism (see Matt 10:1, 8). This is consistent with Matthew's description of Jesus as the "savior" of Israel (1:21). For some interpreters it also highlights the initiative of God working through Jesus, thereby emphasizing the element of grace and giving proper balance to Matthew's characteristic emphasis on good deeds that will dominate the Sermon on the Mount.[5]

THE SERMON ON THE MOUNT (5:1–7:28)

The Sermon on the Mount is undoubtedly the most famous passage of Matthew's gospel. No interpreter of the gospel could ever ignore this compelling and complex discourse. Much of the material in the sermon is drawn from Q and parallels Luke's "Sermon on the Plain" (Luke 6:17-49), but Matthew's discourse is much more extensive, gathering other material from Q and adding his own expansions and editing.[6] The discourse is presented as the first and defining moment of Jesus' teaching, probing to the heart of what it means to be a faithful child of God in the world.

Setting and Structure

Matthew carefully sets the stage for the discourse. The foregoing scene portrays the full impact of Jesus' redemptive mission, as crowds stream to him from every quarter seeking and finding healing (4:23-25). The sight of the crowds prompts Jesus to ascend the mountain and sit down in the manner of a Jewish teacher to address his disciples. As we will note, although the disciples are the ones directly addressed, Matthew conceives of the Sermon as addressed through them to the crowds (see the reaction of the crowd in 7:28). All of these elements—the crowds, the disciples, Jesus' magistral manner, and the mountaintop location (a traditional place of revelation)—give a sense of expectation for what is to follow. Although Matthew does it subtly, the comparison is inevitable with Moses' ascent to Sinai to receive from God the revealed Torah (see Exod 19:16-25).

The discourse is neither the transcript of a single, cohesive speech nor a loose collection of independent sayings. It has a discernible order of four sections, a preamble followed by three main parts, but resists any reduction to a single overarching theme:

1) *5:3-16.* The first section is taken up with the Beatitudes and serves as a preamble to the overall discourse.

2) *5:17-48.* Jesus' interpretation of the Torah commands this section, first in the programmatic sayings of 5:17-20 and then in a series of antitheses, 5:21-48.

3) *6:1–7:12.* The thematic verse about authentic piety (6:1) explains the grouping of most of this material around issues of almsgiving, prayer, and fasting (see 6:1-18). The sayings that follow in 6:19–7:12 are more difficult to incorporate but certainly take up motifs of the sermon and Matthew's theology as a whole. The so-called golden rule with its characteristic emphasis on fulfillment of the law punctuates the section and recalls the preceding material of 5:17-48.

4) *7:13-27.* The sermon concludes with exhortations to authentic action and warnings of judgment. Verses 7:28-29 provide the transition to the next section, which portrays the healing ministry of Jesus.

Fundamental Motifs of the Sermon

Each section of the Sermon contains important themes not only for the discourse itself but for Matthew's gospel as a whole.

1) *The Beatitudes (5:3-16).* This introductory segment alerts the reader to the scope of Matthew's theological vision. Through the beatitudes the Matthean Jesus links the promises of the end time with the status and dispositions of the present. Beatitudes or blessings on certain people or virtues are found in the Bible, particularly the Wisdom literature, and in other ancient writings.[7] In Deuteronomy Moses directs both blessings and woes to the Israelites as they are about to cross the Jordan into the promised land (see Deut 27–28). Luke seems to follow this pattern of beatitudes and woes in his Sermon on the Plain (see Luke 6:20-26). Matthew, however, lists only beatitudes here, expanding Luke's list and reserving "woes" for his critique of the religious leaders in chapter 23.

The Beatitudes cluster in two roughly discernible groups. The first four (5:3-6) bless those whom the Bible typically saw as defended by God: the poor, those who mourn, the meek, and those who hunger and thirst for justice. These are promised the liberating experience of God's Kingdom whose advent was already announced by Jesus. To the explicit promise of the first beatitude—"theirs is the kingdom of heaven"—are added those experiences typically expected for the end time when God would rule: comfort, the security of land, satisfaction from hunger and thirst. The second set of beatitudes underscores the kind of virtuous action that will be taught by Jesus in the sermon and throughout the gospel: acting mercifully (already illustrated in the "righteous man" Joseph; see 1:19), being pure of heart, working for reconciliation and peace, enduring persecution for the sake of justice.

But Matthew's strong ethical inclination blurs the distinction between the two sets of beatitudes. He is not content, for example, with blessing simply the "poor" as in Luke 6:20 but adds "poor *in spirit.*" The blessing on those who hunger in Luke 6:21 becomes hunger and thirst *"for righteousness"* in Matthew. This does not mean, as some interpreters seem to imply, that Matthew waters down Luke's strong prophetic stance on behalf of those in need by espousing a more abstract spiritual view. Rather, Matthew's bias throughout the sermon is to underscore human response to the gospel by means of authentic virtue and good deeds. As indicated in Jesus' first words of the gospel (3:15), this is what being "just" or "righteous" *(dikaios)* means. Blessing those who are "poor in spirit" or those who "hunger and thirst for justice," that is, emphasizing an interior disposition or stance and not simply a particular circumstance or status, reflects that ethical perspective.

Equally important is the eschatological perspective of the beatitudes because it underwrites the entire discourse and is the foundation for the ethical teaching of the gospel as a whole. For Matthew—as for most of the New Testament—the full experience of the reign of God was in the future. Then the full promise of God would be realized and humanity would live as God had intended. But through the teaching and example of Jesus, one could anticipate the reality of the kingdom of God *now* and live a life reflective of that ultimate truth to be revealed in the fullness of God's reign. Therefore acts of mercy, of reconciliation and peacemaking, of seeking justice were in accord with the intent of God and with the true nature of the human person created by God and redeemed by Jesus.

The concluding beatitudes turn into exhortation for the disciples, shifting from the third person to the second ("Blessed are *you . . .*") and indicating the rhetorical purpose of the sermon as a whole. The disciples are to be "salt" and "light" for others (5:13-16). Matthew views the sermon as first of all formative of the community itself and then, through the community's example and teaching, given to the world.[8]

2) *The Fulfillment of the Law (5:17-48).* Coming as the first segment of Jesus' inaugural discourse and touching on an issue of capital importance to Matthew and his community, this section is a fundamental expression of the gospel's theology. A series of keynote sayings (5:17-20) are followed by six antitheses (5:21-48) comparing the teaching of Jesus with the demands of the law and other interpretations of it.

The saying of Jesus in 5:17, a text unique to Matthew (although with echoes in Luke 16:16-17), is programmatic for this gospel: "Do not think that I have come to abolish the law or the prophets;

I have come not to abolish but to fulfill." This accords with Matthew's conviction, already illustrated in the opening scenes of the gospel and explicitly confirmed in his fulfillment quotations, that Jesus is the full flowering of Israel's hopes forged in its history and expressed in its Scriptures. Jesus' teaching does not run counter to the law but fulfills its very intent and purpose.

This perspective runs throughout the sermon and into the gospel as a whole. The sayings about the enduring validity of the law and the exhortation to attend to even its "least commandment" (5:18-19), as well as the demand for "greater righteousness" on the part of Jesus' disciples (5:20), flow from the conviction that the teaching of Jesus represents the full revelation of what God intended through the law and that the advent of God's reign is now urgently present.

The six antitheses of 5:21-48 vividly illustrate the spirit of Jesus' teaching and what "greater righteousness" requires. Each of them begins with a phrase—"you have heard that it was said . . . , but I say to you"—that contrasts the teaching of Jesus with either explicit statements of the law (as, for example, permission to divorce as expressed in Deut 24:1 or the law of "talion" from Exod 21:24) or traditional interpretations of the law. All of the points of law have to do with human relationships: anger and reconciliation; adultery; divorce; true speech; retaliation; love of enemies. And in each instance the teaching of Jesus asks for a more demanding and a more interiorly rooted response. As the term "antitheses" implies, some interpreters emphasize the contrast between Jesus' teaching and that of the law. However, Matthew 5:17 suggests that in the eyes of the evangelist, Jesus' teaching "fulfilled" rather than abolished the law, even if in some instances his teaching exceeded the demands of the law and in so doing seemed to contravene it.

Both the first antithesis calling for reconciliation with an alienated brother or sister (5:21-26) and the last calling for love of enemies (5:43-48) stress the importance of acting out of love rather than enmity and thereby encase this section with a theme of great importance to Matthew's gospel. The final antithesis of 5:43-48 is most notable. Here Matthew lays out diametrically opposed human responses to an enemy's provocation: hatred or love. The follower of Jesus responds with love rather than hatred because this is how one's "Father in heaven" acts. The greater righteousness of the disciple means seeking to be "perfect" or "complete" (the sense of the Greek word *teleios* used in 5:48) as God is "perfect"; in this context Matthew describes God's characteristic action as indiscriminate, gratuitous love toward the enemy.[9]

This remarkable emphasis on reconciliation and love points to a fundamental principle of law for Matthew's gospel. The formulation of the "golden rule" in 7:12, the enunciation of the principle of mercy in the controversy stories of 9:10-13 and 12:1-8 (see the citation of Hosea 6:6 in 9:13 and 12:7), and especially the emphasis on the love command as the principle for interpretation of law in 22:40 (contrast Mark 12:33) flow from this same perspective. The law is to be respected, not abolished, but its interpretation is to be ruled by the love command. This conviction is eloquently stated in 23:23 as the Matthean Jesus attacks the scribes and Pharisees for their false teaching and inauthentic lives: "You tithe mint, dill, and cummin, and have neglected the weightier matters of the law: justice and mercy and faith. It is these you ought to have practiced without neglecting the others."

3) *Authentic Piety (6:1–7:12).* The "greater righteousness" demanded of the disciples is illustrated in a new way in this section of the discourse. The opening verse of the chapter provides the key; literally, it reads: "Beware of practicing your righteousness before others in order to be seen by them" (6:1). In the subsequent verses Matthew singles out three traditional expressions of Jewish piety—almsgiving, prayer, and fasting (6:1-18). In each case negative examples are used as a foil to illustrate authentic piety, either on the part of the "hypocrites" whose actions are done merely for show and do not reflect their interior spirit, or "Gentiles" who are ignorant of authentic piety (6:7, 32). The piety of the disciple must spring from an interior bond with God and not be calculated for gain or human praise. God knows the human heart intimately and can read its spirit. The intriguing emphasis on giving, praying, and fasting "in secret" reflects this emphasis of Matthew (6:4; 6:6; 6:18).

At the heart of this section is the Lord's Prayer (6:9-13), which is presented by Matthew as the model for all Christian prayer: "Pray then in this way" (6:9).[10] Matthew's version is more elaborate than that of Luke (cf. Luke 11:2-4) and echoes some of the language and themes found in ancient Jewish prayer texts.[11] Above all, it is a distillation of motifs that run through the sermon and the gospel as a whole. The prayer addresses God in characteristic Matthean terms as "our Father in heaven." The first three "you" petitions of the prayer call for reverence for God's name, for the coming of the Kingdom, and for God's will to be done—the latter emphasis reflective of the powerful ethical thrust of the sermon itself. The latter half expresses raw human need: for sustenance, for forgiveness, and for protection from the power of evil. Reliance on God when under assault from evil was precisely the example given by Jesus in his own desert test (4:1-11), and that same source of strength would be the object of Jesus' prayer in Gethsemane (see 26:36-46). The need for bread and God's desire to feed the hungry would be dramatically illustrated in Jesus' feedings of the multitudes (14:13-21; 15:32-39). The verses that follow the conclusion of the prayer (6:14-15) amplify the theme of forgiveness that is a special preoccupation with Matthew already evident in the antitheses (see 5:21-26, 43-48) and to be reinforced in 7:12 as well as in the community discourse of chapter 18.

The remaining portion of this section (6:19–7:12) contains sayings somewhat loosely strung together but still focusing on the bond of love and trust between God and the disciple that underwrites all authentic piety and right action. Thus one's heart is to be placed "where neither moth nor rust consumes and where thieves do not break in and steal" (6:20). The eye is to be kept clear and the heart undivided (6:22-23, 24). Rather than expending one's energy on useless worry, the disciple should take wisdom from the birds and the lilies to know that God will provide what is needed for life (6:25-34). The saying in 6:33 drives home the lesson that much of the discourse proclaims: "Strive first for the kingdom of God and its righteousness, and all these things will be given to you as well." The disciples are urged not to judge others harshly but rather to be aware of their own weakness (7:1-5). The section ends emphasizing the themes of God's loving attentiveness to his children and urging the disciple to pray confidently for what is needed (7:7-11).

4) *Doing the Will of the Heavenly Father (7:13-27).* The return to the theme of "the law and the prophets" in the transition verse 7:12 directs the sermon to its closing section where the disciples are urged to put Jesus' teaching into practice. A string of metaphors confronts the reader with alternative choices: There is a wide or a narrow gate, an easy or hard road, false or true prophets, bad or

good trees, foolish or wise builders of houses. The fundamental message of each is the same: The words of Jesus must be translated into the commitments and actions of one's life. It is not enough simply to know and say the right words—"Lord, Lord"—one must also do the will of the heavenly Father (7:21).

The mixture of exhortation to action and threat of judgment found here at the conclusion of the discourse is typical of Matthew.[12] The threat of judgment is in a sense the flip side of the gospel's emphasis on action. The disciple is to be responsible and to live out the reality of the gospel. Failure to do so runs counter to the fundamental reality of life intended by God and therefore necessarily has disastrous consequences. Hence the judgment texts are warnings about the inherently destructive nature of evil conduct.

Interpreting the Sermon

Few gospel passages have challenged interpreters more than the Sermon on the Mount. How is the Christian reader to absorb its specific and seemingly radical demands? In the history of Christianity two key questions emerged: (1) To whom is the sermon directed—to all Christians or only to select ones? and (2) How are the specific injunctions of the sermon to be understood, as "laws" or impossible ideals or in some other way?

At some periods in Christian history, the force of the sermon was blunted by narrowing the scope of its audience. The radical demands of the sermon were meant for not all disciples but only those who had vowed a life of perfection as a monk or religious sister or for Christians who did not have to live public lives or "hold office" in a world filled with compromise. Few would defend this view today and from the perspective of Matthew's gospel there is no hint that the discourse is meant for a select group within the community. As we have noted, in the narrative setting of Matthew the sermon is given most immediately to the "disciples" who ascend the mountain with Jesus (5:1). At this point the "crowds" are in the background. But Matthew clearly indicates that Jesus' discourse is not meant solely for the disciples; at the conclusion of the sermon the crowds marvel at Jesus' teaching and his authority (7:28-29). Therefore the sermon is directed first to the community of disciples called by Jesus (see 4:18-22) but not confined to them. From Matthew's perspective Jesus reveals God's truth intended for all. Jesus' teaching fulfills the intent of the Law, which Judaism and early Christianity saw as written on the human heart (see Paul's expression of this in Rom 2:14-16). Jesus reveals the ways of God and therefore the very structure of ultimate reality.

If the sermon is directed to all, the followers of Jesus first of all and then all humanity, how is one to respond to its specific and concrete demands such as taking no oaths, going an extra mile, or offering no resistance to injury? For some interpreters the injunctions of the sermon should be understood as "ideals," which describe the heroically virtuous human being. As such the demands of the sermon are meant to prod and inspire the ordinary Christian but are not meant as specific requirements or norms. Others, in the classical Protestant tradition, have suggested that the very purpose of the sermon was to confront the sinful disciple with the impossibility of virtue short of the transformation of God's grace. Reflecting on Jesus' demands in the sermon should lead sinners to throw themselves on God's mercy in a spirit of humble repentance. A variant on this was to conclude that Jesus' teaching was a kind of "emergency ethic" based on the conviction that the end of the world was approaching and thereby demanding an urgent and heroic response on the part of the disciple. But here, too, reading the text of Matthew gives no indication that these kinds of conditions were assumed. Jesus' teaching is laid before the reader without qualification or hesitation.

How, then, is the reader to gauge the moral authority of the sermon? Some things are clear:

1) Matthew builds the sermon around a theological vision. The God of Israel is close to his children, attentive to human need, gracious with forgiveness, and intent on bringing creation to its full life. This experience of God is to be the pattern for all human behavior.

2) Equally compelling is the gospel's conviction that in Jesus God's will for humanity is being revealed in a definitive and urgent way. Matthew uses the metaphor of God's reign, the metaphor that undoubtedly the historical Jesus used as the keynote of his own ministry. Thus Matthew works from a decidedly eschatological perspective; that is to say, the fullness of redemption awaited for the end time is beginning to be actually experienced in the ministry of Jesus and in those characteristic human responses of justice or righteousness that will typify the end time.

3) The specific instructions of the sermon draw on these theological assumptions. Acting with compassion, using honest speech, marital love that will not dissolve, sexuality that is not exploitative, reconciliation and love rather than retribution and enmity—all are, from the gospel's perspective, characteristic actions of those who live under God's reign.

4) Therefore the specific instructions of Jesus are not "impossible ideals," although they do reflect what will characterize sons and daughters of God only in the fullness of the Kingdom. They are not meant simply to reveal human sinfulness, even though the gospel is very aware that the disciples of Jesus are weak and fallible as they make their way toward to the fullness of God's reign. Nor does the concreteness of these teachings disqualify them as ethical demands, even though they are not in a legal format and require thoughtful interpretation.

5) The teachings of the sermon, therefore, are best understood as "ethics by example" or "focal instances," revealing to the Christian how the teaching of Jesus is to be lived.[13] As Lisa Cahill has noted, the specific character of many of Jesus' injunctions in the sermon stands in deliberate tension with the way we usually live and think. Jesus' sayings prompt the reader to extend the perspective of the gospel to other such instances. The commands to "love the enemy," to "pray for the persecutor," or "to turn the other cheek," prompt the disciple to ask what among several courses of action available to me is the one that is truly meaningful and forgiving—in other words, the "examples" of the sermon have moral force, guiding the follower of Jesus to find similar ways of responding that reflect the values and vision of the gospel.

Therefore, the gospel of Matthew sees these teachings of Jesus not as mere examples or ideals but as moral imperatives, as revelatory examples or "focal instances" that instruct the Christian on how one is to live in the world—even while conscious that the capacity of each Christian to respond to the gospel is something that develops over time and that the array of alternative moral actions available will always be limited.

JESUS THE HEALER (8:1–9:34)

Matthew signals a new turn in the gospel story by means of a transitional phrase that will find echoes at the end of each of the five great discourses of the gospel (7:28; see 11:1; 13:53; 19:1; 26:1). At the conclusion of the discourse, the compelling words and commanding authority of Jesus the teacher leave the crowds astounded. Now Matthew will illustrate the other dimension in his majestic portrayal of Jesus—his power to heal. The "crowds" had first come to Jesus for healing (see 4:24-25), and he will not disappoint them.

As we have noted, many interpreters see a topical arrangement of the ten miracle stories Matthew places in these two chapters.[14] As Hans Joachim Held and others have pointed out, themes of christology (i.e., Jesus' power to heal) dominate in 8:1-17, that of discipleship in 8:18–9:17 and faith in 9:17-34. But the motifs are not neatly confined to respective sections, and other currents are detectable such as Matthew's concern with the response of Israel's leaders and glimpses of the mission to the Gentiles.[15]

At the outset, Matthew sets the scene in Capernaum, the town in Galilee that will be the centerpoint of Jesus' ministry (see 4:13). He is on his way to Capernaum when the first story, the healing of the leper, takes place (8:2). Jesus will leave Capernaum to go "to the other side" of the sea for the healing of the Gadarenes (8:18) but later will return to "his own town" (9:1).

Matthew draws all but one of the miracle stories from Mark; the cure of the centurion's servant comes from Q (compare Matt 8:5-13 and Luke 7:1-10) as does the material on discipleship in Matthew 8:18-22 (cf. Luke 9:57-62). Matthew makes some changes in the sequence of Mark's material but still shows contact with his source. Besides grouping Mark's stories in one continuous section, Matthew also substantially abbreviates most of them. Many of Mark's narrative details are omitted with the focus of the story falling hard on the dramatic action of Jesus and his decisive words. Thus the concisely narrated stream of Jesus' mighty works in these two chapters draws the reader into Matthew's characteristic perspective.

1) *Jesus the Healing Servant (8:1-17).* The first segment has a clear personality: Three miracles, each of them illustrating the majestic power and extraordinary compassion of Jesus the healer, lead into the fulfillment text of 8:17. As Jesus comes down from the mountains the crowds surge forward (8:1), recalling the scene at the beginning of the Sermon on the Mount (see 4:23-25). The story of the leper is the first to be narrated (8:1-4). More powerful

than even the great prophet Elisha who had cleansed Naaman the Syrian, Jesus heals this man from a malady that reminded the biblical peoples of the very power of death (see the detailed discussion of leprosy in Lev 13–14). Matthew's version of the story puts the spotlight on the words of Jesus: "I do choose. Be made clean!" (8:3). The cure of Simon's mother-in-law is similar. No word is exchanged—the focus is entirely on Jesus' power and commitment to heal. Jesus enters Peter's house, sees the sick woman, and immediately restores her to health (8:14-15).

The intervening story about the centurion and his servant is more complex (8:5-13). The exchange between Jesus and the centurion forcefully stresses Jesus' unique authority: He can heal with simply a word. But the fact that this man is a Roman centurion and Jesus' amazement at his faith leads the story into another set of Matthean concerns, the response of Israel and the mission to the Gentiles.[16] The faith of this Gentile outshines what Jesus has experienced from his own people (9:10). This inspires Jesus to a vision of the future: "Many will come from east and west and will eat with Abraham and Isaac and Jacob in the kingdom of heaven, while the heirs of the kingdom will be thrown into the outer darkness" (8:11-12; cf. Luke 13:28-29). The motif of the procession of the nations to Israel was well known in biblical and Jewish literature (see, e.g., Isa 2:2-4; 25:6; Mic 4:1-14). But usually this motif assumed that the Gentiles would stream to Zion as captives or at least to do homage to triumphant Israel. This saying of Jesus puts a new twist on the motif; the Gentiles will come not with head bent but to partake of the banquet of the kingdom of God. Jesus, the Son of Abraham (1:1), foresees a new people gathered around the table of the patriarchs. Thus the story of the centurion is another instance, along with the Magi of the infancy narrative and stories still to come, where Matthew prepares the reader both for Israel's rejection of Jesus and the mission to the Gentiles.

This first segment of the healing stories concludes with a summary of Jesus' ministry (8:16) and a decisive fulfillment quotation. The work of Jesus as healer fulfills the prophecy of Isaiah 53:4: "He has borne our infirmities / and carried our diseases." Just as Jesus' teaching fulfills the law (5:17) so his healing is also part of God's redemptive plan. It is significant that Matthew envelops Jesus as healer in the mantle of Isaiah's Suffering Servant. Through his healings the Matthean Jesus not only takes away the sufferings of God's people but bears them himself. Here is a subtle reference to the opposition and eventual death that Jesus would endure in the fulfillment of his mission.

2) *Across the Sea (8:18–9:1).* Matthew now changes the scene dramatically, and motifs of discipleship seem to dominate. Prompted once again by the sight of great crowds, Jesus decides to go to the other side of the Lake (8:18). Matthew introduces the crossing of the sea with two encounters with would-be disciples (8:19-22; cf. Luke 9:57-62), clearly suggesting that the sea journey and the mission to the Gadarenes were harbingers of the community's challenging mission yet to come. The commitment of each of those who comes forward is tested. Following the master meant leaving everything behind and made a claim on every allegiance, even one as sacred as burying one's father. Here again Matthew signals teachings on discipleship that will be even more explicit later on in the gospel.[17]

The sea story itself (8:23-27) continues Matthew's focus on the power of Jesus: He is addressed as "Lord" (8:25; cf. "teacher" in Mark 4:38) and is capable of calming the wind and the sea, evoking Old Testament motifs of God's own power over the chaos of nature.[18] The disciples' question is meant to be echoed by the reader: "What sort of man is this, that even the winds and the sea obey him?" (8:27) At the same time, this story also continues this section's reflection on discipleship. In the midst of their distress the disciples implore Jesus for relief (8:25), yet their faith remains weak. The notion of "little faith" (8:26) is a characterization of the disciples favored by Matthew.[19] As here, the symptoms of that weakness are often fear and hesitation; another sea story involving Peter and the disciples will have similar motifs (see discussion to come, 14:22-33).

The liberation of the two Gadarenes from the fierce demonic powers that hold them in their grip (8:28-34) once again demonstrates Jesus' messianic authority but now shows that this power extends beyond the boundaries of Israel, picking up a motif begun with the cure of the centurion's servant. Matthew's rendering of the story confines it to being a vivid preview of the Gentile mission that will be fully engaged only in the age of resurrection. The demons themselves seem to chide Jesus for tormenting them "before the time" (8:29, *pro kairoû*). Unlike Mark's account where Jesus interacts with the Gadarene at the conclusion of the story and actually sends the man out on mission in the Decapolis, Matthew concludes the story abruptly, with the townspeople begging this disturbing healer to leave their region (cf. Matt 8:34 and Mark 5:17-20). Only at the end of the gospel will Jesus commission the disciples to go to the nations (28:16-20).

3) *Return to Capernaum (9:1-34)*. Matthew brings the story back across the sea to Capernaum (9:1; note also that here Matthew picks up again the thread of Mark's narrative, using stories from chapter 2 of Mark's account). The string of incidents included in this segment continues the gospel's focus on themes of christology and discipleship, with new emphasis on faith.

The story of the paralytic (9:2-8, greatly simplified from Mark's version) illustrates Jesus' authority as "Son of Man" to forgive sins, a liberating power confirmed in his healing of the paralytic and acclaimed by the crowds (9:8).[20] But it is also a story that praises the faith of those who brought their disabled friend to Jesus (9:2). The hostility of the religious leaders serves as a foil to highlight Jesus' authority. But the scribes' silent accusation that Jesus "blasphemes" by claiming to forgive sins is the first direct evidence of hostility, other than Herod's attack on the infant Jesus (2:1-18), we have encountered in the gospel to this point.

The next story (9:9-13) alerts the reader to the full meaning of the healing stories. Passing by the tax booth Jesus encounters "Matthew" and calls him to be a disciple.[21] Once again the religious leaders—this time the "Pharisees"—serve as a hostile foil by complaining to the disciples about Jesus' association with "tax collectors and sinners" (9:11). This draws from Jesus another programmatic statement of his mission. He is called to be "physician" for the "sick," not for those who are well (9:12). This salvific mission of Jesus was signaled in his God-given name "Jesus" (1:21) and prophesied in the scriptures (8:17). The weight of scriptural authority is applied by Matthew once more in the conclusion of the story: The leaders are challenged to learn the meaning of the text of Hosea 6:6, "I desire mercy, not sacrifice" (9:13; see also 12:7). By means of this story Matthew extends the meaning of "healing" to Jesus' inclusive ministry to tax collectors and sinners. The healing stories are not simply a physical transformation of sick or possessed people; they extend beyond physical cures to profound spiritual transformation and healing whereby those who had been isolated or excluded are now drawn into the community and partake of its life. At the same time, the community of the "healthy"—here represented by the religious leaders who protest Jesus' actions—are challenged by Jesus' inclusive ministry. Not only Gentiles but now "the lost sheep of the house of Israel" are embraced by God's Messiah.

The encounter between the disciples of John and the disciples of Jesus confirms both the messianic authority of Jesus' mission and its radical impact (9:14-17). Jesus' disciples need not fast because the time of the messianic banquet is already here and Jesus is the "bridegroom" (although the gospel is also aware that the death of Jesus looms and, for a time, the bridegroom will be "taken away," 9:15). To use another metaphor, new wine requires fresh wineskins so that both the wine and the wineskins will be preserved (9:16-17). Matthew underscores here what his narra- tive has already clearly proclaimed: Jesus is the Messiah and God's people must respond accordingly.

More healing stories conclude this large section of the gospel. Following Mark's lead Matthew pairs the story of the cure of the woman with the hemorrhage with that of raising Jairus' daughter, abbreviating both stories and editing them in his usual way (cf. Matt 9:18-26 and Mark 5:21-43). Both the leader of the synagogue who trusts in Jesus to raise his daughter from death (even though the crowd derides the possibility, 9.24) and the woman deter- mined just to touch Jesus' cloak exhibit exemplary faith that leads to healing. So do the two blind men who cry out for mercy to the "Son of David" (9:27). This is the first time the title has been used in Matthew since its appearance in the opening verse of the gospel. This "Son of David," perhaps different from expectations of a powerful political leader in the mold of King David, exercises his messianic authority in compassion and healing.

The enthusiastic reporting of their cure by the blind men seems to prompt Jesus to leave Capernaum for other regions (9:30-31, 35). But one last healing will conclude this section, leading as it does to the contrasting reactions of the crowds and the Pharisees. Jesus' healings bring the crowds to the brink of faith: "Never has anything like this been seen in Israel" (9:33). But the Pharisees remain hostile and draw a very different conclusion: "By the ruler of the demons he casts out the demons" (9:34). Matthew prepares the reader for the fierce wind of opposition that will sweep through the gospel in the next large section of the narrative.

THE MISSION DISCOURSE (9:35–10:42)

The mission discourse of chapter 10 brings this section of the gospel to a close by spelling out the intrinsic connection between the mission of Jesus and that of the community. In a pattern by now familiar, Matthew weaves this discourse together from his principal sources Mark and Q. However, the overall structure of the discourse, much of its content, and its entire perspective are decidedly Matthean.[22]

Matthew prepares for the discourse with a transitional scene in which Jesus urges the disciples to pray that the Lord of the harvest would send out laborers to relieve the distress of the crowds (9:35-38). The summary of 9:35, identical with 4:23, recalls for the reader the whole span of the intervening chapters where Jesus has been portrayed as teacher and healer. And once again the crowds are present, as they were at the beginning and conclusion of the Sermon (4:24–5:1 and 7:28-29) and at the beginning and end of the section on healing (8:1 and 9:33). Their urgent need for redemption is described with two traditional biblical metaphors, "sheep without a shepherd" and the plentiful "harvest" (9:36-37). Both images subtly evoke Matthean themes. That of sheep abandoned by their shepherds recalls Ezekiel's prophetic indictments of the leaders of Israel (see Ezek 34) and prepares the reader for the sharp clashes still to come in the gospel. That of the harvest ties into Matthew's eschatological perspective already stated in the beatitudes and further proclaimed in the parable chapter (see 13:24-30, 36-43) as well as in the discourse of chapters 24–25. By urging the disciples to pray to the "Lord of the harvest" to send out laborers (9:38), Matthew adds another strong theological note to the discourse that follows. Jesus himself and his commissioning of the Twelve is God's answer to the disciples' prayer.

The structure of the discourse itself is not easily discernible. It begins with the formal call of the Twelve (10:1-4) followed by a long series of instructions for their mission (10:5-42). The sayings group around some basic themes: instructions for the journey (10:5-15); warnings about persecution and divisions in the course of the mission (10:16-23); an exhortation not to fear but to trust in God's care (10:26-33); and a final call for commitment to following Jesus and his mission (10:34-39). Two other segments, one in the center of the discourse (10:24-25) and the other at the conclusion (10:40-42), express the fundamental perspective of the discourse: The mission of the disciples is an extension of Jesus' own mission. Therefore the disciples should not be surprised when they experience what Jesus did. At the same time, even the least of Jesus' disciples deserve to be treated with reverence and respect because they are sent in his name and through them Jesus is present.

A more baffling challenge for interpreters has been the issue of the precise force of this discourse. The instruction "Go nowhere among the Gentiles, and enter no town of the Samaritans, but go rather to the lost sheep of the house of Israel" (10:5-6) seems, at first reading, to make Jesus' instructions archaic, meant for the original disciples perhaps but not for Matthew's community.[23] The same might be said for 10:23 where Jesus predicts that they will not have gone through all the towns of Israel before the coming of the Son of Man. On the other hand, Matthew's incorporation of material from Mark 13 referring to the experience of the community beyond the lifetime of Jesus (see, e.g., Matt 10:16-22) implies that the instruction was indeed meant for the community who received the gospel and not confined to characters within the story.

The dilemma for interpretation posed by this chapter is really no different from that for any other part of the gospel. Matthew's narrative consistently works on two levels: one confined to the time, space, and particular characters that fill the narrative world of Matthew's story and the other reaching beyond the immediate world of that story to include the implied readers of the text.[24] Thus within the confines of Matthew's narrative world the Sermon on the Mount is addressed to the disciples and through them to the crowds that follow Jesus, but the readers know that these teachings of Jesus are also directed to them. The paralytic is healed and forgiven at Capernaum within the narrative world of Matthew, but Matthew's readers are meant to understand that the authority of Jesus to heal and forgive extends to them.

So, the restriction of the mission to Israel fits within the confines of Matthew's narrative world; only after the death and resurrection will the risen Christ send the community to the nations (28:16-20). Yet virtually all the content of the mission discourse extends to the post-Easter community and from Matthew's perspective bears the authority of the risen Christ. Note, too, that in

Matthew's formulation two streams of the gospel converge: Israel and the nations. The disciples are sent to the "lost sheep" of the house of Israel. Matthew has already provided the reader with examples of such "lost sheep," particularly in the miracle stories of chapters 8 and 9: the leper, Matthew the tax collector, the woman with a hemorrhage. The Matthean Jesus works the periphery of Israel, with the sick and the social outcasts. From this periphery to those beyond the boundaries is not such a long step, as the cure of the centurion's servant and the healing of the Gadarene demoniacs have already alerted the reader.[25]

Matthew draws the mission discourse to a close with the standard transitional formula we first observed at the end of the Sermon on the Mount (11:1; cf. 7:28-29). Although the Twelve have been commissioned, Matthew does not describe them as actually going out on mission (contrast Mark 6:12-13 where the apostles do go out and begin their mission); rather, it is Jesus who continues his ministry (11:1). Within the framework of Matthew's narrative, the mission of the community must await the conclusion of the gospel (28:16-20).

CHAPTER 10

RESPONDING TO JESUS: REJECTION AND UNDERSTANDING
(11:1–16:12)

Jesus' ministry of teaching and healing, so powerfully described in the foregoing section, continues in the chapters that follow. But another motif surfaces, that of response to Jesus' message. Matthew portrays the religious leaders as intransigent and utterly opposed to Jesus. The crowds continue to react favorably while the disciples now move closer to center stage. Even though fearful, hesitant, and often baffled, they ultimately show they are capable of understanding the mystery of Jesus' person and the meaning of his mission.

Typical of Matthew, this section is a blend of materials from Mark, Q, and the evangelist's own editorial contributions. With the parable discourse of chapter 13, Matthew will bring to a close the long stretch of narrative where he is most independent from the sequence of Mark's story line. From chapter 14 to the end of the gospel, with very few exceptions, Matthew follows closely the sequence of Mark's gospel and incorporates virtually all of its content even as he gives it his characteristic editing.

JOHN AND JESUS (11:2-30)

Matthew opens this new section of the gospel by returning to the ministry of John that had inaugurated Jesus' own mission (3:1-17). Matthew's point is not simply to compare John and Jesus but to illustrate that both messengers of God experienced rejection. The contents of this section are almost exclusively from Q (cf. Matt 11:2-27 and Luke 7:18-35; 10:12-15, 21-22). A notable exception is the beautiful passage in 11:28-30 that is unique to Matthew and portrays Jesus in imagery drawn from Israel's reflections on Wisdom.

At the outset the reader is reminded that John is in prison (see 4:12), and the question about Jesus' identity raised by John and his disciples enables the evangelist to review the messianic works of Jesus: "The blind receive their sight, the lame walk, the lepers are cleansed, the deaf hear, the dead are raised, and the poor have good news brought to them" (11:4-5). The ominous beatitude: "And blessed is anyone who takes no offense at me" (11:6) alerts the reader to the theme of response that will dominate much of the chapters to come.

This section also echoes the contrast between John and Jesus that was found in the inaugural scene by the Jordan (esp. 3:11-12). John is the greatest of the prophets; he is Elijah returned in expectation of the end time. Like the prophets of old he would experience rejection just as Jesus would (11:7-19). But John only foreshadows Jesus and the advent of God's reign; therefore the least in the kingdom of heaven is greater than John (11:11). Jesus alone is God's Messiah and unique son, and in his teaching and compassion one could find rest (11:25-30). Yet John and Jesus equally experience rejection by "this generation": John the ascetic prophet because he is deemed insane; Jesus, because he eats and drinks with sinners and tax collectors (11:16-19).

The saying that punctuates the comparison between Jesus and John shows that Matthew intends to portray Jesus through the biblical metaphor of "wisdom," the embodiment of God's presence in Israel: "Wisdom is vindicated by her deeds" (11:19). The messianic "deeds" of Jesus cited in response to John's inquiry demonstrate that this compassionate teacher and healer is indeed the messenger of God, the visible manifestation of God's own loving presence in Israel.[1]

This portion of the text closes with a series of vivid contrasts. The mocking rejection experienced by Jesus from "this generation" (i.e., the religious leaders within the narrative world of Matthew's story) provokes a series of "woes" on the Galilean towns where Jesus exercised his ministry: Chorazin, Bethsaida, and even Capernaum, his hometown. The "deeds of power" (11:20, 21, 23) Jesus performs on their behalf do not lead to repentance. Once again the contrasting response of the Gentiles looms on the horizon: The Gentile cities of Tyre and Sidon or even wicked Sodom would have repented if they had seen Jesus' works, and, therefore, it will be more tolerable for them on the day of judgment.

Jesus' prophetic lament and threat of judgment contrast sharply with the hymn of thanksgiving that erupts in 11:25-30. In one of the gospel's most memorable passages, the Matthean Jesus thanks God for revealing the mysteries of the Kingdom not to the wise and intelligent but to mere infants. The bond between Father and Son is inseparable and intimate; God's unique son Jesus reveals God to those whom he chooses. While the poetic language of this text seems exceptional in the gospel, the underlying theology portraying Jesus as "Son of God" has been demonstrated by Matthew at every turn.[2] It is this christology that underwrites the authority of Jesus as messianic teacher and healer and ultimately is the basis for the very existence of the Matthean community.

The segment ends with another text steeped in wisdom imagery. The weary and burdened are invited to find rest in Jesus, an invitation already enacted in previous scenes of the gospels where the sick and harassed flock to Jesus for healing (see 4:23-24; 8:1, 16-17; 9:35-36). Unlike the religious leaders who impose heavy burdens (23:4), the teachings of Jesus refresh the soul, and therefore his yoke is easy, his burden light (11:28-30).

JESUS IN CONFLICT (12:1-50)

With the lines now drawn, the next section narrates a series of healings that provoke bitter controversy with Jesus' opponents. The evangelist seems to set the scene in and around Capernaum, although this has to be inferred. We learn at the conclusion of the section that he is in a house "beside the sea" (12:46; 13:1). This is probably to be thought of as Capernaum since Matthew has already described it as "Capernaum by the sea" (4:13) and we had a sequence in Capernaum where there was mention of the synagogue (9:18), the house (8:14; 9:10), and the sea (9:1).

Matthew draws most of this material from chapters 2 and 3 of Mark's gospel, which is also dominated by conflict (see Mark 2:1–3:6). The segment concludes with the leaders' demand for a sign, a story found in chapter 8 of Mark (cf. Matt 12:38-42 and Mark 8:11-12). As in Mark's account, the story of Jesus' true family—"those who do the will of my heavenly Father"—leads into the parable discourse (cf. Matt 12:46-50 and Mark 3:31-35).

Matthew paints these scenes with clashing colors. On the one hand Jesus continues his ministry of healing and compassion, giving this messianic work priority even over observance of the sabbath. He defends his disciples as they satisfy their hunger by picking grains of wheat on a sabbath (12:1-8). Jesus is "lord of the sabbath," and once again he interprets the law compassionately (12:8, citing Hos 6:6). On that same sabbath he heals the man with a withered hand (12:9-14), defending the principle that "it is lawful to do good on the sabbath." Along with many other sick who follow Jesus and are cured (12:15), a blind and mute demoniac is brought to Jesus and he heals him (12:22). This ministry of Jesus fulfills the words of Isaiah concerning God's compassionate servant (Matt 12:17-21, quoting Isa 42:1-4) and inspires the amazed crowd to ask, "Can this be the Son of David?" (12:23).

Yet this same ministry of Jesus provokes bitter opposition from the leaders. They take offense when his disciples pull off heads of grain to eat on the sabbath (12:1-2), and they challenge the propriety of healing on the sabbath (12:10). In 12:14, Matthew notes that the Pharisees resolve to destroy Jesus. The cure of the blind and mute demoniac that inspires the crowd to acclaim Jesus drives the Pharisees to conclude that Jesus himself is possessed by Beelzebul, the ruler of the demons (12:24). For their intransigence, the leaders earn Jesus' bitter denunciation (12:33-37). Jesus' exorcisms, and indeed all of his ministry, are a sign that God's reign is present (12:28), yet the leaders cannot comprehend this fundamental reality.

The leaders now clearly assume their assigned role as implacable foes of Jesus, serving as a vivid counterexample to Jesus himself and to the positive responses of the disciples and the crowds.

THE PARABLE DISCOURSE (13:1-53)

The narrative setting Matthew gives this third great discourse of the gospel provides a clue to its fundamental meaning. At the beginning Matthew notes that Jesus leaves the house where he has been teaching (see 12:46) and sits "beside the sea" (13:1). The crowds are so great that he gets into a boat to address them from offshore as they gather on the beach (13:2). But midway through the speech Jesus will leave the crowds at the seaside and enter a house alone with his disciples (13:36). That movement from the crowds to the disciples reflects the gathering focus of this entire part of the gospel, as in the wake of mushrooming opposition Jesus concentrates his attention on instructing his disciples.

The content of the parable discourse also revolves around the entwined themes of revelation and response. Typically Matthew draws much of the material from Mark. This is especially true of the first part of the discourse where the parable of the sower and its explanation dominate (13:1-23; cf. Mark 4:1-20). But in the latter half of the discourse, especially when Jesus turns his attention to the disciples, Matthew includes several parables that are unique to his gospel and strongly reflect his theology: the parable of the wheat and the tares along with its explanation (13:24-30, 36-43); the parables of the hidden treasure and the pearl (13:44-46); and the parable of the net (13:47-50).

The very notion of "parable," those metaphors and stories of Jesus that reveal the reign of God yet demand perception and understanding, helps explain the diverse reactions to Jesus' ministry. The opening parable about the seed falling on different types of soil (and the explanation that follows in 13:18-23) emphasizes not only the indomitable power of the word but the radically different ways that people will respond. Taking his cue from Mark 4:10-12 but with his own characteristic interpretation, Matthew has the disciples ask Jesus: "Why do you speak to them in parables?" (13:10; cf. Mark 4:10). The answer is that the mystery of the Kingdom is revealed to the disciples but not to those who oppose Jesus, because "seeing they do not perceive, and hearing they do not listen, nor do they understand" (13:13). Matthew goes on to cite the quotation from Isaiah 6:6-9 that inspires this imagery (13:14-15). In Matthew's gospel images of perception—"seeing," "hearing," and, above all, "understanding"—are very important metaphors for active faith.[3] Despite their weakness and hesitation, the disciples—in contrast to the leaders who remain "blind guides"—are ultimately able to "understand" Jesus and respond to him. At the end of the parable discourse, the question will be put to them directly: "Have you understood all this?" and they will reply "yes" (13:51).[4] For this their eyes and ears are blessed (13:16).

Jesus' proclamation of the reign of God in parables also fulfills the prophecy of Psalm 78:2 about the revelation of hidden mysteries (13:35; in some textual variants Matthew attributes the prophecy to Isaiah!). As Jesus had acclaimed to his father earlier in the gospel, his mission is to reveal what has been hidden from the beginning of the world (cf. 11:25-27). In addition to the fundamental theme of response to God's word, the parables included here by Matthew sound other themes of the gospel: the ultimate triumph of the reign of God (the parable of the mustard seed, 13:31-32; the parable of the yeast, 13:33); the final judgment that will come at the end of the world (the parable of the wheat and the tares, 13:24-30, 37-43; the parable of the net, 13:47-50); the call to committed discipleship for the sake of the Kingdom (the parable of the treasure, 13:44; the parable of the pearl, 13:45).

As was the case with the mission discourse, the reader must be aware of different levels at work in the parable discourse in order to interpret it properly. On one level, that of Matthew's narrative world, the interaction is among Jesus, the disciples who understand Jesus, and the "others" who do not (implicitly the Jewish religious leaders who have been opposing Jesus and remain blind to his message). The narrative framework of the discourse moves accordingly from the wider audience of the crowds to a focus on Jesus and the disciples. For the reader of the gospel, however, the horizon encompassed by this parable discourse (and by the gospel itself) expands to another level: Now it is no longer simply a historically past interaction between Jesus, his disciples, and the Jewish authorities who opposed him, nor even the struggle between the Christian community and Israel contemporary with the immediate history of Matthew's community, but the discourse also opens out to the "world" and its future. As Jesus explains to the disciples, the "field is the world" (13:38), and the drama is a cosmic one involving the "children of the kingdom" and the "children of the evil one" (13:38), all leading up to judgment "at the end of the age" (13:49). From Matthew's perspective all peoples now stand accountable before the mystery of the reign of God.

The discourse concludes on another characteristically Matthean note. Jesus confirms that the disciples indeed "understand" what he is teaching them (13:51).[5] Thereby they earn the title "scribe trained for the kingdom of heaven" as noted in a verse that in many ways can be considered a signature verse of the gospel (13:52). The scribe trained for the Kingdom is like the "head of the household" who brings out of his "treasure" things that are "new and old." Endowed with the kind of profound understanding that enables one to absorb and act on the teaching of Jesus, the disciple is a "scribe"—thoughtful, wise, skilled—one who is dedicated to the reign of God. This scribe is set over the "household" of God, the community itself. This scribe draws from his "treasure." As defined in Matthew's gospel, the "treasure" or "treasure house" (the term *thesaurion* implies the latter) is the place of one's deepest convictions, the place where "one's heart is" (6:21). It is one's most precious possession placed carefully where neither moth or rust can consume nor thief break in and steal (6:20). It is that which one earnestly desires, like the treasure hidden in the field and for which one joyfully sells all to purchase it (13:44). From such a "treasure" the understanding scribe draws out for the household things that are both "new and old."

Do we have here a subtle description of the ideal disciple or leader in Matthew's view? Perhaps even an unwitting self-portrait of the evangelist, who through his interpretation of Jesus and his teaching at a critical moment of transition for the members of his community was ministering to them as a good and understanding scribe, retrieving the "old" from the sacred heritage of Judaism yet opening to them "new" horizons as well?

THE MISSION RESUMED (13:54–16:12)

The parable discourse concludes with Matthew's characteristic transition phrase (13:53; cf. 7:28; 11:1), and now the narrative of Jesus' ministry in Galilee resumes. The focus remains on the mystery of differing responses to the gospel. From now on Matthew follows closely the narrative sequence of Mark, but still gives the

125

narrative his own characteristic touch. The corresponding section in Mark (from 4:35 to 8:21) has a strong expansive mission context.[6] Jesus ranges back and forth across the sea and to the borders of Tyre and Sidon, ministering on both the Jewish and Gentile sides of the Lake. Much of this aura remains in Matthew's narrative, but the mission focus is more diffuse and concentration falls more heavily on the contrasting responses between the leaders of Israel and the disciples.

Rejection in Nazareth (13:54-58)

The action begins with Jesus' return to Nazareth and his teaching in "their synagogue" (13:54-58). Following the lead of Mark, Matthew calls this Jesus' "native city" (the literal sense of the Greek word *patris* used by Matthew), the one he had left at the beginning of his public ministry (4:13) and distinct from Capernaum, which is labeled Jesus' "own city" (9:1). In Nazareth Jesus' own people reject him, taking "offense" at him (13:57)—the very reaction Jesus had warned of in his response to John's emissaries (11:6). This story about his hometown, coming on the heels of the parable discourse, has intriguing parallels with the "family" story that precedes the discourse (12:46-50). Informed that his family was outside wanting to speak with him, Jesus had pointed to his disciples as his new family, "Here are my mother and my brothers! For whoever does the will of my Father in heaven is my brother and sister and mother" (12:49-50).

The Death of John (14:1-12)

The note of rejection in the Nazareth story leads into a final scene about John the Baptist (14:1-12), one that alerts the reader to the ultimate price of Jesus' prophetic ministry. The wedge into the story line is the threat of yet another Herod, this time Herod Antipas, the son of Herod the Great and the brother of Archelaus, whom Matthew has also portrayed as a threat to Jesus (2:22). Antipas, like others (see 16:14), believes that Jesus may be John come back from the dead. The narrative then gives the reader a flashback to John's death, filling in what remains of the Baptist story: In 4:12 the reader learned that John had been arrested; in 11:2 we hear of John in prison inquiring about the deeds of the messiah; now his ultimate fate is reported.

The death of John, the courageous prophet, clearly serves as a portent of Jesus' own destiny. Herod's hesitancy to execute John for fear of the crowd "because they regarded him as a prophet" anticipates the same fear the leaders will have regarding Jesus (21:46; see also 21:26; 26:5); the arrest, binding, and imprisonment of John evoke what will happen to Jesus in his passion (14:3; 26:50, 57; 27:2); the hesitancy of Herod and the persistence of Herodias to condemn John are reminiscent of a similar drama between Pilate and the leaders concerning Jesus; John is buried by his disciples just as Jesus will be buried by Joseph of Arimathea whom Matthew identifies as a "disciple" (14:12; 27:57).

Two Great Signs (14:13-36)

The narrative now turns to two great signs around and on the sea that will both illumine the profound authority of Jesus and his bond with the disciples. The first of these is the miraculous feeding of more than five thousand (14:13-21). This great work is laden with biblical symbolism and therefore serves Matthew's accustomed pattern of wrapping Jesus in the mantle of Old Testament symbols and typology. It recalls Moses and the Exodus story of the manna (Exod 16) where God fed the multitudes in the desert (the setting of the multiplication story in a "deserted place" and the presence of the hapless, hungry crowds coincide with this; 14:13, 14-15). It recalls the prophetic work of Elisha who miraculously fed the hungry (2 Kgs 4:42-44). And it also summons up the vision of the end time when all of Israel would be gathered for the messianic banquet on Zion (Isa 25:6-10).

As the reader continues through the gospel, this story, along with its twin in chapter 15:32-39, will also connect with Jesus' final meal with the disciples on the eve of his passion (26:26-29). Virtually the same gestures of taking the loaf, blessing, breaking, and distributing it to the disciples are present in all three accounts. In the first two stories Jesus the Messiah feeds the hungry people their provisions of bread (as had been prayed for in the Lord's Prayer, 6:11). In the last feeding story, Jesus gives his very being to the community through his death and resurrection. The connection of the Last Supper with the early community's celebration of the Lord's Supper implies that Matthew's readers would see in the feeding stories an anticipation of their own experience of the Eucharist in which the presence of the risen Christ was felt within the community. Therefore the ensemble of feeding stories connects with a time line that spans the whole of salvation history: Israel's sacred past; the narrative present of Jesus' own ministry; the experience of the community to whom the gospel was addressed; and the eschatological future gathering of God's people.

Unlike Mark's story where the disciples seem to remain intransigent and speak ironically to Jesus ("Are we to go and buy two hundred denarii worth of bread, and give it to them to eat?" Mark 6:37; omitted by Matthew), in Matthew's story Jesus employs the disciples in feeding the crowds—he gives the multiplied loaves to the disciples, and the disciples, without protest, distribute them to the crowds (Matt 14:19). As we noted in the introduction to the Sermon on the Mount, Matthew seems to conceive of the disciples as an inner core of the community and through them Jesus' words are also directed to the "crowds." Here, too, the feeding of the crowds is "mediated" through the hands of the disciples.

The second of Matthew's sea stories adds yet another great sign in Matthew's portrayal of Jesus and his bond with the disciples (14:22-26; see foregoing, 8:23-27). A close comparison with Mark's account illustrates Matthew's particular interest in the story (see Mark 6:45-52). In Mark's version, the apparition of Jesus walking upon the sea provokes terror in the disciples, and yet this mysterious and powerful epiphany is unable to penetrate their lack of understanding and "hardness of heart," the sober note on which the story ends (Mark 6:52). While retaining the nucleus of the story, Matthew has completely transformed it. Now Jesus' awesome epiphany on the sea leads to full confession of him as Lord and Son of God, both by the community and, dramatically, by Peter. The significant changes are Matthew's injection of the Peter story in the midst of the account (14:28-32) and the episode's radically different conclusion (14:33).

Matthew leaves intact the theophany implicit in this story. Jesus mysteriously exercises divine power over the chaos of the sea, treading upon its windswept surface, and manifesting himself to the awestruck disciples. Treading upon the sea was a divine prerogative in the Old Testament (see Job 9:8; 38:16; Ps 77:19; Isa 43:16; Hab 3:15; Sir 24:5-6), and in both Mark's and Matthew's accounts, Jesus seems to bear the divine name: "Take heart, it is I *(egō eimi)*; do not be afraid" (Matt 14:27; Mark 6:50). The formulation

"I am" *(egō eimi)* evokes the divine name (see Exod 3:14; Deut 32:39; Isa 41:4; 43:2, 10-11; 45:18; 51:12).

To this profound christology, Matthew will attach his strong interest in discipleship that runs throughout this section. The vivid story of Peter is told in typical Matthean vocabulary and is an intense summation of his theology of discipleship.[7] Peter's request to walk on the water as Jesus is able to do reflects the gospel's conviction that the disciples have, in fact, been entrusted with the same messianic powers as Jesus (see the words of the commissioning of the Twelve in 10:1, 7-8). At the same time, Matthew consistently tempers this conviction about the authority of the community with a realistic assessment of its inherent weakness and its complete dependence on the power of Jesus. Peter experiences the terrifying power of the wind and is overwhelmed with fear, earning from Jesus Matthew's characteristic description, "You of little faith." Yet the apostle exemplifies what the gospel requires in the midst of crisis—he prays, "Lord, save me!" (14:30). In response Jesus "reached out his hand," a gesture reminiscent of his healings,[8] to rescue Peter from the terrifying abode of the deep and his paralyzing fear.

The story concludes with a dramatic confession of Jesus on the part of the entire group of disciples. As Jesus and Peter get into the boat, the wind ceases. Matthew notes that those in the boat "prostrate" themselves before Jesus in an attitude of profound reverence (the meaning of the term *proskuneō* used by Matthew in 14:33[9]) and acclaim: "Truly you are the Son of God." Coming as it does in the midst of a section of the gospel where response to Jesus has been at the center of attention and in the awesome setting of Jesus' mastery over the chaotic forces of nature and his rescue of the apostle, this confession of Jesus reveals that for the evangelist and his community the term "Son of God" exceeds the traditional messianic meaning it held in Jewish tradition. The risen Jesus is imbued with divine power and is the object of prayer and worship on the part of the community. Both signs—the miraculous feeding and the sea story—show strong connections with the worship experience of Matthew's community.

The powerful christology and strong confessional tone of this section carry over into the transitional verses that Matthew uses to conclude this segment around the sea (14:34-36). When the boat comes ashore at Gennesaret on the western side of the sea, people recognize Jesus and, once again with Matthew's characteristic emphasis on the healing power of Jesus, they bring to him "all who were sick," "begging" him even to let them touch the fringe of his garment. All who touched it were healed. Few scenes in the gospel are more transparent than these for glimpsing the profound christology of Matthew.

A Dispute with Israel; An Opening to the Gentiles (15:1-28)

The clash with the Pharisees and scribes over interpretation of the purity laws is a jarring contrast with the undisputed confession of Jesus in the previous two stories (15:1-20). Matthew's casting of the scene moves it in an ever-narrowing focus from a discussion with the religious authorities (15:1-9), to interaction with the crowds (15:10-11), then with the disciples (15:12-14), and finally to an instruction prompted by Peter's question (15:15-20, an aspect of the story not found in Mark). Although the original issue concerning defilement is not lost, Matthew's real interest in this scene, as indicated by his addition of verses 12b-14, is his indictment of the Jewish leaders as "blind guides" who lead others astray (see 23:16, 17, 19, 24, 26). Their interpretation of law is not in accord with God's intent (15:3, 6) and their words and actions have no integrity (15:7-9).

While Matthew's community surely ascribed to Jesus' teaching that real defilement emanated from the human heart and that eating with unwashed hands was insignificant in comparison to this more profound sense of purity (the point of the saying in 15:14 and the explanation in 17-20), they may have hesitated to draw the radical conclusion found in Mark's text: "Thus he declared all foods clean" (Mark 7:19), a comment not found in Matthew's version. The Jewish Christians of Matthew's community probably continued to keep the Jewish purity laws but interpreted them in accord with Jesus' teaching.

The story of the Canaanite woman (15:21-28) is a remarkable text, one that is laden with Matthean theology and one to which the evangelist gives considerable attention. Once again a comparison with Mark's version of this same story (Mark 7:24-30) underscores the distinctive features of Matthew's perspective.

Jesus' departure from the foregoing scene and his travel toward the district of Tyre and Sidon set the stage for a contrast with the reception he had just received from the Jewish leaders. Matthew seems to place the action near the border with Tyre and Sidon but not truly beyond the boundaries: Jesus withdraws "toward" or "to" (the sense of the Greek preposition *eis* here) the district of Tyre and Sidon, and suddenly a Canaanite woman from that district "came out *(ekselthousa)* . . ." In Mark's version there is no ambiguity: Jesus goes to the region of Tyre and Sidon and enters a house to avoid the crowds; the "Syrophoenician woman" comes into the house and confronts him (7:25). As we noted earlier Matthew has somewhat muted the missionary crossing of borders that are clearly present in this section of Mark's account; for Matthew the mission beyond Israel is yet to come, as this very story proclaims (Matt 15:24).

Matthew also calls the woman a "Canaanite" in contrast to Mark's designation, "a Greek, a Syrophoenician by birth" (Mark 7:26). Perhaps with this more archaic designation Matthew wished to recall the salvation history of Israel and its struggle with the nations, a point that will be at the center of the story.

Even more significant, Matthew rachets up the tension of this story by having three exchanges between the woman and Jesus rather than simply two as in Mark, by having the disciples enter into the drama, and by adding dialogue.

In the first encounter (15:22-24, material unique to Matthew), the Gentile woman addresses Jesus in strong confessional terms: "Have mercy on me, Lord, Son of David . . ." But this entreaty on behalf of her daughter is met with silence by Jesus, to the point where the disciples, disturbed by her cries, ask Jesus to send her away. Responding to them and not to her, he replies: "I was sent only to the lost sheep of the house of Israel." This reinforces what the Matthean Jesus had already stated in the mission discourse (a mission only "to the lost sheep of the house of Israel," 10:5).

For a second time the woman approaches Jesus, this time prostrating in worship (*prosekunei,* the same word used to describe the demeanor of the disciples as they confessed Jesus as "Son of God" in 14:33). Just as Peter had done, this Gentile couples her remarkable confession of Jesus as Lord with a prayer for mercy: "Lord, help me" (15:25). Yet again Jesus rebuffs her entreaty with a statement of Israel's privilege, but now couched in startling terms: "It is not fair to take the children's bread and throw it to the dogs" (15:26). The image of bread makes a connection with the multiplication of the loaves in 14:13-21 as well as with the dispute

131

with the scribes and Pharisees about eating "bread" with unwashed hands (15:2; the same word "bread," *arton*, is used in both cases). Another feeding story will follow in 15:32-39.

But for a third time the Canaanite woman will not be denied her request on behalf of her ill daughter: "Yes, Lord, yet even the dogs eat the crumbs that fall from their masters' table." With this third acclamation of faith, Jesus' refusal to extend his mission beyond the boundaries of Israel dissolves. As was the case with Matthew's story about the centurion of Capernaum (see Matt 8:10), it is the extraordinary faith of this Gentile woman that amazes Jesus: "Woman, great is your faith!" (this is much more emphatic than Mark's formulation: "For saying that, you may go," Mark 7:29).

By means of this intriguing story Matthew advances the motif that runs throughout this central section of his gospel. Whereas the leaders of Israel plot against Jesus, declare him to be in league with Satan, and protest his interpretation of the law, this Canaanite woman tenaciously and boldly proclaims her faith in Jesus as "Lord" and "Son of David." The healing of this woman's daughter in response to her great faith is clearly another sign of the future mission to the nations, a sign quite similar to previous encounters with the centurion (8:5-13) and the Gadarene demoniacs (8:28-34).

But there is another dimension to the Canaanite woman story not found in the others. Here Jesus himself emphatically resists extending his mission to this Gentile. Only in the face of the woman's tenacious faith, driven by the plight of her daughter and her conviction that Jesus had the power to heal her, do Jesus' hesitations—based on Israel's privilege and the restriction of his mission to Israel—dissolve. It is highly probable that this story is a window to the very struggles that Matthew's community had experienced in resolving the issue of outreach to the Gentiles.[10] While fully recognizing the historical privilege of Israel as the children of God's household and admitting that Jesus' own ministry was restricted to Israel, the community was still called to respond to the faith and need of the Gentiles. By portraying Jesus himself—rather than a negative character within the gospel drama—as the one who initially resists this extension, Matthew's gospel shows exquisite pastoral sensitivity toward those in his community who struggled to accept this new situation.

Healing and Feeding the Multitudes and the Demand for a Sign (15:29–16:12)

Matthew concludes this main section of the gospel with yet another powerful display of Jesus' mission that contrasts sharply with disbelief and rejection on the part of the religious leaders.

In 15:29-31, Jesus returns to the area around the Sea of Galilee and to an epic scene of healing, strongly reminiscent of the introduction to the Sermon on the Mount (see 4:23–5:1; see also the summary of Jesus' ministry in 11:5). Once again Jesus climbs to a mountaintop and sits in the position of authority. And yet again the crowds stream to him bringing the sick for healing. Jesus' extraordinary compassion and authority to heal move the crowds to "praise the God of Israel" (15:31; see also 5:16; 9:8).

Jesus' final great work in the course of his Galilean ministry is to feed the multitudes once again (15:32-39), a story parallel with Mark's (8:1-10). As before, it is Jesus' compassion for the ever-present crowds that triggers the miracle (15:32; cf. Matt 14:19), and again he draws the disciples into an active role in satisfying the hunger of the people (15:36), signifying the strong ecclesial connections of this story.

The rationale for a second feeding story is clearer in Mark, who situates this incident in the Decapolis, that is, on the Gentile side of the Sea of Galilee (see Mark 7:31). But in Matthew's version the story does not seem to be situated in Gentile territory; it follows immediately upon Jesus' healing of the multitudes near the sea on the western (i.e., Jewish) shore (15:29, 32). As we have seen consistently in Matthew, he is reluctant to portray Jesus as moving beyond the boundaries of Israel. Even though signs are erupting in Matthew's account about the eventual mission to the Gentiles and Jesus has been met with consistent rejection by the Jewish leaders, within the narrative world of the gospel Jesus holds true to his mission to Israel. Only under his authority as the risen Christ will the community be sent to the nations (28:16-20).

From a story of startling faith, the pendulum swings back, as it has throughout this section of the gospel, to a story of disbelief and rejection on the part of the Pharisees and Sadducees (16:1-12). Matthew augments the account found in Mark's parallel (Mark 8:11-13) with material from Q (Matt 16:2-3; cf. Luke 12:54-56). In the face of Jesus' extraordinary ministry, the leaders, as a "test" for Jesus, demand a sign from him. But no sign will be

133

given, except the "sign of Jonah." In a previous dispute with the leaders the Matthean Jesus had already interpreted the meaning of this sign: "For just as Jonah was three days and three nights in the belly of the sea monster, so for three days and three nights the Son of Man will be in the heart of the earth" (12:40).

The section concludes with Jesus leaving the religious authorities and crossing the sea with his disciples (16:1-12). In Mark's account, this scene evolves into a strong critique of the disciples themselves, who remain obtuse, unable to understand Jesus' warnings about the "leaven" of the Pharisees and Herod, and their hearts and minds closed to the significance of his miraculous feedings of the multitudes (see Mark 8:14-21). But for Matthew the focus remains, as in the previous incident, on the failures of the religious leaders. The disciples' initial confusion about the meaning of Jesus' metaphor about "the yeast of the Pharisees and Sadducees" is a sign of the disciples' "little faith" (16:8). But once instructed by Jesus, they come to "understand" that he was warning them about "the teaching of the Pharisees and Sadducees" (16:12). Matthew's portrayal of both the disciples and the leaders remains consistent.

CHAPTER 11

THE JOURNEY TO
JERUSALEM (16:13–20:34)

The movement of Jesus and his disciples from the region around the sea to the "district of Caesarea Philippi" (16:13) and the dramatic encounter that will take place there signal another turning point in the gospel story. Jesus will conclude his ministry in Galilee and with his disciples begin the fateful journey to Jerusalem. His messianic work of healing and teaching continues, but now there is a much stronger concentration on instructing his disciples, a motif that had begun to emerge in the preceding section. Virtually every scene involves only Jesus and the disciples or private instruction of the disciples following encounters with others (see, e.g., 17:19-21; 19:10-12; 19:23-30; 20:24-28). The crowds are still present (17:14; 19:2; 20:29), as are Jesus' opponents (17:24; 19:3), but they play a decidedly minor role. Another new element is the focus on the passion of Jesus and its meaning for those who would follow him, as for the first time in the gospel Jesus openly predicts his death and resurrection. Thus Matthew continues his focus on christology, inviting the reader to reflect on yet another dimension of Jesus' identity.

Throughout this section Matthew follows closely the story line provided by Mark (cf. Mark 8:27–10:52). Two sinews bind this section together in both gospels: The first is the journey from Galilee to Jerusalem, and the second is the set of three solemn predictions of the passion that punctuate the journey and give it its meaning.

1) *The Journey.* Through editorial insertions Matthew (generally following the lead of Mark) shapes the material into a deliberate journey of Jesus and the disciples from Galilee to Jerusalem. While in the northern region of Caesarea Philippi, Jesus announces to the disciples that he "must go to Jerusalem" (16:21). Matthew adds to the solemnity and deliberation of the journey by noting that Jesus and the disciples "gather" in Galilee as Jesus once again predicts his impending passion (17:22; contrast Mark 9:30, "They went on from there and passed through Galilee . . ."). Then at the conclusion of the community discourse, Matthew notes Jesus' departure from Galilee and his travel to the region of "Judea beyond the Jordan" (19:1). The reader is again reminded about the continuing journey in 20:17 ("While Jesus was going up to Jerusalem . . ."). Finally the departure from Jericho (20:29) and the approach to Bethphage and Jerusalem itself (21:1) bring the journey to its destination. (See figure 2.)

2) *The Passion Predictions.* Again following Mark's lead, Matthew has Jesus three times solemnly predict his sufferings and exaltation. The first occurs at Caesarea Philippi immediately following the confession of Peter (16:21); the second as they move from the region of Caesarea back to the area of Capernaum (17:22); and the third and most detailed of the predictions near the climax of the journey (20:17-19).

These predictions are coupled with discipleship instruction, and this is what gives this segment of the narrative its characteristic tone. The exhortations to "take up the cross" and "lose one's life" (16:24-26), the exacting demands of the community discourse (18:1-20), and the warnings about abuse of power (20:20-28) follow in the wake of Jesus' disclosures about the suffering he would have to endure. Similarly the teaching on divorce and remarriage (19:3-12) and renunciation of possessions (19:16-30) also sharply portray the demands of discipleship. As Jesus had already instructed his disciples in the mission discourse, the destiny of the disciple would be the same as that of the master (10:24-25).

The insertion of the community discourse (18:1-35) into the

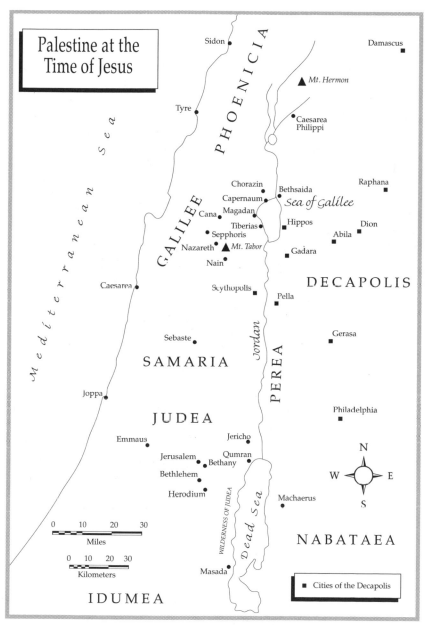

Figure 2

journey narrative is the most substantial change Matthew makes in Mark's pattern in this part of the gospel. Introduced by the uniquely Matthean incident of the temple tax (17:24-27), the discourse takes as its starting point the question posed by the disciples, "Who is the greatest in the kingdom of heaven?" (18:1). Matthew's inspiration for this undoubtedly comes from Mark 9:33-34, where it is noted that during the journey the disciples had been arguing about "who was the greatest." Instead of an exchange between Jesus and his uncomprehending disciples—a typical feature of Mark—Matthew uses the question as the jumping off point for the gospel's fourth great discourse. The content of the discourse is Matthew's typical blend of Marcan material (18:1-5, 6-9; cf. Mark 9:33-37, 42-50), Q (18:10-14, 15, 22; cf. Luke 15:3-7; 17:3, 4), and traditions unique to Matthew (18:16-18, 19-20, 21-22, 23-35).

One remaining feature special to Matthew in this section is the parable of the laborers in the vineyard (20:1-16), although its concluding saying has parallels in Mark and Luke (cf. Matt 20:16; Mark 10:31; Luke 13:30).

CONFESSION AT CAESAREA PHILIPPI (16:13-28)

The meaning of this scene in Matthew's narrative calls for careful consideration. The confession of Jesus' messianic identity at Caesarea Philippi is clearly an important transition in the gospel story.[1] Undoubtedly the fundamental question Jesus poses to the disciples is also directed at the reader: "Who do you say that I am?" And Peter's full response—"You are the Messiah, the Son of the living God"—recapitulates the christological perspective evident throughout Matthew's narrative to this point. If in Mark's account the reply of Peter ("You are the Messiah," Mark 8:29) and Jesus' own reaction are somewhat ambiguous, that is not the case in Matthew's version.[2] Despite their "little faith," the Matthean disciples do understand who Jesus is and had already confessed their faith in him as "Son of God" in the remarkable conclusion to the miracle of Jesus' walking on the water (14:33). In Mark's story, by contrast, the disciples have not yet been able to understand Jesus or confess him as Messiah and Son of God. Thus coming on the heels of that important confession, the scene at Caesarea Philippi seems to lose some of its dramatic punch in Matthew's narrative. In a sense, the disciples have already answered Jesus' question in an emphatic manner at an earlier stage in the gospel story.

This suggests that Matthew has shifted the focus of this scene from the disciples as a whole to *Peter* and Jesus' words to him. Simon's full confession of Jesus as "Messiah and Son of the living God" is rewarded with a solemn blessing of the disciple and his investiture with authority (16:17-19). Peter is one of those entrusted by the Father with an authentic revelation of Jesus' identity, reminiscent of the great prayer of Jesus in 11:25-27. For this he is appointed by Jesus as foundation stone of his "church" *(ekklêsia)*, which will endure the threats of the demon.[3] Furthermore, Peter is designated as the one entrusted with the "keys of the kingdom," a sign of Peter's authority reminiscent of the passage in Isaiah where Shebna is appointed prime minister of the royal household and "the key of the house of David" is placed on his shoulders (Isa 22:22). And Peter is also given the power to "bind and loose," terms used in later rabbinic texts to describe authority over a variety of matters, including doctrinal issues and questions of membership.[4]

Matthew's portrayal of Peter falls short of idealization, however. When Jesus concludes his blessing of the disciple he begins to describe the passion that awaits him (16:21). Compared with Mark, Matthew amplifies Peter's response to Jesus' prediction just as he had augmented Peter's confession and Jesus' words to him (cf. Matt 16:22-23 and Mark 8:32-33). Ironically Peter addresses Jesus as "Lord" *(Kurie)*, but not in a spirit of confession or supplication (as in 14:28, 30) but as part of an exclamation attempting to dissuade Jesus from enduring the sufferings destined for him. Jesus' rebuke of Peter is also put more intensely in Matthew's version: Peter is called not only "Satan" by Jesus but a "stumbling block" *(skandalon)* because he thinks according to human rather than divine standards (16:23). Peter thus falls under the warning that Jesus had directed to John's disciples: "Blessed is one who does not find me an obstacle" *(skandalisthē;* Matt 11:6). Matthew may well intend to play on the images of *petron* (rock) and *skandalon* (obstacle or stumbling block) attributed to Peter in this remarkable scene. In any case, Matthew portrays Peter with the kind of mixed terms applied to the disciples as a whole: They understand Jesus and confess him as Son of God but are also fearful, doubting, and of "little faith."

As we discussed earlier, Matthew's portrait of Peter has been a challenge for interpretation throughout the centuries.[5] Is Peter in this scene simply a "representative disciple" whereby the narrative illumines the power (and weakness) of the followers of Jesus by fleshing out these qualities in one specific character? Or, as Kingsbury and others have argued, does Matthew portray Peter not simply as a "representative disciple" but as one who had a singular role within salvation history? Peter's post-resurrection confession of Jesus witnessed in such early traditions as 1 Corinthians 15:3-5 as well as his actual leadership role as a bridge figure between Jewish Christianity and Gentile Christianity made him, in fact, a "foundation stone" of the community and one who had a unique role in helping the community decide issues of membership (as Acts 10–11, 15, and even Paul's negative reaction to Peter's withdrawal from table fellowship with Gentiles in Gal 2:11-14 imply). Or, finally, as many Roman Catholic interpreters would suggest, does Jesus' emphatic blessing of Peter and the entrusting to him of signs of authority indicate that the gospel portrays Peter not simply as a revered historical figure from the past but as a symbol of continuing leadership developing within the Matthean community itself? The blessing of Peter as well as Jesus' rebuke to him may serve as affirmation and warning to those entrusted with the leadership of the community.[6]

The scene concludes with an instruction to all the disciples (16:24-26). The disciple who would follow Jesus must be prepared for the way of the cross. Matthew's gospel had already emphasized the demands of discipleship. The would-be disciples who sought to follow Jesus were reminded that "the Son of Man has nowhere to lay his head" and that no other obligation, even that of burying one's father, could take precedence over the commitment required (8:18-22). In the mission discourse, the disciples had been warned to expect persecution and suffering in the course of the mission (10:16-25) and that "whoever does not take up the cross and follow" Jesus is not worthy of him and "those who lose their life for my sake will find it" (10:38-39). These same instructions are repeated here after the first passion prediction, taking on new urgency as Jesus and his disciples begin their journey to Jerusalem.

Throughout this section the mysterious title "Son of Man" is applied to Jesus with increasing frequency.[7] Used to describe the sufferings and humiliation of Jesus (17:12; 22) as well as his exaltation and triumphant return (16:27-28; 17:9; 19:28), the title fits well into this section of the gospel where the reader's attention is turned toward the death and resurrection of Jesus.

TRANSFIGURATION (17:1-21)

A temporal notice, "six days later," moves the reader to a new scene in which the identity of Jesus as God's Son will be luminously revealed to the disciples. Coming on the heels of the first passion prediction, the transfiguration anticipates the exaltation of Jesus and reaffirms his messianic authority, with the emphatic "Listen to him" (17:5) underscoring the crucial discipleship instruction that is the focus of this section of the gospel. The link to Moses and Elijah fits neatly into Matthew's characteristic emphasis on Jesus' continuity with the law and the prophets.

In general Matthew's version of the story is close to that of Mark, with the only notable difference being his treatment of Peter and the disciples. Instead of the incomprehension typical of the disciples' response in Mark's story (Mark 9:6, 10), Matthew portrays Peter and his companions in tones reminiscent of the story of the walking on the sea (Matt 14:22-33). Their genuine homage is mixed with fear and Jesus compassionately rescues them from their terror.

Peter's response to Jesus is with the strong confessional address, "Lord," rather than the term "Rabbi" used by Mark here but consistently avoided by Matthew (Matt 17:4; cf. Mark 9:5), and the deferential "if you wish" is added.[8] Peter's dumbfounded response in Mark's version ("He did not know what to say, for they were terrified," Mark 9:6) is omitted in Matthew so that the reader has no impression that Peter's offer to build three tabernacles is inappropriate.

Thus once again in Matthew Peter takes a leadership role within the community of the disciples. His offer of homage will be overwhelmed by the voice from heaven that speaks to the three chosen disciples and fills them with fear (17:6). In a gesture reminiscent of the healing stories and the walking on the water, Jesus approaches his awestruck disciples, touching them and reassuring them: "Get up and do not be afraid" (Matt 17:6-7).

The wondrous vision concluded, Jesus and his three disciples descend the mountain. On the way, Jesus again alludes to his impending death and resurrection (17:9) and responds to the disciples' question about Elijah (17:10-13). More emphatically than Mark, Matthew identifies John the Baptist with Elijah redivivus, the one expected before the end time (17:13; note, too, that the Matthean disciples "understand" this). This portrayal of the Baptist fits with Jesus' teaching in 11:7-19. John was the last and greatest of the prophets, the one whose advent signaled the messianic age fulfilled in Jesus.

The descent from the mountain completed, Jesus and the disciples encounter yet again another waiting crowd (see 8:1, 18; 9:36; 14:14; 15:30) and a man pleading for a cure of his epileptic boy (17:14-21). As in Mark the interest of this story falls on the issue of faith rather than on the miracle itself (cf. Mark 9:14-29), but Matthew has considerably edited this story, shaping it to his perspective. In Mark's version the focus is on the exchange between Jesus and the father of the epileptic boy. The inability of the disciples to cure the boy exposes their lack of faith and contrasts with both the power of Jesus and the ardent faith of the parent: "I believe; help my unbelief!" (Mark 9:24). In Matthew the father virtually drops out of the story after his initial request to Jesus and the attention remains on Jesus and the disciples, characteristic of this entire section of the gospel. The failure of the disciples to cure the man's son earns Jesus' sharp condemnation of this "faithless and perverse generation," words that evoke Moses' lament about Israel in Deuteronomy 32:5. In the private instruction of the disciples that follows the cure of the boy (Matt 17:19-20), Matthew returns to the more nuanced term that best describes his "mixed" image of the disciples: It is because of their "little faith" (17:20) that they were unable to liberate the boy from the demonic power destroying his life.

LIFE WITHIN THE COMMUNITY OF THE KINGDOM (17:22–18:35)

Another milestone on the journey is marked in 17:22, as Jesus and his disciples "gather" in Galilee and for a second time he solemnly predicts his passion and resurrection. In contrast to the disciples in Mark's story who remain baffled by Jesus' words, the Matthean disciples are deeply saddened (contrast Mark 9:32 and Matt 17:23).

This reminder of the passion leads into the curious incident about the temple tax (17:24-27) and the discourse on community (18:1-35). The story about the tax, found only in Matthew, seems at first reading to have no connection to its context. Before the temple's destruction in AD 70, payment of the half-shekel tax for the upkeep of the Temple was an important sign of solidarity for all Jewish families, even those in the Diaspora outside Palestine. After the destruction of the Temple, the Romans continued to levy the tax but applied the revenue to the Temple of Jupiter in Rome. Payment of the tax, therefore, posed something of a dilemma for the Jewish Christians of Matthew's community both before and after AD 70.

This story provides the Jewish Christians a rationale for paying the tax without separating themselves too radically from their Jewish neighbors (prior to AD 70) or creating problems with Roman authorities (after 70). Once again in Matthew's story Peter plays a leading role on behalf of the community, becoming in effect the spokesperson for this community policy.

On another level, the theology of this story provides the lead into the discourse that follows.[9] Although Jesus concludes that the tax should be paid "not to give offense," both he and the disciples are exempt because "the children of the king are free" (17:26). Even though the seeds of the kingdom are planted in the "world" (13:38) and the teaching and healing of Jesus will be directed beyond the perimeter of the community, Matthew considers the disciples a core group, privileged to have full access to and understanding of Jesus' teaching, to witnessing his great works, and to a share in his messianic power. By the same token, however, the disciples are required to respond with full faith and greater righteousness. The discourse on community life that immediately follows, keyed by the disciples' question about "who is the greatest in the kingdom of heaven?" (18:1), concentrates on the qualities that should characterize those privileged to be called disciples of Jesus.

The discourse itself is a collection of sayings and parables that in combination offer remarkable insight into the conditions and aspirations of Matthew's community. Although there is some debate about its precise structure, certain features are clear. Two key sayings about the "heavenly Father" recapitulate two important themes of the discourse: (1) 18:14—"So it is not the will of your Father in heaven that one of these little ones should be lost"—draws a conclusion to the exhortations of 18:2-13; and (2) the concluding saying of 18:35—"So my heavenly Father will also do to every one of you, if you do not forgive your brother or sister from your heart"—drives home the exhortation to limitless forgiveness that dominates 18:21-35. The central segment on how to deal with a recalcitrant member and the authority to do so given to the community (18:15-20) both stands in tension with the admonitions to compassion and forgiveness that surround it and is tempered by them.

The interpreter should keep in mind the viewpoint of this discourse. A close reading of its content, particularly in the first half of the discourse, suggests that it is directed to the inner core of the community, perhaps even its leadership. Those addressed are members of the community capable of placing an "obstacle" in the way of the "little ones" (18:6-9), those tempted to "despise" the "little ones" (18:10), and those positioned to search for the "stray" (18:12-13). The second half, too, speaks not to the recalcitrant or offending members of the community but to those who have been "sinned against" (18:15, 21).

The content of the discourse emphasizes virtues extolled by Matthew's gospel.

1) Jesus challenges his disciples to "turn" and become humble like a child (18:2-5). The Matthean Jesus had already blessed the meek (5:5) and praised his Father for revealing the mystery of the kingdom of God to "infants" (11:25; see also 19:13-15). Later in this part of the gospel, Jesus again reminds his disciples of the conversion of spirit demanded by the reign of God so that the "first will be last and the last will be first" (19:30; 20:16).

2) Care for the weak or seemingly insignificant members of the community (18:6-14) reflects Jesus' own attentive compassion for the crowds of sick and the "lost sheep" of Israel, which has been a hallmark of Matthew's narrative and illustrated in the stories of healing throughout the gospel (esp. chaps. 8–9). Matthew subtly switches terminology in the discourse from the image of the "child" *(paidion)* to that of "little one" *(mikron)*. The latter refers to the person's status in the community (see, for example, 10:42, where the persecuted disciples on mission are called "little ones" and the "least" in the parable of the sheep and the goats, 25:31-46).

3) The emphasis on forgiveness in the concluding section of the discourse is a characteristic Matthean theme already taught by Jesus in the Sermon on the Mount (e.g., 5:21-26, 38-42, 43-48; 6:12, 14-15). The correspondence between the material in the Sermon, particularly 5:43-58, and the uniquely Matthean parable of the unforgiving servant (18:23-35) is based on remembering God's own indiscriminate graciousness. In both instances the disciple must be willing to offer forgiveness to an injuring party because the disciple has experienced such remarkable graciousness from God.

4) The procedure suggested for dealing with an erring and recalcitrant member of the community (18:15-17) is reminiscent of a similar procedure within the sectarian community of Qum-

ran.[10] Even though ultimately severe in its consequences, the procedure does exhibit the qualities called for in the rest of the discourse. The erring member is treated with respect and discretion, and every effort is made to find a solution before the member is expelled. The injunction to treat the offender as one would a "Gentile and a tax collector" is intriguing. At times, Matthew refers to Gentiles and tax collectors as indicative of those outside the community and who do not share its values (e.g., 5:46-47). But Jesus also befriends both tax collectors and Gentiles in the gospels and they ultimately become the object of the community's mission (8:5-13; 9:9-10; 11:19). Does the saying—"Let such a one be to you as a Gentile and a tax collector"—imply that the expelled member, although now outside the community, becomes an object of the community's earnest search?

The issue of expulsion from the community also reveals the authority that Matthew's gospel assigns to the "assembly" or "church" *(ekklêsia)*. The same power of "binding and loosing"— in this instance clearly referring to the power of deciding membership—that had been given to Peter in 16:19 is also entrusted to the community assembly (18:18-19). The basis of that power is the abiding presence of the risen Christ in the community (18:20). Here the discourse catapults into the life of the reader of the gospel; the promise to remain with the community is the final promise that Jesus-Emmanuel will leave with the eleven apostles at the conclusion of the gospel (28:20).

This eloquent discourse, therefore, channels some of the gospel's most pointed teaching on discipleship and human relationships into a community exhortation. One can only guess whether the concentration on care for those on the margin, on dealing with disputes, and on forgiveness reflects some of the actual tensions within the Matthean community.

TEACHINGS ON THE JOURNEY (19:1–20:16)

With a transition phrase similar to those at the end of each of the great discourses, Matthew turns the reader back to the continuing journey to Jerusalem (19:1). There is a fleeting reference to the ever-present crowds of the sick and Jesus' healing of them (19:2), but the focus of this segment like that of the journey narrative as a whole is on instruction for the disciples. Other characters—some

145

Pharisees (19:3), the children (19:13), and a rich young man (19:16)—enter onstage at different times, but in each instance the words of Jesus they provoke are ultimately turned to the disciples. With the exception of the parable of the laborers in the vineyard, which is unique to Matthew's gospel (20:1-16), the material in this part of the narrative is drawn from Mark.

Marriage and Divorce (19:3-12)

Matthew carefully edits the discussion on divorce and remarriage (19:3-9), aligning it with Jesus' teaching in the Sermon on the Mount (5:31-32) and tying it clearly into a Jewish context. The Pharisees test Jesus by asking if it is lawful for a man to divorce his wife *for any cause*—the precise point of debate in rabbinic circles.[11] Unlike Mark, who may reflect a Roman context and speaks also of the woman's initiating divorce (Mark 10:12), Matthew retains the law's focus on the role of the man. Matthew arranges the flow of the discussion so that the fundamental point is more clearly expressed: The original and abiding intent of God regarding marriage is expressed in the ideal of man and woman united through marriage in an inseparable bond of "one flesh" (Gen 1:27; 2:24). The permission for divorce (Deut 24:1) was only a concession because of "your hardness of heart," Jesus tells the Pharisees (19:8).

In accord with 5:32, Matthew's version of Jesus' saying on divorce seems to include an exception in the case of *"porneia"* (19:9). The precise meaning of this Greek term, which basically means something "unclean" or "unlawful," is much debated, and translations range from "unchastity" (NRSV) to an "illicit" (NEW JERUSALEM BIBLE) or an "unlawful" marriage (NEW AMERICAN BIBLE). In the interpretation chosen by the NRSV ("unchastity"), the exception is broad and undefined and might apply to infidelity or a whole range of other serious causes. This would mean a true "exception" presumably introduced by the Christian community as a moderation of the radical teaching of Jesus still preserved in Mark's version where no exception clause exists (Mark 10:11-12).[12] In the interpretation suggested by the NAB and NJB translations, Matthew's phrase would not actually be an "exception" to the prohibition of divorce at all since *porneia* would be referring to an unlawful or invalid marriage. A possible situation in view would be Gentile converts who desired to enter the Matthean community yet were in an unlawful marriage (perhaps married within forbidden bloodlines); they would be expected to dissolve such marriages before entering the community. Thus understood the "exception" clause in Matthew would in no way reduce the radical demands of Jesus' original teaching on marriage.[13]

Choosing which of these possibilities the text intends is difficult and probably impossible. Here is an obvious example where ecclesial practice—permitting divorce or not—can incline a reader or a community to prefer one interpretation over another. In any case, Matthew's point is that in his teaching on marriage and divorce Jesus "fulfills" the meaning of the law by forcefully proclaiming God's will expressed in the "one flesh" ideals of Genesis. As in the antitheses of the Sermon on the Mount and in Jesus' teaching about pastoral care for the stray and mutual forgiveness in the community discourse of chapter 18, the thrust of Jesus' teaching in Matthew consistently emphasizes unity and reconciliation.

The discussion on divorce and remarriage concludes with a private exchange between Jesus and his disciples (19:10-12), a text found only in Matthew. The radical demands of Jesus' teaching lead the disciples to exclaim that it may be better "not to marry." Jesus' answer suggests that a range of responses to the call of the kingdom are possible, depending on the capacity of the disciple. Some may choose to be "eunuchs for the sake of the kingdom of heaven"; presumably this refers to those who would not remarry in virtue of Jesus' teaching on divorce and remarriage or others who would remain celibate because of their radical commitment to the Christian mission. As the mission discourse of chapter 10 suggests, the ideal of the itinerant who renounces family life and possessions for the sake of the mission was still honored in Matthew's community.[14] Though in Judaism marriage was strongly endorsed as the normal and God-intended way of life, at least some groups within Palestinian Judaism contemporary with Jesus and the early Christian community also chose a radical and celibate way of life.[15]

The Children (19:13-15)

Once again the child is lifted up as a sign of the kingdom of God (see 11:25; 18:1-5). In Mark's version, Jesus sharply rebukes the disciples when they prevent people from bringing their children to Jesus to have him "touch them" (Mark 10:14). In Matthew's less turbulent scene, the people bring their children to Jesus to have the Master "lay his hands on them and pray," a gracious gesture of blessing (Matt 19:13; cf. Mark 10:13). He does not rebuke the

disciples but instructs them, "it is to such as these that the kingdom of heaven belongs" (19:14).

On Leaving Behind One's Possessions (19:16-30)

The challenging portrayal of discipleship that is the hallmark of
this part of the gospel continues in this section dealing with possessions. In Matthew's version of the story of the rich young man,
Jesus' respect for the law is again underscored (19:16-22). When
the young man asks what "good deed" he must do to inherit everlasting life, Jesus reminds him of the heart of the Jewish law: "If
you wish to enter into life, keep the commandments" (19:17; cf.
Mark 10:18-19). To the summary of the commandments found in
Mark, Matthew adds his characteristic emphasis, "You shall love
your neighbor as yourself" (Matt 19:19; see 22:34-40).

As in the antitheses of the Sermon on the Mount and other
instances of his teaching, the Matthean Jesus offers a more radical
possibility beyond adherence to the law. If the rich young man
wishes to be "perfect," he should sell his possessions, give the pro-
ceeds to the poor, and follow Jesus in his itinerant mission. The term
"perfect," a translation of the Greek work *teleios*, meaning to be
complete or whole, was also held out as the ultimate goal for the disciples in 5:48. There, being "perfect" meant striving to love even the
enemy in the pattern of God's own indiscriminate graciousness. In
19:21 it means putting aside one's possessions and following Jesus.

Are such invitations addressed to an elite group of disciples, as
some have suggested? Or does Matthew consider the invitation to
a radical following of Jesus another "focal instance" meant to give
compelling direction for the lives of all disciples, no matter what
array of choices may be possible for them at a given moment of
their journey?[16]

The tenacious lure of possessions and the difficulty of what Jesus
asks are driven home by the response, both of the rich young man
and the disciples. The young man goes away grieving because "he
had many possessions" (19:22), and the disciples wonder out loud,
"Then who can be saved?" (19:25). Only the power of God, not
human determination, can provide the grace of discipleship (19:26).

Once again Peter steps forward on behalf of the disciples to ask
what will be the fate of those who do leave all things for the sake
of Jesus (19:27-30). To Mark's version of the "hundredfold,"
Matthew adds a new promise: At the triumphant return of the Son

of Man the faithful disciples will "sit on twelve thrones, judging the twelve tribes of Israel" (Matt 19:28; cf. Mark 10:29-30). Matthew's strong eschatological perspective breaks through here. The community that follows Jesus and obeys his teaching will bring to completion God's promise of a reassembled and renewed Israel.

The Parable of the Laborers (20:1-16)

The last of Jesus' teachings in this segment takes the form of a parable, one unique to Matthew's gospel. The parable is framed by and presumably illustrates Jesus' enigmatic saying that the "first will be last, and the last will be first" (19:30; 20:16). This provocative story overturns the expectations of those hired first who have "borne the burden of the day" that they would receive a greater wage than the laborers brought in at the last hour. They are not to be jealous, because the landowner is generous (20:15).

To whom does this Matthean parable apply and what is its meaning? In its present setting, the immediate referent for the saying and for the parable framed by it would seem to be those who follow Jesus. Even though they have left all to follow Jesus and are promised to be exalted as judges over the tribes of Israel, they should not take pride in their status. Matthew stresses the importance of response and good deeds, but his gospel does not lose sight of the fact that ultimately God's generosity alone is what counts, not human achievement. In response to Peter's alarm about the demands of discipleship, Jesus had assured the disciples that ". . . for God all things are possible" (19:26). That, ultimately, is the message of this parable as well.

The fact that this story involves a "vineyard," a traditional symbol for Israel (see Isa 5 and the parable of the wicked tenants in Matt 21:33-44), suggests another level of meaning to some interpreters. Does Matthew also see this story applying to the situation of the religious leaders of Israel, who are, in a sense, the "first hired," and the later workers as a reference to those tax collectors, sinners, and even Gentiles who will ultimately share in the kingdom of God on an equal basis with the righteous of Israel? Here, too, God's indiscriminate and abundant generosity is what counts, not one's status or history. Whether or not this kind of salvation history perspective is intended here, it will emerge clearly in later parables such as Matthew's story of the two sons (21:28-32) and in his conclusion to the parable of the tenants (21:43).

THE CONCLUSION OF THE JOURNEY (20:17-34)

The final passion prediction—the most detailed of them all—
alerts the reader to the continuing journey of Jesus, which is
about to reach its destination. A final instruction about the use of
power (20:20-28) and the gospel's last healing story (20:29-34)
complete this large section of the narrative.

The story of Zebedee's sons' quest for power (20:20-28) continues the gospel's emphasis on the humility and care for others that
is to characterize the disciples.[17] An interesting Matthean touch,
perhaps reflective of his more positive treatment of the disciples
compared with Mark, is the fact that the request comes from their
mother rather than directly from the two disciples themselves
(although in his response Jesus addresses them, not the mother).
As this section of the gospel has repeatedly stressed, the lot for
those who choose to follow Jesus is suffering and persecution (the
probable meaning of the "cup" symbol), not grand exaltation.

The disciples' quest for power prompts more of Jesus' teaching.
The community is not to imitate the oppressive power exercised
by Gentile rulers; within the community power is expressed as
humble service toward the other. The exemplar of such power is
the crucified Messiah; although endowed by God with overwhelming power, Jesus, the Son of Man, exercises that power
through giving his life for others (20:24-28).

Following Mark's lead, Matthew concludes his journey narrative with a story in which Jesus heals blindness.[18] As they leave
Jericho, "two blind men" (Mark's story has only one, "Barti-
maeus") cry out to Jesus for healing, addressing him with
Matthew's favored title, "Son of David." In the face of the crowd's
attempt to still their cries, the blind men only intensify their plea,
addressing Jesus as "Lord" and "Son of David." Since "seeing" has
already been used by Matthew as a metaphor for faith (e.g., 13:10-
17), the symbolic dimension of this story is apparent. Faced with
the extraordinary challenge of following Jesus on his journey to
the cross, the community can only make its own the urgent pleas
of these blind men: "Lord, let our eyes be opened" (20:33). Jesus'
compassionate and healing response encourages the members of
the community that the master would indeed provide them with
the grace needed to follow the way of Jesus.

CHAPTER 12

IN THE HOLY CITY: CONFLICT, DEATH, RESURRECTION
(21:1–28:15)

The arrival of Jesus and his disciples at the Mount of Olives and the preparations for his triumphant entry into the Holy City signal another important turning point in Matthew's gospel, one that will lead the story to its conclusion. The concentration on Jesus and his disciples that dominated the journey narrative now dissolves into a broader focus. Jesus' opponents are back in the picture, as are the crowds and new characters in the story, the Romans. Looming over much of this section is the shadow of the Temple: Jesus' teaching will take place in and around the temple and the fate of the temple will be a leitmotif of the apocalyptic discourse and reemerge in the passion story.

Matthew continues to demonstrate his dependence on Mark's

151

story line and content. Apart from some small adjustments to Mark's dramatization of the entry into Jerusalem and the omission of Mark's story of the widow's mite (Mark 12:41-44), Matthew follows exactly the Marcan sequence. Typical of the evangelist's inclination throughout the gospel, however, Matthew injects additional discourse material into the narrative including the parable of the two sons (21:28-32), the parable of the wedding feast (22:1-14; cf. Luke 14:15-24), the condemnation of the scribes and Pharisees (23:1-39), and the string of parables added to the apocalyptic discourse (24:37–25:46).

In the passion narrative Matthew again follows Mark closely but does add some significant and characteristic material, such as the instruction of the disciples at the moment of Jesus' arrest (26:52-54), the story of Judas' death (27:3-10), the appearance of Pilate's wife (27:19), and the acclamation of the crowd during the trial of Jesus (27:24-25), the cosmic events triggered by the death of Jesus (27:51-53), an appearance of the risen Jesus to the women who come to the tomb (28:9-10), and the polemical material about the guards at the tomb in 27:62-66 and 28:11-15. The Jerusalem setting is the thread that binds together the sequence of narrative and discourse that runs through this climactic part of the story.

THE MESSIAH AND THE TEMPLE (21:1-17)

By binding together into one event what Mark had cast as two, namely the entry into the city on one evening (Mark 11:1-11) and the cleansing of the Temple the next day (Mark 11:12-19), Matthew amplifies the power and force of this scene.[1]

The focus is on Jesus, the very drama of the entry scene enabling Matthew to reaffirm the messianic authority of Jesus. His command sends the disciples without hesitation to prepare for the entry, instructing them to procure a donkey and a colt simply by noting that "the Lord needs them" (Matt 21:1-3). The acclamations of the crowds that process into the city with Jesus confirm that this is the Messiah coming to take possession of his city and exercise authority over the temple (21:8-9). With a distinctive touch, Matthew notes that "the whole city was in turmoil," reminiscent of the fear that ran through Jerusalem at the announcement of his birth (see Matt 2:3). As a zealous prophet Jesus purifies the temple, which, in Matthew's perspective, is a sign of its eventual destruction. That fate will be explicitly cited at the beginning of the apocalyptic discourse (24:1-2) and a sign of it given at the moment of Jesus' death when the temple veil is torn in two (27:51). Matthew respects the sacred history of the temple, designating it as the "temple of God" (26:61) and God's "house" (citing Jer 7:11 in 21:13), but from the vantage point of his post-AD 70 community, he is aware of its eventual destruction and interprets this as part of God's punishment for the sins of Israel, particularly its rejection of the Messiah.

Matthew also portrays Jesus with his favored title "Son of David," a messianic title but one that for Matthew paradoxically underscores the humility and compassion of God's servant.[2] Thus the Messiah who enters the city does so humbly mounted on a donkey and a colt (21:5) and, even in the temple, continues to minister to the sick with compassion and healing (21:14).

Matthew also emphasizes his characteristic theme of scriptural fulfillment throughout this scene. The procurement of the animals prompts the fulfillment text from Zechariah 9:9 in 21:5, underscoring the humility of Jesus, the Son of David. The typical Semitic paralleling, "on a donkey, and on a colt, the foal of a donkey" in the quotation leads Matthew to refer to two animals in the scene, emphasizing the literal fulfillment of the text (21:2, 7; contrast Mark 11:7). As in Mark, Jesus justifies his prophetic action in the temple by appealing to a combination of Isaiah 56:7 and Jeremiah 7:11 (Matt 21:13; Mark 11:17). And Jesus counters the objections of the chief priests and scribes by quoting Psalm 8:2 (Matt 21:16).

THE TEACHER AND HIS OPPONENTS
(21:18–22:46)

A new day (21:18) leads the reader into another segment where Jesus will spar with a series of his opponents. The story of the condemned fig tree that served in Mark's account as an interpretative frame around the cleansing of the temple is left somewhat freestanding in Matthew and becomes an instruction to the disciples on the importance of strong and confident faith (21:18-22). By contrast, the chief priests and elders—the first of several groups to confront Jesus—demonstrate a lack of faith in Jesus by their challenge to his authority (21:23-27).

Their intransigence draws from Jesus a series of parables, most of them pointed at the leaders' lack of faith and its consequences. The parable of the two sons (21:28-32) is unique to this gospel and typical of Matthew's perspective: What counts is not just saying the right words but actually doing the will of God, and this axiom finds its illustration in the tax collectors and prostitutes who respond positively to Jesus while the leaders refuse to believe or act.

The parable of the wicked tenants is already found in Mark, where the vineyard as a traditional symbol for Israel gives the story evident allegorical meaning (Mark 12:1-12; Matt 21:33-44; see Isa 5:1-10). Matthew enhances the parable's portrayal of salvation history from his vantage point. The *kairos*, the time of judgment, is near (21:34, 40). The first two series of messengers sent by the "owner of the vineyard" (21:40) are treated badly and, in Matthew's version, some of them are even killed, reflecting the persecution of the prophets before Jesus (see 23:34-38). Finally the owner sends his son, whom the tenants first cast outside the vineyard and then kill (reversing the order of events in Mark's story and possibly reflecting the passion account where Jesus is crucified outside Jerusalem, 21:39). For this act, the owner of the vineyard brings judgment upon the tenants: They are put to a "miserable death" and the vineyard itself is given over to other tenants "who will give him the produce at the harvest time" (21:41). Matthew drives home this point by his addition of verse 43: "Therefore I tell you, the kingdom of God will be taken away from you and given to a people that produces the fruits of the kingdom." The reaction of the leaders validates the intent of the parable: They realize that Jesus is speaking about them, and their determination to destroy Jesus continues (21:45-46).

This parable offers a clear insight into Matthew's interpretation of the opposition to Jesus. The rejection suffered by Jesus is in line with that endured by the prophets. Because Jesus is the last and definitive messenger of God—God's own son—the consequences for rejecting him are bound to be dire. For Matthew that conviction was confirmed in the terrible events of the destruction of Jerusalem in AD 70. He also sees traces of God's overarching plan of salvation in the midst of this tragedy: If Israel fails to respond to God's message of repentance and salvation, the Gentiles will respond. Therefore the privileged role of the tenants will be handed over to others who will produce a harvest.

The following parable of the wedding banquet is drawn from Q, but Matthew adds his own special emphasis (Matt 22:1-14; cf. Luke 14:15-24). Once again the basic story in both Matthew's and Luke's versions is a thinly veiled allegory of salvation history: The king extends invitations to the wedding feast but those first invited reject the invitation. The king then opens the invitation to all who would respond. In Luke this story emphasizes Jesus' mission to the poor and the marginalized (see Luke's description of the invitees— "the poor and maimed and blind and lame," 14:21). For Matthew, however, the story focuses on the differing responses of Israel and the Gentiles. The ones first invited not only reject the invitation but, as in the case of the messengers to the vineyard (21:35), abuse and kill the servants who bear the invitation (22:6). In response the king exercises swift and severe judgment: Troops are sent "to destroy those murderers and burn their city" (22:7). It is probable that Matthew alludes here to the destruction of Jerusalem and, as he had in the previous parable, interprets this catastrophe as divine retribution for the rejection of Jesus.

To this grim parable Matthew appends another sober lesson on judgment, this time applicable to the Gentiles (see Matt 22:11-14, which has no parallel in Luke's version). Those invited to replace the first set of intended guests include "both good and bad" (reminiscent of Matthew's parable of the wheat and the tares, 13:24-30, 36-43). And when the king enters the banquet hall he discovers a guest without a wedding garment, most likely a symbol of repentance and good deeds. This hapless guest also falls under the king's judgment and is thrown "into the outer darkness" (22:13). Matthew's theology is utterly consistent: The same criterion of repentance and good deeds is applied to both Jews and Gentiles. For Matthew, the Gentiles are not a new privileged class who take over from Israel in the history of salvation. For both Jew and Gentile the same truth holds: Belonging to God's people means doing the will of God (12:50).[3]

Throughout this section Matthew presents the religious leaders as antagonists. The setting of these conflicts in the Temple, the very center of Jewish teaching authority and orthodoxy (21:23), adds a sense of drama and finality to the conflict. Matthew notes the utter frustration of Jesus' opponents—none of them is successful as they seek to entrap him in his teaching (22:15). Their failure only serves to highlight Jesus' authority as the Messiah

155

standing in God's house. The disciples of the Pharisees and some Herodians cannot trap him with their question about tribute to Caesar and they go away "amazed" (22:22). The Sadducees question him about the resurrection (22:23-33), but Jesus refutes their logic and his answer leaves the crowds "astounded" at his teaching (22:33) and "silences" the Sadducees (22:34). Then it is the Pharisees' turn: They "test" him with a question about the greatest commandment of the law (22:34-40), only to have Jesus turn the tables and ask them a question about the messiah that leaves them speechless. From that point on, Matthew notes, no one "dared to ask him any more questions" (22:46).

Through all of these conflict stories Matthew's distinctive portrayal of Jesus continues to be affirmed. While escaping the trap of the question about taxes, Jesus reaffirms that everything belonging to God should be rendered to God (22:21), just as he had from the moment of his initial testing in the desert (4:1-11). Deflecting the ploy of the Sadducees, he pays homage to the "God of the living," anticipating the source of his own triumph over death that would conclude the gospel. The test put to him by the Pharisees about the greatest commandment of the law (22:34-40) concludes with a reaffirmation of the principle of interpretation taught by Jesus throughout the gospel: On the command to love God and neighbor "hang all the law and the prophets," a conclusion to this story found only in Matthew (Matt 22:40; cf. Mark 12:31; Luke 10:27).[4] And in his final parry with the Pharisees, Jesus pointedly asks them the decisive question reminiscent of that put to the disciples at Caesarea Philippi: "What do you think of the Messiah? Whose son is he?" (Matt 22:42; contrast Mark 12:35; Luke 20:41). The Messiah is not only "Son of David" but also one David must call "Lord"—the mysterious and compelling authority of Jesus that Matthew has affirmed throughout the gospel goes beyond the traditional messianic expectations. The reader cannot forget that the disciples had called upon Jesus as "Lord" in moments of danger and need (see, e.g., 8:25; 14:30; 15:25).

CONDEMNATION OF THE SCRIBES AND PHARISEES (23:1-39)

The string of conflicts throughout this section of the gospel culminates in a bitter denunciation of the leaders in chapter 23.

Some interpreters see this as part of one great discourse that will run through chapters 24 and 25. But the change of setting and mood in 24:1-4 clearly shows that for Matthew chapters 24–25 form a distinct discourse of Jesus. Although this prophetic critique of the leaders may not rate as one of the five principal discourses of the gospel, it is a significant speech of the Matthean Jesus and offers important insight into the gospel's perspective.[5] The fact that it is addressed to the disciples is an important clue about the ultimate purpose of this speech. While obviously intended as a critique of the scribes and Pharisees, it is primarily intended as instruction for the followers of Jesus.

This prophetic speech of Jesus is most likely triggered by a brief passage in Mark where at the end of his teaching in the temple Jesus warns his disciples not to be like the scribes who make a pretense of piety but also devour the houses of widows. The extraordinary generosity and devotion of the widow entering the temple is praised by Jesus and offers a sharp contrast to the false piety of the leaders (see Mark 12:38-44). Matthew completely reconfigures this conclusion of Jesus' teaching in the temple. The story of the widow is omitted but Jesus' denunciation of the scribes is vastly expanded into a full-blown discourse condemning the "scribes and Pharisees." Much of the material is from Q and appears at various places in Luke's gospel, but by assembling it here and developing it into a prophetic speech of Jesus, Matthew makes it the final expression of judgment on the leaders that has been building throughout the gospel and stoked to white-hot intensity in the temple section we have been considering.

The discourse falls into three segments. In the first segment (23:1-12), the leaders' authority as legitimate teachers is duly noted (23:1-3) but they are condemned for the kind of failings the Matthean Jesus has denounced throughout the gospel: failure to act justly; a lack of compassion in laying heavy burdens on others; false piety and arrogant pride.[6] In contrast to the arrogance and status-seeking of the religious leaders, Jesus presents an alternative vision for the community. No one should be called "rabbi" or "Father" or "instructor"—in each instance such titles of honor and status within the community are nullified by the realization that only God and God's Messiah hold such authority. Everyone else in the community is on the same basis—fellow students, brothers and sisters, fellow servants.

This extraordinary portrayal of an egalitarian community is an important ingredient in Matthew's ecclesiology, one that echoes the spirit of the community discourse in chapter 18 where authority resided in the entire community and where leadership was to be characterized by humility, respect for others, attention to the weaker members, compassion for the stray, and active forgiveness.[7]

The second section of the discourse (23:13-36) continues and even intensifies the critique of the leaders but now uses the traditional literary device of "prophetic woes." In so doing, Matthew portrays Jesus in the familiar role of the prophet, denouncing the sins of the leaders.[8] The seven sets of woes are tied to characteristic Matthean concerns: being obstacles and corrupters of others (23:13-15; cf. 18:6-9); taking insincere oaths (23:16-22; cf. 5:33-37); wrong priorities in their interpretation of law (23:23-24; cf. 15:3-9); being hypocritical, that is, masking inner corruption with a pious exterior (23:25-26, 27-28; cf. 6:2-18).

The woes culminate in an ominous reminder of the fate of the prophets and a dire prediction of the future (23:29-36). As Matthew interprets history and had already signaled in his parable of the tenants and the parable of the wedding feast (21:35; 22:6), the prophetic messengers to Israel were rejected and even killed. A similar fate awaited the messengers that Jesus the Messiah would send out in his name: These "prophets, sages, and scribes" would meet persecution and even death "in your synagogues" (23:34). The rejection of Jesus and his messengers would ultimately bring judgment upon "this generation" (23:36).[9]

The third and concluding segment of the discourse moves from the rhetoric of the prophetic "woes" to that of lament (23:37-39; cf. Luke 13:34-35). Now Jerusalem, "the city that kills the prophets and stones those who are sent to it" is the object of Jesus' words. In the infancy narrative (2:3) and at the moment of Jesus' entry into the holy city (21:10), Matthew had personified the city and characterized it as profoundly disturbed by Jesus. Now Jesus poignantly predicts that its "house" (probably meaning the temple) would be desolate. As he had done in the preceding parables of the tenants and the wedding feast, Matthew has Jesus foretell the destruction of Jerusalem and interprets this catastrophe as punishment for its rejection of the Messiah.

The final verse of the discourse is significant (23:39). This is

Jesus' last moment in Jerusalem and its temple prior to his passion (see 24:1). The Holy City will not see a visitation of its Messiah again "until" it is prepared to receive him with acclamation. The words of the acclamation—"Blessed is the one who comes in the name of the Lord"—are from Psalm 118:26, the very words with which the crowds greeted Jesus as he entered Jerusalem for the first time (21:9). What is Matthew's view about the future of Israel? Does Matthew, as suggested in the definitive tones of 21:43, believe that Israel is forsaken because of its rejection of Jesus? Or, as the conditional "until" implies here, is it still possible that eventually Israel would receive its Messiah?[10]

The bitter invective of this discourse poses a challenge for the interpreter of Matthew's gospel who cannot afford to be unaware of the legacy such a text has for feeding anti-Semitism. Several points should be kept in mind:

1) Undoubtedly within the historical setting of his own ministry, Jesus encountered opposition, as prophetic figures before him had. And the strong tone of Jesus' words to his opponents is not dissimilar to the prophetic denunciations that prophets such as Amos or Jeremiah hurled at the leaders in their day. The tension between Jesus and his opponents described in the gospel has its origin in this historical basis but does not stop there.

2) Matthew's strong critique of the Jewish leaders in this passage and elsewhere in the gospel also reflects the tension between his largely Jewish Christian community and the Pharisaic leadership of formative Judaism, as both communities were attempting to define themselves in the period prior to and contemporary with the composition of the gospel. Such tension and debate, while often hostile in tone, remained essentially an intra-Jewish debate and cannot be understood as "anti-Semitic" in the sense the term is used today.

3) Even within these perimeters, Matthew's critique in chapter 23 and elsewhere is presented not as a blanket condemnation of the "Jews" but mainly of their leaders for what the gospel judges as specific failings within a specific time frame ("this generation"). The gospel text does not condemn all Jews for all times.

4) In casting the leaders in uniformly negative tones, Matthew's gospel offers a stereotyped view of such groups as scribes, Pharisees, Sadducees, and others. The historical reality was such that not *all* the leaders were hypocritical or corrupt. In fact, other

sources suggest that the Pharisees had many goals in common with Jesus.[11]

5) Matthew's purposes in a passage such as chapter 23 are multiple—not only a critique of the Jewish leaders but also defining the distinctive identity and values of the Christian community; not simply attacking those outside the community but instructing the Christians themselves on what attitudes and practices they should avoid, and at the same time underscoring the integrity and authority of Jesus as the sole legitimate teacher and leader of the community.

All this said, the potential of these Matthean passages to be read and interpreted as an unqualified attack on Jews and Judaism remains, and Christian teachers bear the responsibility for preventing such a toxic reading of the gospel.

THE COMING OF THE SON OF MAN AND THE JUDGMENT OF THE WORLD (24:1–25:46)

Jesus' departure from the Temple for the Mount of Olives signals another change of scene in Matthew's story (24:1-3). So, too, does the narrowing of the focus to now just Jesus and his disciples, who come to him "privately" on the Mount of Olives (24:3). The crowds and the opponents drop from sight. Matthew is about to present for the reader the fifth and last of Jesus' great discourses, one that will cover chapters 24 and 25 and lead into the passion story itself (26:1).

Jesus' prophecy concerning the fate of the temple ("not one stone will be left here upon another . . .") and the disciples' double question ("When will this be, and what will be the sign of your coming and of the end of the age?") set the topic for this discourse about the end time and the stance the disciple is to take in the face of it. The setting of the discourse on the Mount of Olives, a location associated with the end of the world in Jewish tradition, also helps color the mood (see Zech 14:4).

The initial section of the discourse proper (24:4-36), which parallels Mark 13, speaks of the signs of the end time and the coming of the Son of Man (see esp. 24:30-31). Both Mark and Matthew draw on stock Jewish apocalyptic imagery, particularly as modeled in the book of Daniel.[12] This view of history, born in crisis, believed that the end of the age was at hand and that God would sweep away the remnants of the old order and create a new one.

From that vortex would emerge a new Israel, redeemed and exalted by God, freed from the humiliation and oppression it had experienced and restored to peace and dignity. This Jewish perspective was also important for early Christianity, which saw the death and resurrection of Jesus as well as the community's own place in history through such an apocalyptic perspective.

Thus Jesus' discourse foretells of the chaos to be experienced in history as the end nears. Matthew adds some characteristic touches: False prophets would arise to "lead many astray" and "because of the increase of lawlessness, the love of many will grow cold" (24:11-12). In the community discourse, Jesus asked the disciples to care for those that "were led astray" (18:12-14). And the followers of the Matthean Jesus who had insistently taught obedience to the law and the centrality of the love command should not be surprised at warnings about "lawlessness" (see 7:23; 13:41; 23:28) and a lack of love (see 22:33-44). So, too, Matthew adds that the disciples should pray their flight may not be in winter "or on a sabbath" (24:20; cf. Mark 13:18), another glint of evidence that the Matthean community still revered their Jewish traditions.

The first part of the discourse proclaims a twofold message about the future, and both dimensions are fundamental to Matthew's theology. On the one hand, the Matthean Jesus firmly proclaims that the Son of Man will come in triumph at the end of history to gather the elect from the four corners of the earth (24:30-35). As we noted earlier, the "Son of Man" title in Matthew describes both Jesus' humiliation and suffering as well as his final exaltation and triumph.[13] In this discourse the focus is solely on the final triumph of Jesus as the Son of Man. But, at the same time, Matthew emphasizes that no one can be sure when this final moment will come; anyone who claims to know is a false prophet (24:36-44). The disciple of Jesus, therefore, must live in history confident of its triumphant conclusion with the coming of the Son of Man yet watchful and ready for this unknown and unpredictable moment.

Defining this stance commands the rest of the discourse. The disciple is to be "awake," expectant, and ready for the coming of the Son of Man. The discourse uses a profusion of images and stories to convey this: the owner of the house being alert if he knew the thief was coming (24:43-44); the faithful and wise slave awaiting the master's return—in contrast to the wicked slave who is irresponsible and negligent and thus caught off guard (24:45-51); the five wise bridesmaids who have their lamps ready for the return of the bridegroom (undoubtedly an allusion to Jesus, who had already spoken of himself as the "bridegroom" earlier in the gospel; see Matt 9:14-15)—in contrast to the five foolish bridesmaids, who are unprepared and shut out of the wedding feast (25:1-13); and the differing reaction of the slaves, who either prudently develop their talents and are thus rewarded upon their master's return or, in the case of the hapless servant who buries it in a hole, experience condemnation (25:14-30).

Through this set of stories the Matthean Jesus not only teaches the disciples to be watchful but further defines such "watchfulness" in terms of proper action. Here Matthew fuses on to typical apocalyptic concerns about the end time the ethical focus characteristic of his gospel. Thus the faithful servant gives food to the other servants and is found "at work" when the master returns (24:46); the oil in the lamps of the wise virgins may also suggest a life of good deeds (25:4);[14] and those who increased the talents entrusted to them did not prove "wicked and lazy" (25:26). In Matthew's perspective, "watchfulness" concerning the end time is not defined by speculation about the end time (which is expressly discouraged) but precisely in doing the will of God as taught by Jesus, the consistent ethical message of the gospel as a whole.

All of this leads into the final segment of the discourse, the famous story of the sheep and the goats (25:31-46). The parable is not simply one more illustration in the string of images and parables in the discourse. Matthew signals that something different is at stake by recalling at the very beginning of the parable the vision of coming of the Son of Man that was the climax of the first part of the discourse (25:31; cf. 24:30). Popular interpretation of this Matthean parable sees it as an eloquent call for charity and justice to those most in need. We will be judged on how we respond to the "least." Although this fundamental Christian message is by no means an invalid interpretation of Matthew's parable, a close reading of Matthew's text suggests that the evangelist may have had a more specific focus in mind.[15] One of the keys for the interpretation of this parable is the identity of those assembled before the throne of the Son of Man. "All the nations," namely the Gentiles, are now gathered for judgment. The previous set of parables were stories about how the *community* itself would be judged—that is, on its alertness for the coming of the Son of Man and its perseverance in doing good deeds. Now Matthew turns his attention beyond the immediate boundaries of the community to the "nations" or Gentiles who will be the object of the community's mission in the time remaining before the end of the world (24:14). The parable, therefore, answers the question of how *they* will be judged.

One other element of the parable has to be considered before drawing any conclusions. The Gentiles are to be judged on how they treat the "least of my brethren" (25:40, 45). Who are these "least"? From Matthew's vantage point these "least brethren" are the members of the Christian community, more specifically the missionaries who go out and encounter the Gentiles. In the mission discourse, Jesus had spoken of the disciples sent on mission in similar terms: These were the "little ones" sent in Jesus' name (10:42). Even more important, the missionaries represent Jesus and, therefore, whoever welcomes them welcomes Jesus (10:40). The parable, therefore, suggests that in treating the missionaries of the community with respect and compassion, the Gentiles are in effect so treating Jesus himself—something which, understandably, the Gentiles are not yet able to recognize. They will be judged on their instinctive application of Jesus' teaching about compassion and justice to these apparently insignificant strangers who come to them with the message of the gospel.

Thus for everyone the ultimate criterion of judgment is the love command. In chapter 23, the scribes and Pharisees had been condemned for their "hypocrisy" in not carrying out the very commands they themselves taught. In chapters 24 and 25, the disciples have been warned that while awaiting the coming of the Son of Man they are to be doing good deeds. And in the final parable of the sheep and the goats, the Gentiles are held to the same criterion, as illustrated in the specific instance of how they treat the emissaries of the community. Here is where the broader more popular interpretation of the parable as an exhortation to compassion and justice intersects with Matthew's specific application. Even though Matthew may have in mind a very particular encounter of Gentiles with Christian missionaries, he sees their instinctive response to these "least brethren" as indicative of their fundamental values and therefore the basis of God's just judgment.

To the criterion of good deeds, Matthew had added one more

norm for the members of the community: They are also to be alert for the coming of the Son of Man, even though the precise time of that coming cannot be known. In his portrayal of the foolish servants and bridesmaids who ignore the end time, Matthew may intend to critique those members of his community whose hopes for Jesus' triumphant return had grown dim. He may also have in mind factions within the Jewish community who had become leery of apocalyptic fever, particularly in the wake of the Jewish revolt when some Jewish apocalyptic groups had created a self-destructive atmosphere on the basis of their expectations that God would miraculously destroy the Romans and exalt Israel.[16] But the apocalyptic theology Matthew proposes was not a destructive fanaticism. While awaiting with confidence and hope the triumphant return of Jesus, the community was not to expend its energy on useless speculation but be committed to its mission of proclaiming the gospel to the world and living in accord with Jesus' teaching.

THE PASSION AND RESURRECTION OF JESUS
(26:1–28:15)

Matthew's story now mounts to its summit. The eschatological discourse ends with another of the evangelist's transition formulas, but this time he notes "when Jesus had finished saying *all* these things." All of the great speeches of Jesus are now concluded; there remain only the climactic events of the passion and resurrection. Matthew follows Mark's passion account closely without swerving from its sequence of events, yet through his characteristic changes and the introduction of some special material Matthew's version of the passion and resurrection is distinct from that of Mark.[17]

Three dominant motifs—each of them characteristic of the gospel as a whole—weave their way through the various scenes of Matthew's passion story:

1) *Christology.* The attention of the passion story falls mainly on *Jesus* who even in the midst of suffering and death remains a figure of majesty and authority. Matthew colors the christology of the passion story with the same strong tones found throughout the gospel. Thus right from the start the Matthean Jesus foretells the events of the passion and prepares his disciples for its onslaught (26:1-2). At

the Passover meal he predicts Judas' betrayal, the denial of Peter, and the flight of the rest of the disciples (26:20-25, 30-35). In the blessing of the bread and the cup, the Matthean Jesus interprets his death as expiation "for the forgiveness of sins," echoing the promise of his God-given name "Jesus" (1:21) and affirming that beyond the frontiers of death he would drink the wine of the Kingdom anew with his disciples (26:26-29). His prayer in Gethsemane is anguished, but, even more emphatically, it is a prayer of obedience to the Father, fitting perfectly with Matthew's consistent portrayal of Jesus from the moment of the baptism (3:15) and desert test (4:1-11) and throughout the narrative. At the moment of the arrest Jesus is not taken by surprise: He anticipates his betrayal (26:20-25, 45-46), and as Judas plants his treacherous kiss, Jesus already knows his intention (26:50). Jesus refuses to be rescued by violence, consistent with his teaching in the Sermon on the Mount (5:38-48) even though as God's beloved, legions of angels could be at his disposal (26:52-54). Jesus' arrest, as well as the entire passion and his whole life, fulfill the scriptures (26:54), as the gospel had noted from the moment of his birth.[18]

In the face of the high priest's question (26:63-64), Jesus affirms—as the gospel earlier already had—that he is the Christ and the Son of God but also the Son of Man who would ultimately come in triumph at the end of the world (a strong tie to the preceding discourse; see 24:30-31). Though the soldiers and the passersby mock Jesus for his supposed pretensions to kingship (27:27-30), the reader knows that he truly is the royal Son of God. In a final act of mockery found only in Matthew, his tormentors hurl at Jesus the words of Psalm 22:8, "He trusts in God; let God deliver him now, if he wants to; for he said, 'I am God's Son'" (27:43).[19] Therefore immediately before the moment of Jesus' death, Matthew again calls the reader's attention to the issue of Jesus' obedient trust in God, even in the face of death. Jesus dies with the words of Psalm 22 on his lips—"My God, my God, why have you forsaken me?"—a prayer of anguish and ultimate trust from the obedient Just One at the final moment of his life.

God's vindication of Jesus' trust and obedience is confirmed in the miraculous signs that follow immediately upon Jesus' death (27:51-53).[20] The veil of the temple is torn in half (a confirming sign of the destruction Jesus had predicted in 24:2), and in imagery drawn from Ezekiel's vision of the dry bones revivified

(Ezek 37), events of the end time begin to happen immediately upon Jesus' death as the earth shakes and the holy ones are liberated from their tombs (27:51-53). The centurion's testimony— "Truly this man was God's Son!" (27:54)—dramatically confirms what the reader of the gospel has long known (see 14:33; 16:16). Through his death Jesus, God's obedient Son, has liberated those trapped in the darkness of Sheol, freeing them from the grip of sin and death and thus fulfilling the promise of his name (see 1:21) and confirming Jesus' own prophecy that his death would bring forgiveness of sin (26:28).

2) *Ecclesiology.* Matthew's "mixed" portrayal of the disciples as being of "little faith" is also confirmed in the passion narrative. As the narrative begins, the "Twelve" remain the privileged companions of Jesus, celebrating the last Passover with him and being the first to share in the meal that promised forgiveness of sins (26:28). At that meal, Jesus also promised that he would drink the fruit of the vine "with you [i.e., the disciples] in my Father's kingdom" (26:29).

But most of the passion story reveals the weakness and failure of the disciples in the face of suffering and death. Despite Jesus' warnings earlier in the gospel they seem unprepared: They chide the woman who anoints Jesus (26:8); they sleep in Gethsemane despite Jesus' instruction to stay awake (26:38, 40, 41, 43, 45; see also 25:13); and at the moment of the arrest all of them abandon Jesus and flee (26:56).

In Matthew's account the characters of Judas and Peter illustrate the failure of discipleship in grim detail. Judas stands for utter failure, as Jesus himself predicts (26:20-25). He aligns himself with Jesus' opponents (26:14-16), calls Jesus "Rabbi" (26:25, 49), and betrays his master with a kiss (26:49). Matthew alone follows Judas' story to its tragic conclusion. Stricken by remorse when Jesus is condemned, the betrayer hurls the blood money into the temple sanctuary and then takes his own life (27:3-20). Peter, too, models failure in the passion story but his fate is different. Peter insists that he will never desert Jesus, ironically underscoring the enormity of his eventual denial (26:33). Despite his bravado he sleeps in the Garden during Jesus' anguished prayer (26:40). Matthew, following the device of Mark, plays out the denial of Peter in slow motion. Unlike the others, Peter does not flee at the moment of the arrest but follows Jesus "at a distance" (26:58). At the very moment Jesus fearlessly confesses his identity before the high priest, Peter swears "with an oath" that he did not even know Jesus—the taking of the oath a Matthean touch coinciding with Jesus' condemnation of oath taking in the Sermon on the Mount (26:74; see 5:33-37). Even though his sin is grievous, Peter will be restored to discipleship as his grief upon remembering Jesus' words already signals (26:75). The reader of the gospel recalls Jesus' blessing of Peter at Caesarea Philippi (16:16-19) and the instruction the disciples had received about limitless forgiveness (18:21-35). Thus the figures of Peter and Judas vividly illustrate for Matthew's community two different responses to failure: One continues to align himself with Jesus' opponents and despairs, the other is stricken with remorse and will be reconciled.

As has been the case throughout the gospel, other seemingly minor characters display the traits of genuine discipleship even when the chosen twelve do not. The insight and devotion of the woman who anoints Jesus at Bethany is one obvious example (26:6-13). Pilate's wife, a character found only in Matthew's account, defends Jesus as a "just" *(dikaios)* man even as the religious leaders seek to have him crucified (27:19).[21] The Roman centurion and the other soldiers who keep watch over the crucified Jesus confess him as "Son of God" (27:54). Joseph of Arimathea, a "rich man" and a "disciple of Jesus," proclaims his continuing loyalty by offering the crucified Jesus the homage of a proper burial in his own new tomb (27:57-61). And while the other disciples have fled, women who had "followed Jesus from Galilee and had provided for him" remain by the cross (27:55-56). Some of their number, "Mary Magdalene and the other Mary" witness his burial (27:61) and are the first to discover the empty tomb and encounter the risen Jesus (28:1-10), thereby becoming the ones who proclaimed the resurrection to the disciples (28:10-11).[22]

Through his portrayal of the disciples in the passion story, Matthew reaffirms the warnings found in the mission discourse and the apocalyptic discourse about the struggles the community had to face as it carried out its mission in history (see esp. 10:16-42; 24:9-14). The passion of Jesus was, in effect, a preview of the passion of the community.

3) *Theology of History.* The passion story also illumines what we can call Matthew's "theology of history."[23] The death and resurrection of Jesus form the decisive turning point in the history of salvation. Several features of Matthew's account illustrate this.

The opposition of the Jewish leaders to Jesus reaches its climax in the passion and serves multiple purposes. Their negative portrayal is only intensified in the passion story. They conspire "to arrest Jesus by stealth" (26:3-5) and pay Judas thirty pieces of silver to betray his master (26:14-16). They engineer his arrest (26:47) and seek "false testimony" against Jesus (26:59). The high priest, in the name of the council, rejects Jesus' testimony about his identity and labels it blasphemy (26:65). The entire council declares that Jesus is worthy of death (26:66; 27:1) and they themselves mock and abuse him (26:67-68). The story of Judas' death becomes an even more insistent indictment of them. Although the ill-fated disciple finds remorse that he has betrayed "innocent blood" (27:3-4), the priests and elders rebuff him and take up the blood money themselves—ironically signaling their own complicity. Through the last of the gospel's fulfillment quotations, Matthew emphasizes that even this tragic moment falls within God's plan (27:9-10).

Matthew's rendition of the trial before Pilate is calculated to further underscore the leaders' rejection of Jesus. They take the lead in accusing him before the governor (27:12), and despite the attempts of both Pilate and his wife (27:19) to release Jesus, the leaders persuade the crowd to choose Barabbas (27:20-23). As Jesus hangs on the cross, the leaders mock the very affirmations that the gospel has repeatedly directed at Jesus: his role as savior of others; his identity as the Messiah ("the King of Israel") and God's beloved son (27:41-43). Alone of all the evangelists, Matthew extends the hostility of the leaders beyond the death of Jesus. They insist that a guard be set at the tomb to prevent the disciples from taking away Jesus' body (and then falsely claiming that he was raised from the dead) and then, even in the face of the guards' testimony about the miraculous events at the tomb, bribe the guards to lie (27:62-66; 28:11-15). In one of the clearest signs that Matthew reads the current experience of his community into the events of the gospel, he concludes his account by noting that the false testimony about the resurrection of Jesus continues "among the Jews to this day" (28:15).

On one level this negative portrayal of the leaders serves as a foil to Matthew's portrayal of Jesus. Their ill will and hostility throw into relief the integrity and majestic authority of Jesus as the Messiah and suffering Son of Man. But the comportment of the leaders has a more fundamental significance for Matthew's theology, illustrating the rejection of Jesus and the Christian mission by Israel and paving the way for the mission to the Gentiles. This turn of events was, in Matthew's perspective, not simply a tragic accident of history but was entwined with God's own mysterious will. Just as the mission of Jesus fulfilled the Scriptures, so, too, did all the events of the passion (26:54), even the betrayal of Judas and the complicity of the leaders in the shedding of Jesus' innocent blood (27:9-10). Matthew's story had already hinted at this turning point in history: the coming of the Magi to do homage to Jesus while Herod and the leaders responded hostilely (2:1-12); the faith of the centurion in Capernaum leading Jesus to foresee Gentiles sitting at Abraham's table while the heirs of the Kingdom are banned to the outer darkness (8:11-12); Jesus' acknowledgment of the "great faith" of the Canaanite woman at the border of Tyre and Sidon (15:28); the blunt conclusion to the parable of the vineyard directed at the Pharisees which predicted that the vineyard would be "taken away from you and given to a people (*ethnos*) that produces the fruits of the kingdom" (21:43); and Jesus' prediction that the temple would be destroyed (24:2).

Now this turning point in history would reach its apex in Jesus' death and resurrection. For Matthew the passion of Jesus was an eschatological event, bringing to an end the old age and ushering in the new. As the Passover eve approached, Jesus had referred to the passion as the *"kairos,"* the decisive end time (26:18).[24] And at the very moment of Jesus' death, Matthew fills the scene with portents of the end time: The sky darkens (27:45), the veil of the temple is torn in two (27:51), the earth quakes, and events expected for the end of the world begin to take place: the opening of the tombs and the resurrection of the just Israelites.[25] Thus Matthew portrays the very moment of Jesus' death as a triumph, an anticipation of the resurrection. In the empty tomb story, too, Matthew will include this kind of eschatological coloring: There is a great earthquake and an angel of the Lord clothed in shining white rolls back the stone from the tomb (28:2).

For Matthew's theology, the rejection of Jesus by the leaders and, through their influence, by the people themselves, is only one side of a coin: From rejection comes new life; from the broken hopes of the mission to Israel, comes the mission to the Gentiles. This is why Matthew describes the decisive choice of the leaders and the people at the Roman trial with such solemnity. Throughout the dialogue with Pilate, Matthew emphasizes the choice that faces the leaders (27:17, 21, 22, 23). While the Gentile governor and his wife affirm Jesus' innocence, the leaders sway the crowds to reject Jesus and choose Barabbas. The climax comes in an episode unique to Matthew's account. Evoking an Old Testament ritual (see Deut 21:1-8), Pilate washes his hands and declares his innocence for the shedding of Jesus' blood. In response the "whole people" *(pas ho laos)*, invoking another biblical formula, accept responsibility, declaring "his blood be on us and on our children" (27:24-25).

Few New Testament texts have had a more controversial history than these words of Matthew's gospel.[26] Their meaning within the narrative world of Matthew's gospel should be fairly clear to readers who have worked their way from the beginning of the story to this point. For most of the gospel the crowds were neutral and often positive in their responses to Jesus. But the leaders were consistently hostile, and now that hostility engulfs the entire people as the leaders persuade them to reject Jesus. Matthew had already warned about the corrosive influence of the leaders in the indictments of chapter 23 (23:13-14) and now it comes true. Thus Matthew is much harder on the leaders than he is on the people, blaming them for Jesus' rejection. As we have already seen, the evangelist believed that the terrible events of the destruction of Jerusalem and its Temple were punishment for this sin. Therefore, the people who rejected Jesus "and their children"—that is, the generation that experienced the fall of Jerusalem—experienced retribution for shedding the innocent blood of Jesus.

As difficult as this theology of Matthew may be for interpretation, it is a far cry from the devastating interpretation often given to 27:24-25 as a blank check for anti-Semitism, understanding the cry of the people as a perpetual curse on the Jewish people of all generations. Such was not Matthew's perspective. For him the rejection of Jesus by Israel was one unfathomable component of the mysterious providence of God (and so, too, was the paradoxical fact that through the shed blood of Jesus God would forgive sins, 26:28). Although he believed that it involved human responsibility—that of the leaders first of all and to some extent of those generations of Jews in Jesus' day and in the period leading up to the destruction of Jerusalem—Matthew's greatest interest was in interpreting what for him and many in his community was a tragic and inexplicable turn in history. Instead of acclaiming allegiance to the one Matthew's community considered the Messiah, Israel had rejected him; instead of a successful mission to Israel, Matthew's community met opposition; instead of a successful completion of God's age-long mission to Israel, Gentiles, not Jews, were streaming into the community and defining its future. Matthew's goal was to find the guiding hand of God's providence within these tortuous and unexpected twists of history. For him and his community, the death and resurrection of Jesus was the key: From death came new life. At the defining moment of Jesus' death and vindication, an old era of history was completed and the new and final age begun.

CHAPTER 13

FINALE (28:16-20)

A decisive change of setting signals another turning point in the story and sets this final scene off from what had taken place in Jerusalem. Although composed of only five verses, this concluding scene can be considered a distinct and important section of Matthew's gospel.[1] Here the evangelist will bring his majestic story of Jesus to a close and direct the message of the gospel out into the future of the community. This scene is unique to Matthew; its language and content suggest that it is a composition of the evangelist. Scholars have debated what literary form this passage may be patterned after, describing it for example as a "theophany" or as similar to an Old Testament commissioning text.[2]

Following the directive communicated to the women at the tomb by an angel of the Lord (28:7) and the risen Jesus himself (28:10), the disciples now gather in *Galilee*. They go to a *mountain* where the gospel has situated so many powerful scenes of revelation: the desert test (4:1-11), the first of Jesus' great teachings (chaps. 5–7), the place where the transforming power of Jesus' healings was revealed (15:29-31), the place where Jesus had been transfigured before the dazzled eyes of his disciples (a scene reminiscent of this final moment, 17:1-8). Now on this

Galilean mountain the final manifestation of Jesus to his disciples will take place, and strong themes that have run throughout the gospel will be reaffirmed. Jesus and the disciples are the only characters in this scene and are the focal points for its contents.

THE FIGURE OF JESUS

A clear purpose of this scene is to underscore the authority of the risen Jesus, catching up affirmations that the reader has encountered throughout the gospel. Jesus declares that "all authority in heaven and on earth has been given to me" (28:18), words that evoke the exaltation of the Son of Man in Daniel 7:14: "To him was given dominion / and glory and kingship, / that all peoples, nations, and languages / should serve him. / His dominion is an everlasting dominion / that shall not pass away." As we saw throughout the gospel, Matthew portrays Jesus as the Son of Man, bearing authority to heal, to forgive sins, and holding sway over the sabbath and the Temple. But this Son of Man was also to be humiliated and endure suffering, only to be exalted at the end time. The triumphant return of the Son of Man at the end time had been an important motif of the apocalyptic discourse immediately prior to the passion narrative (24:30-31, 37, 39, 44; 25:31). In a sense Matthew anticipates the final appearance of the Son of Man in this concluding scene of the gospel. As the signs at the death and resurrection of Jesus had signaled (27:51-53; 28:2), Matthew's view is that the final age of the world has already begun.

Jesus' identity as the triumphant Son of Man is not the only way Matthew has portrayed Jesus in the gospel.[3] Jesus is also God's Son who knows the will of the Father and was uniquely entrusted by God with the revelation of that will to whomever he chose (11:25-27). Jesus therefore is the consummate teacher whose interpretation of the law brings it to its "fulfillment" (5:17) and whose authority had enthralled the crowds (7:28-29) and silenced his opponents (22:46). In this final scene of the gospel, the risen Jesus once more assumes the mantle of the messianic teacher, instructing his disciples to "make disciples of all nations . . . and teaching them to obey everything that I have commanded you" (28:19-20).

Jesus had also been endowed with the name "Emmanuel," God-with-us (1:23), and here, again, that mysterious identification

174

of Jesus with the community is reaffirmed and extended into the future: "I am with you always, to the end of the age" (28:20). This aspect of Matthew's christology was asserted in the infancy narrative as the child and his family recapitulated the anguish and suffering of Israel through persecution, exile, and dislocation. In the body of the gospel, the Matthean Jesus has spoken of his identification with the "little ones" (10:42; 18:1-14) and the "least" (25:46-51) within the community. Wherever two or three of the community would gather, Jesus, Emmanuel, would be with them (18:20). This feature of Matthew's christology gives his gospel a most distinctive conclusion. Whereas in Mark the promise of the future remains as yet unfulfilled (Mark 16:1-8) and in Luke, Jesus ascends to heaven in order to send the Spirit to the community (Luke 24:49; Acts 1:1-12), the ending of Matthew focuses solely on the abiding presence of the risen Christ and triumphant Son of Man in the midst of the community, underwriting its teaching authority and motivating its universal mission.

THE DISCIPLES

Matthew's final portrayal of the disciples is also characteristic of the gospel. Even here the evangelist refuses to idealize the disciples. The reader is reminded of the fresh wound of Judas' betrayal by the number "eleven" (28:16). Curiously, Matthew also continues to portray the disciples as hesitant. Despite the majesty of the scene, he still notes that although they "worship" Jesus, "some," at least, are doubtful (28:17).[4] Without using his favored term "little faith," Matthew still characterizes the community as a mixture of faith and weakness.

THE MISSION

Particularly strong is the emphasis on mission. With the final and decisive age of salvation now here, the disciples' mission is no longer restricted to the "lost sheep of the house of Israel" (10:5-6; 15:24) but now extends to "all nations" (28:19). For Matthew the rejection of Jesus by the leaders throughout the gospel and then tragically by "all the people" (27:24-25) shifts the focus of the community's mission from Israel to the nations (21:43). In Matthew's perspective does this final mission instruction therefore definitively exclude any mission at all to Israel? Or is he simply widening the scope of the mission to now include the Gentiles and Samaritans, who were previously excluded? In fact, the words of Jesus do *not* say, "Don't go to Israel" in the model of the previous prohibition against the Samaritans and Gentiles in 10:5, yet the transfer implied in 21:43 ("Therefore . . . the kingdom of God will be taken away from you and given to a people that produces the fruits of the kingdom") makes difficult to determine Matthew's view of this issue.[5]

Matthew gives content to the mission of the community. They are to "make disciples," that is, form followers of Jesus in the manner affirmed throughout the gospel of Matthew, particularly in the section where Matthew had focused on Jesus' instruction of his disciples (see, esp., 16:13–20:4). They are to "teach" these new followers to "obey everything I have commanded you" (28:20). In the mission discourse of chapter 10, the disciples had been entrusted with the tasks of proclamation and healing but not teaching (10:1, 7-8). Perhaps Matthew held this dimension of Jesus' mission until all of Jesus' instructions to the community had been completed. Now they were equipped to be "teachers" of disciples.

One final element in their commission has little precedent in the foregoing narrative: They are to baptize "in the name of the Father and of the Son and of the Holy Spirit" (28:19). This formula, similar to that in the Didache (7:1-3), is probably drawn from the liturgical practice of Matthew's community. Matthew's concern with the formation of the "church" was evident in chapter 16 where Peter was constituted as the "rock" on which the community was to be built and given authority within the community. Similar concerns are found in the discourse of chapter 18, which deals with issues of pastoral care and community discipline in the "church" (18:17). The forming of a people who will "produce the fruits of the kingdom" (21:43) becomes, therefore, the object of the disciples' mission. The presence of the risen Christ with the community as it goes out on its mission and the abiding truth of his word to the community are the sources of its strength and the basis of its authority. This, too, had been the message of the mission discourse (10:40-42) and Jesus' final instructions in the apocalyptic discourse (24:3-35).

The gospel concludes, therefore, with a concentration on christology, discipleship, and mission—the same concerns that kept pace with the story from the beginning. By ending his narrative with a commissioning text, that is, with the full authority of the risen Christ sending forth the community into its future and with Jesus' promise to remain with the community until the end of time, Matthew ties the narrative world of the gospel to the unfolding history of the readers and hearers of the gospel within his own community.

In the opening chapter of his story, Matthew engulfed the reader in the world of his gospel, by first rooting Jesus' origin in the mystery of God's relationship with Israel. As the story unfolded, the reader became a privileged observer of Jesus' messianic mission first and foremost to Israel and only by anticipation to the Gentiles in his encounters with striking individuals. Now the story concludes on a mountain in Galilee with the gospel turning its face to the future and to the nations. But in a very real sense, it does not conclude at all. Through the final words of Jesus to his disciples, Matthew projects the gospel story out into the time and space of the reader's world, and even farther, to those in the future who would accept the message of Jesus' missionaries, be baptized by them, and through them be schooled in the way of Jesus. Jesus' message to the disciples is now clearly a message directed to the church.

NOTES

PREFACE

1. An important study of the influence of Matthew's Gospel on early patristic writers is that of Edouard Massaux, *The Influence of the Gospel of Saint Matthew on Christian Literature Before Saint Irenaeus*, New Gospel Studies 5, 3 vols. (Leuven: Peeters; Macon, Ga.: Mercer, 1990). Some scholars, however, are less confident than Massaux about the direct influence of Matthew's Gospel on the earliest patristic writings, suggesting that these writers made direct contact not with Matthew but with oral traditions similar to those that also emerge in Matthew's Gospel.
2. For such a survey, see Donald Senior, *What Are They Saying About Matthew?* rev. ed. (New York: Paulist, 1996).
3. For a list of commentaries on Matthew, see the bibliography at the end of this volume.

1. THE SOURCES AND STRUCTURE OF MATTHEW'S GOSPEL

1. The assumption that the first of the four canonical gospels would necessarily be more "historical" is not valid. Each of the gospels is an interpretation of Jesus' life based on traditional materials and the particular theological perspective of the evangelist and his community. None of the gospels is necessarily either more—or less—historical than the others because of its order of composition.
2. See the discussion in Christopher M. Tuckett, *The Revival of the Griesbach Hypothesis*, SNTSMS 44 (Cambridge: Cambridge University, 1983).
3. For most scholars the unique features of John's Gospel in comparison with the other three gospels eliminated it from this discussion, although the relationship of John to the Synoptic gospels continues to be debated by scholars today.
4. Compare, e.g., the parable of the mustard seed as found in Mark 4:30-32,

Matt 13:31-32, and Luke 13:18-19, or the betrayal by Judas in Mark 14:10-11, Matt 26:14-16, and Luke 22:3-6.

5. See, e.g., the story of John's challenge of those who come for baptism in Matt 3:7-10 and Luke 3:7-9 (an incident not found in Mark). A few scholars contend that there is no literary relationship among the synoptics at all. The apparent similarities among the three are due to access to a common pre-synoptic gospel tradition. This theory has not had much support in current biblical scholarship.

6. A full discussion of the synoptic problem is not intended here; a clear exposition of the issues and a compelling case for the two-source hypothesis can be found in Frans Neirynck, "Synoptic Problem," *The New Jerome Biblical Commentary* (Englewood Cliffs, N.J.: Prentice Hall, 1990), 587-95.

7. These categories are suggested by Ulrich Luz, *Matthew 1–7* (Minneapolis: Augsburg Fortress, 1989), 35-36; for a more detailed analysis of this issue, see David Bauer, *The Structure of Matthew's Gospel* JSNTSup 31 (Sheffield: Almond Press, 1989); Donald Senior, *What Are They Saying About Matthew?* rev. ed. (New York: Paulist, 1996), 25-37.

8. The five discourses are (1) the Sermon on the Mount (chaps. 5:1–7:28); (2) the Mission Discourse (10:1-42); (3) the Parable Discourse (13:1-52); (4) the Community Discourse (18:1-35); (5) the Apocalyptic Discourse (24:3–25:46). Each of them is treated in detail in Part 2.

9. Benjamin W. Bacon, *Studies in Matthew* (London: Constable, 1930); "The 'Five Books' of Matthew Against the Jews," *The Expositor* 15 (1918): 55-66.

10. Dale C. Allison, Jr., "Matthew: Structure, Biographical Impulse and the *Imitatio Christi*," in Frans Van Segbroeck et al., eds., *The Four Gospels 1992*, Festschrift Frans Neirynck; BETL (Leuven: Leuven University, 1992), 2:1203-21.

11. On this point see Luz, *Matthew 1–7*, 38.

12. See Peter F. Ellis, *Matthew: His Mind and His Message* (Collegeville, Minn.: Liturgical Press, 1974); H. Benedict Green, "The Structure of St. Matthew's Gospel," in Frank L. Cross, ed., *Studia Evangelica IV:* Papers Presented to the Third International Congress on New Testament Studies (Berlin: Akademie, 1968), Part One: *The New Testament Scriptures*, 47-59.

13. See the discussion in Bauer, *Structure of Matthew's Gospel*, 36-40.

14. In his recent commentary, M. Eugene Boring proposes that Matthew has devised a chiastic pattern in the first twelve chapters of the gospel, where he drastically intervenes, but after chapter 12 adopts the story line of Mark as his basic structure; see "The Gospel of Matthew," in the *New Interpreter's Bible*, vol. 8 (Nashville: Abingdon, 1995), esp. 14-118.

15. Jack Dean Kingsbury, *Matthew: Structure, Christology, Kingdom* (Philadelphia: Fortress, 1975); Edgar Krentz, "The Extent of Matthew's Prologue: Toward the Structure of the First Gospel," *Journal of Biblical Literature* 83 (1964): 409-15. Krentz returns to his consideration of the structure of Matthew in his later article, "More Than

Many Lessons: On Preaching Matthew," *Currents in Theology and Mission* 19 (1992): 440-52, esp. 441-45. In his more recent writings Kingsbury has utilized the methods of literary criticism to trace the "plot" of Matthew's gospel but retains his basic view about Matthew's three-part structure; see, e.g., *Matthew as Story* (Philadelphia: Fortress, 2nd rev. ed., 1988) and "The Plot of Matthew's Story," *Interpretation* 46 (1992): 347-56.

16. Allison, "Matthew," 56.

17. Frans Neirynck, "APO TOTE HRZATO and the Structure of Matthew," in F. Van Segbroeck, ed., *Evangelica II 1982–1991. Collected Essays by Frans Neirynck* (Leuven: University Press, 1991), 141-82.

18. See the more detailed discussion in Donald Senior, "Matthew's Account of the Burial of Jesus Matt 27,57-61," in Van Segbroeck, *The Four Gospels*, 2:1433-48, esp. 1441-42.

2. MATTHEW'S USE OF THE OLD TESTAMENT

1. Playing upon the word "Nazareth," Matthew may be referring to the "Nazirites" in the Old Testament such as Samson, who was dedicated to God (see Judg 13:5-7), or, more probably, the Hebrew word "nazir" meaning "shoot" or "sprig," which is found in Isaiah 11:1, "A shoot shall come out from the stump of Jesse . . . ," emphasizing Jesus' identity as the Davidic messiah in a moment of transition and discontinuity.

2. Matthew quotes the Old Testament some 61 times, more than any other gospel. If one adds to this the number of allusions to Old Testament passages, characters, and events, the instances would number in the hundreds. See further, M. Eugene Boring, "The Gospel of Matthew," in the *New Interpreter's Bible*, vol. 8 (Nashville: Abingdon, 1995), 151-54.

3. For an exhaustive study of Moses typology in Matthew's gospel, see Dale C. Allison, Jr., *The New Moses* (Minneapolis: Fortress, 1993).

4. Krister Stendahl, *The School of St. Matthew and Its Use of the Old Testament* (Philadelphia: Fortress, first American ed., 1968).

5. Stendahl actually named the quotations "formula" quotations since they were attached to a more or less standard introductory formula. Some interpreters have preferred the word "fulfillment" or "reflection" for the quotations, to express their function in the context of Matthew's Gospel. In referring to a "school," Stendahl was thinking not that this would necessarily have been some specific institution but rather a "school" in the sense of a "school of thought," namely a particular milieu that had its own traditions and perspectives about Christian formation. This Christian group would have adapted from Judaism a method of interpreting the Scriptures called the "pesher" method, whereby a passage from Scripture would be interpreted in the light of current events.

6. See Robert Gundry, *The Use of the Old Testament in St. Matthew's Gospel with Special Reference to the Messianic Hope,* NovTSup 18 (Leiden: Brill, 1967). Stendahl himself conceded this possibility in the

preface to the 1968 edition of his book; his study had originally appeared in 1954.

7. See further examples in Graham Stanton, *A Gospel for a New People: Studies in Matthew* (Edinburgh: T & T Clark, 1992), 346-63.

8. See Ulrich Luz, *The Theology of the Gospel of Matthew*, New Testament Theology (Cambridge: Cambridge University Press, 1995), esp. 37-41.

9. Some debate whether 26:56 should be included. If the number of fulfillment quotations is restricted to those with the standard introductory formula followed by an explicit Old Testament quotation (this would exclude 26:56) then the total is 10. Of these, all but two (21:5 and 27:9-10) are confined to chaps. 1–13. Five of the remaining eight are found in chaps. 1–4.

10. See above, pp. 31-32.

11. Matt 4:14-16 draws on Isa 8:23; 8:17 on Isa 53:4; 12:17-21 on Isa 42:1-4; 13:14-15 on Isa 6:9-10. In 13:35, Matthew quotes Ps 78:2, but, in some manuscript traditions, the quotation is attributed to Isaiah. Some commentators believe that this is the original reading, another instance in which Matthew uses a biblical quotation from one source but attributes it to another for theological purposes (see, e.g., 27:9-10 where a quotation from Zechariah is attributed to Jeremiah).

12. Frans Van Segbroeck, "Les citations d'accomplissement dans l'Evangile selon saint Matthieu d'après trois ouvrages récents," in M. Didier, ed., *L'Evangile selon Matthieu*, BETL 29 (Leuven: Leuven University Press, 1972), 107-30.

13. J. D. Kingsbury, *Matthew as Story*, 35.

14. D. B. Howell, *Matthew's Inclusive Story*, JSNTSup 42 (Sheffield: Sheffield Academic Press, 1990), 189-90.

3. MATTHEW'S UNDERSTANDING OF THE JEWISH LAW

1. See, e.g., Matt 9:9-13 (esp. the addition of the quotation from Hos 6:6 in Matt 9:13); 9:14-17; 12:1-8 (with another appeal to Hos 6:6); 12:9-14; 15:1-20; 17:24-27; 19:3-9; 22:15-22; 22:34-40 (this story is not a conflict in Mark's version; see Mark 12:28-34); and the sharp polemic of chap. 23.

2. See, e.g., Gerhard Barth, "Matthew's Understanding of the Law," in *Tradition and Interpretation in Matthew* (Philadelphia: Westminster, 1963), 58-164; similarly, Robert Guelich, *The Sermon on the Mount: A Foundation for Understanding* (Dallas: Word, 1982). Hans Dieter Betz, who has written extensively on the Sermon, presses this view in an even more significant way (see his *Essays on the Sermon on the Mount* [Philadelphia: Fortress, 1985] and his important commentary, *The Sermon on the Mount* [Hermeneia; Minneapolis: Fortress, 1995]). He believes that the entire Sermon on the Mount comes virtually intact from an earlier Jewish Christian community (probably in Jerusalem in the mid-fifties) and fits uncomfortably into Matthew's overall gospel. He notes that this material in itself has little christo-

logical content. Its literary form is that of an "epitome," or collection of sayings gathered for instructing the community on the essentials of Jesus' teaching. This Jewish Christian community held on to the Jewish law in its entirety, including the purity and ceremonial laws, but understood them in the light of Jesus' teaching. Their emphasis on the validity of the law stood in direct contrast with the Pauline wing of the church. In fact, Betz suggests, the reference to the "least" in the kingdom of heaven who breaks even the minor commands of the law and teaches others to do the same (5:19) is a veiled criticism of Paul. Matthew incorporates this earlier and stricter view of the law into his overall gospel, appreciating its strong ethical emphasis but in the main holding a view of the law that was more moderate than this older source. Betz's contention that the Sermon is devoid of christology and is not well integrated into Matthew's overall theology has been strongly contested by many scholars; see, e.g., Graham Stanton, *A Gospel for a New People* (Edinburgh: T & T Clark, 1992), 307-25. We will illustrate the relationship of the Sermon to Matthew's structure and theology in Part 2, pp. 101-10.

3. See John Meier, *The Vision of Matthew: Christ, Church, and Morality in the First Gospel* (New York: Paulist, 1978), 262.

4. First-century Judaism had a variety of viewpoints on this issue; see Betz, *Sermon on the Mount*, 181-84.

5. Alexander Sand, *Das Gesetz und die Propheten: Untersuchungen zur Theologie des Evangeliums nach Matthäus,* Biblische Untersuchungen 11 (Regensburg: Friedrich Pustet, 1974); see also Klyne R. Snodgrass, who suggests that the reference to the law *and the prophets* implies an emphasis on the justice proclamation of the prophetic literature (as distinct from the cultic), in "Matthew's Understanding of the Law," *Interpretation* 46 (1992): 368-72.

6. See Ulrich Luz, *Matthew 1–7* (Minneapolis: Augsburg Fortress, 1989), 271.

4. MATTHEW AND THE MISSION TO THE GENTILES

1. The story of the "Syrophoenician" woman is already found in Mark 7:24-30. But in Matthew's version of the story, Jesus' resistance to the entreaties of the "Canaanite" woman is much more emphatic (Matt 15:21-28); see Part 2, pp. 130-32.

2. Of the four women mentioned by Matthew, Rahab (Joshua 2:1-21), Ruth (Ruth 1:4), and Bathsheba, whom Matthew identifies as the "wife of Uriah" (2 Sam 11–12), are clearly not Jews. It is uncertain whether or not Tamar was Jewish (Gen 38:29-30). In any case, they play the role of the "outsider" in biblical history; see Part 2, pp. 88-89.

3. Rolf Walker, *Die Heilsgeschichte im ersten Evangelium* (Göttingen: Vandenhoeck & Ruprecht, 1967).

4. Georg Strecker, "Das Geschichtsverstandnis des Matthäus," *Evangelische Theologie* 26 (1966): 57-74; an English translation appeared in the *Journal of the American Academy of Religion* 35 (1967): 219-30.

5. John Meier, "Salvation-History in Matthew: In Search of a Starting Point," *Catholic Biblical Quarterly* 37 (1975): 203-14; see also Meier, *The Vision of Matthew* (New York: Paulist, 1978), 26-41.
6. David B. Howell, *Matthew's Inclusive Story: A Study in the Narrative Rhetoric of the First Gospel*, JSNTSup 42 (Sheffield: Sheffield Academic Press, 1990).
7. Amy Jill Levine, *The Social and Ethnic Dimensions of Matthean Salvation History. "Go Nowhere Among the Gentiles . . ." (Matt. 10:5b)*. Studies in the Bible and Early Christianity 14 (Lewiston, N.Y.: Edwin Mellen, 1988).
8. Howell, *Matthew's Inclusive Story*, 211.

5. MATTHEW'S CHRISTOLOGY

1. Titles such as "Christ," that is "messiah" or "anointed one," and "Son of David" originate in Israel's experience of the monarchy and have a specific meaning derived from Jewish messianic expectations, namely that the messiah would be a savior and liberator in the idealized image of David; they were not immediately comprehensible to non-Jewish peoples. On the other hand, a title of respect such as "lord" was used as a way of addressing God in the Hebrew Scriptures but could also be used as a more generic title of authority and respect within both Judaism and Hellenistic culture. "Son of God" had a specific application as a title for the king in Israel's history but in Hellenistic culture would also be used with connotations of divinity. On this see further, Pheme Perkins and Reginald Fuller, *Who Is This Christ?* (Philadelphia: Fortress, 1983); Raymond E. Brown, *An Introduction to New Testament Christology* (New York: Paulist, 1994).
2. Jack Dean Kingsbury, *Matthew: Structure, Christology, Kingdom* (Philadelphia: Fortress, 1975); *Jesus Christ in Matthew, Mark, and Luke* Proclamation Commentaries (Philadelphia: Fortress, 1981), 64-73; *Matthew as Story* (Philadelphia: Fortress, 2nd rev. ed., 1988).
3. See the discussion of the threefold structure proposed by Kingsbury, pp. 28-31.
4. Kingsbury, *Matthew as Story*, 52.
5. Ibid., 96.
6. Graham Stanton, *A Gospel for a New People* (Edinburgh: T & T Clark, 1992), 180-85.
7. David Hill, "The Figure of Jesus in Matthew's Gospel: A Response to Professor Kingsbury's Literary-Critical Probe," *Journal for the Study of the New Testament* 21 (1984): 37-52 (Kingsbury responded in "The Figure of Jesus in Matthew's Story: A Rejoinder to David Hill," *Journal for the Study of the New Testament* 25 [1985]).
8. John Meier, *The Vision of Matthew* (New York: Paulist, 1978), 210-19.
9. Dale C. Allison, Jr., *The New Moses: A Matthean Typology* (Minneapolis: Fortress, 1993).
10. See above, pp. 25-26.
11. Allison, *The New Moses*, 277.

12. Ibid., 290.
13. M. Jack Suggs, *Wisdom, Christology, and Law in Matthew's Gospel* (Cambridge: Harvard University, 1970).
14. Suggs' thesis found refinement and amplification in the work of such scholars as Fred W. Burnett and Celia Deutsch. Burnett believes the entire eschatological discourse of Matt 24:3-31 was also influenced by the image of Jesus as Wisdom. The disciples are to be Wisdom's emissaries and, therefore, in his final testament Jesus warns them to prepare themselves for rejection and persecution; see F. W. Burnett, *The Testament of Jesus-Sophia: A Redaction-Critical Study of the Eschatological Discourse in Matthew* (Washington: University Press of America, 1981). Celia Deutsch sees the motif of Wisdom's rejection also influencing Matt 23:34-37; see "Wisdom in Matthew: Transformation of a Symbol," *NovT* 32 (1990): 13-47.
15. Hans Joachim Held, "Matthew as Interpreter of the Miracle Stories," in *Tradition and Interpretation in Matthew* (Philadelphia: Westminster, 1963), 165-299.
16. See the discussion of this section in Part 2, pp. 110-15.
17. Kingsbury, for example, believes there is a fourfold division in these chapters: (1) 8:1-17 focusing on christology (as in Held's proposal); (2) 8:18-34 on discipleship (as in Held); (3) 9:1-17 on the separation of Jesus and his followers from Israel; (4) and 9:18-34 on faith (as in Held); see "Observations on the 'Miracle Chapters' of Matthew 8–9," *CBQ* 40 (1978): 559-73.
18. Birger Gerhardsson, *The Mighty Acts of Jesus According to Matthew* (Lund: Gleerup, 1979).
19. Ibid., 82.
20. See R. T. France, *Matthew: Evangelist and Teacher* (Grand Rapids: Zondervan, 1989), 278-317; Donald Senior, "The Jesus of Matthew," *Church* 5 (1989): 10-13.

6. DISCIPLESHIP IN MATTHEW'S GOSPEL

1. See Charles E. Carlston, "Christology and Church in Matthew," in F. Van Segbroeck et al., eds., *The Four Gospels 1992*, vol. 2, 1283-1304; and David Howell, *Matthew's Inclusive Story: A Study in the Narrative Rhetoric of the First Gospel* JSNTSup 42 (Sheffield: Sheffield Academic Press, 1990), 251-59.
2. Jean Zumstein, *La Condition du Croyant dans L'Evangile selon Matthieu* Orbis Biblicus et Orientalis 16 (Göttingen: Vandenhoeck & Ruprecht, 1977); see also, Richard A. Edwards, "Uncertain Faith: Matthew's Portrait of the Disciples," in F. Segovia, ed., *Discipleship in the New Testament* (Philadelphia: Fortress, 1985), 47-61; Ulrich Luz, "The Disciples in the Gospel According to Matthew," in G. Stanton, ed., *The Interpretation of Matthew* (Edinburgh: T & T Clark, 2nd ed., 1995), 115-48; Michael J. Wilkins, *Discipleship in the Ancient World and Matthew's Gospel* (Grand Rapids: Baker Books, 1995), esp. 225-47, where the author reviews recent literature on discipleship in Matthew.

3. See David E. Orton, *The Understanding Scribe: Matthew and the Apocalyptic Ideal* JSNTSup 25 (Sheffield: University of Sheffield Press, 1989).

4. See, e.g., Eduard Schweizer, "Observance of the Law and Charismatic Activity in Matthew" *NTS* 16 (1969–70): 213-30.

5. See our discussion of this text to come, pp. 130-32.

6. Elaine Mary Wainwright, *Toward a Feminist Critical Reading of the Gospel According to Matthew* (BZNW 60; Berlin/New York: Walter de Gruyter, 1991); and "The Gospel of Matthew," in Elisabeth Schüssler Fiorenza, ed., *Searching the Scriptures: A Feminist Commentary,* vol. 2 (New York: Crossroad, 1994), 635-77.

7. On this point see also the work of Howell, *Matthew's Inclusive Story,* 233-36.

8. See Ulrich Luz, *Matthew in History* (Minneapolis: Fortress, 1994), 57-74.

9. *Catechism of the Catholic Church,* #881.

10. Jack Dean Kingsbury, "The Figure of Peter in Matthew's Gospel as a Theological Problem," *JBL* 98 (1979): 67-83.

11. Kingsbury reaffirms his position in his work, *Matthew As Story* (Philadelphia: Fortress, rev. ed., 1988), 132.

12. Arlo J. Nau, *Peter in Matthew: Discipleship, Diplomacy, and Dispraise* Good News Studies 36 (Collegeville, Minn.: Liturgical Press, 1992).

13. Nau, *Peter in Matthew,* 147.

14. Raymond Brown, *Biblical Reflections on Crises Facing the Church* (New York: Paulist, 1975), 63-83.

15. R. Brown, K. Donfried, J. Reumann, eds., *Peter in the New Testament: A Collaborative Assessment by Protestant and Roman Catholic Scholars* (Minneapolis: Augsburg; New York: Paulist, 1973).

16. On this, see Frances Young, *The Theology of the Pastoral Letters* New Testament Theology (Cambridge: Cambridge University Press, 1994), 122-44.

17. Pheme Perkins, *Peter: Apostle for the Whole Church* (Columbia: University of South Carolina Press, 1994), 66-80.

7. MATTHEW AND HIS COMMUNITY

1. We do not know if Matthew wrote his gospel for a single, geographically bound community or for a cluster of smaller communities or house churches, or even intended it to be circulated more widely among several Christian groups. The reference to a gathering of the "ecclesia" ("assembly" or "church") to hear the case of an errant member (18:17) seems to imply a fairly small group. Yet this is not decisive, since this text could have been meant as instruction to any number of local communities and we cannot be sure it is describing actual local church discipline at the time of Matthew, although most commentators believe that is the case.

2. On first-century Judaism, see Frederick J. Murphy, *The Religious World of Jesus: An Introduction to Second Temple Palestinian Judaism* (Nashville: Abingdon, 1991); Lester L. Grabbe, *Judaism from Cyrus to*

Hadrian, 2 vols. (Minneapolis: Fortress, 1992); Anthony J. Saldarini, *Pharisees, Scribes, and Sadducees in Palestinian Society: A Sociological Approach* (Wilmington: Michael Glazier, 1988); E. Sanders, *Judaism: Practice and Belief 63 BCE–66 CE* (Philadelphia: TPI, 1992).

3. Rabbinic texts are, of course, an important such source. The problem is that these texts were written considerably after the first century, although they often reflect earlier traditions. Rabbinic texts, like the gospels themselves, must be interpreted with great caution in attempting to get an accurate and complete picture of first-century Judaism. On this see Jacob Neusner, *Rabbinic Judaism: The Documentary History of its Formative Age 70–600 CE* (Bethesda, Md.: CDL Press, 1994).

4. W. D. Davies, *The Setting of the Sermon on the Mount* (Cambridge: Cambridge University, 1964). This view is maintained in Davies' important commentary on the gospel; see W. D. Davies and Dale C. Allison, Jr., *Matthew* International Critical Commentary (Edinburgh: T & T Clark, vol. 1 [Matthew I-VII], 1988; vol. 2 [Matthew VIII-XVIII], 1991). On the Jewish revolt and its aftermath, see David M. Rhoads, *Israel in Revolution 6–74 CE* (Philadelphia: Fortress, 1976).

5. See Jacob Neusner, *From Politics to Piety: The Emergence of Pharisaic Judaism* (Englewood Cliffs, N.J.: Prentice-Hall, 1973); see also *First-Century Judaism in Crisis* (Nashville: Abingdon, 1975).

6. See Davies and Allison, *Matthew*, vol. 1, 134, n. 106. On this point, see also J. Andrew Overman, *Matthew's Gospel and Formative Judaism: The Social World of the Matthean Community* (Minneapolis: Augsburg Fortress, 1990), 38-43.

7. Ulrich Luz, *Matthew 1-7* (Minneapolis. Augsburg Fortress, 1989), 88.

8. David E. Garland, *The Intention of Matthew 23* NovTSup 52 (Leiden: Brill, 1979); Sjef Van Tilborg, *The Jewish Leaders in Matthew* (Leiden: Brill, 1972).

9. Reinhart Hummel, *Die Auseinandersetzung zwischen Kirche und Judentum im Matthäusevangelium* (München: Kaiser Verlag, 1963).

10. Overman, *Matthew's Gospel and Formative Judaism*, esp. 6-34.

11. Graham Stanton, *A Gospel for a New People: Studies in Matthew* (Edinburgh: T & T Clark, 1992); see also his article, "The Communities of Matthew," *Interpretation* 46 (1992): 379-91.

12. See above, pp. 46-47.

13. Anthony J. Saldarini, *Matthew's Christian-Jewish Community* (Chicago: University of Chicago, 1994).

14. See Saldarini, *Matthew's Christian-Jewish Community*, 113; Overman, *Matthew's Gospel and Formative Judaism*, 149.

15. "Though Matthew draws his interpretation of Jesus from Jewish tradition, the emphasis on Jesus and the high status accorded him make the gospel different from other Jewish literature. Second Temple literature contains accounts of biblical figures and their final testaments, but none gives as important and unique a role to its central figure as that given to Jesus by Matthew" (Saldarini, *Matthew's Christian-Jewish Community*, 193).

16. Stanton, *A Gospel for a New People,* 160-61; D. C. Sim goes farther to suggest that Matthew's community did not undertake a Gentile mission at all but only tolerated it on the part of other communities; see "The Gospel of Matthew and the Gentiles," *JSNT* 57 (1995): 19-48.

17. On Matthew, for example, see the extensive introductions in the commentaries of M. Eugene Boring, "The Gospel of Matthew," in the *New Interpreter's Bible,* vol. 8 (Nashville: Abingdon, 1995); Davies and Allison, *Matthew,* vol. 1; Luz, *Matthew 1–7.*

18. See extensive discussion in Davies and Allison, *Matthew,* vol. 1, 7-58; Luz, *Matthew 1–7,* 93-95.

19. The hypothesis of an original Hebrew or Aramaic version of Matthew's gospel was also an earlier stance of many Catholic scholars. The hypothesis of a now lost original Aramaic or Hebrew version, followed later by a Greek version, protected the traditional view of Matthew as the first gospel but also accounted for the evidence of Matthean (i.e., the Greek version's) dependence on Mark.

20. J. Kürzinger, "Das Papiaszeugnis und die Erstgestalt des Matthäusevangeliums," *BZ* 4 (1960): 19-38.

21. However, the Evangelical scholar, Robert H. Gundry, defends Matthean authorship. He concedes that the apostle Matthew used both the gospel of Mark and Q as sources but edited and supplemented them on the basis of his own "notes"; see *Matthew: A Commentary on His Handbook for a Mixed Church Under Persecution* (Grand Rapids: Eerdmans, 2nd ed., 1994), 609-22.

22. A few scholars disagree with this kind of assessment and believe that Matthew was not a Jewish Christian but a Gentile who was interested in the Jewish heritage of the Christian movement (see, e.g., John Meier, *The Vision of Matthew: Christ, Church, and Morality in the First Gospel* Theological Inquiries [New York: Paulist, 1979], and more recently his article, "Matthew, Gospel of," *Anchor Bible Dictionary,* vol. 4 [New York: Doubleday, 1992], esp. 625-27). There are a few instances, these scholars believe, where the gospel seems incorrect or uninformed about Jewish matters. For example, Meier points to Matthew's reference to two animals in the story of the entrance of Jesus into Jerusalem (Matt 21:2, 7) and suggests that the evangelist apparently thought that the Old Testament quotation from Zech 9:9 referred to two animals instead of one, a mistake he thinks no Jew would make. However, evidence shows that ancient Jewish authors sometimes underscored literal fulfillment of Old Testament texts; see further, Joel Marcus, "The Role of the Scripture in the Gospel Passion Narratives," in John T. Carroll and Joel B. Green, *The Death of Jesus in Early Christianity* (Peabody, Mass.: Hendrickson, 1995), 204-33.

23. The classic work on the use of the gospel of Matthew in the early church is that of Edouard Massaux, *The Influence of the Gospel of Saint Matthew on Christian Literature Before Saint Irenaeus,* 3 vols., New Gospel Studies 5 (Macon, Ga.: Mercer, 1990).

24. See Raymond E. Brown and John Meier, *Antioch and Rome: New Testament Cradles of Catholic Christianity* (New York: Paulist, 1983); see

also Rodney Stark, "Antioch as the Social Situation for Matthew's Gospel," in David Balch, ed., *Social History of the Matthean Community* (Minneapolis: Fortress, 1991), 189-201.

25. Not everyone agrees that Antioch is the prime candidate for Matthew's location. Other urban contexts that would become important Jewish Christian centers have also been suggested such as Alexandria and Caesarea Maritima, the latter having the advantage of being close to Jamnia (and therefore in touch with its Pharisaic reforms) and a city which would later be identified with Christian scholarship (including Eusebius, who preserved the testimony of Papias); see Benedict T. Viviano, "Where Was the Gospel According to Matthew Written?" *CBQ* 41 (1979): 533-46. Employing sociological models, L. Michael White also chooses a Palestinian location but a settlement somewhere in the border region between lower Galilee (whose border cities such as Chorazin, Bethsaida, and Capernaum Matthew criticizes for being unresponsive to Jesus; see Matt 11:20-24) and Syria. Here, he contends, the identity crisis triggered for both Judaism and Jewish Christianity by the calamity of the Jewish war would have been most acutely felt. See L. Michael White, "Crisis Management and Boundary Maintenance: The Social Location of the Matthean Community," in Balch, *Social History of the Matthean Community*, 211-47.

26. See, e.g., Jack Dean Kingsbury, *Matthew As Story* (Philadelphia: Fortress, rev. ed., 1988), 152-53.

8. THE ORIGINS OF JESUS AND HIS MISSION (1:1–4:11)

1. See the discussion of Matthew's sources in Part 1, pp. 19-24.
2. See above, p. 56.
3. The precise reason for this grouping of women is debated, but in each case the circumstances are unusual and the women are "outsiders" (Gentiles in the cases of Rahab, Ruth, and probably Bathsheba; someone outside the clan in the case of Tamar); see further, Raymond E. Brown, *The Birth of the Messiah* (New York: Doubleday, 1977), 71-74.
4. See the foregoing discussion on Matthew's interpretation of the law, pp. 39-44.
5. On the fulfillment quotations, see above, pp. 33-38.
6. See the discussion in Dale C. Allison, Jr., *The New Moses* (Minneapolis: Fortress, 1993), 140-64.
7. On the importance of Jesus' designation as Son of God in Matthew's christology, see above, pp. 54-57.
8. Matthew's version of the crucifixion scene makes the death of Jesus a test of his obedience and trust in God; see, e.g., his addition of 27:43, a quotation of Psalm 22:8.
9. The classic study of this scene is that of Birger Gerhardsson, *The Testing of God's Son (Matt 4:1-11 and Par.): An Analysis of an Early Christian Midrash* (Lund: Gleerup, 1966).

10. On the symbolic role of mountains as places of revelation in Matthew's gospel, see T. L. Donaldson, *Jesus on the Mountain: A Study in Matthean Theology* JSNTSup 8 (Sheffield: JSOT, 1985).

9. JESUS: MESSIAH IN WORD AND DEED (4:12–10:42)

1. On the audience and intent of the sermon, see below, pp. 108-10.
2. John will reappear in Matthew's story. In 11:2 he sends word to Jesus from prison, and in 14:1-12 Matthew recalls for the reader John's martyrdom.
3. See the discussion of the probable location of Matthew's community, pp. 81-83.
4. As we have seen, some authors consider this verse a turning point in the structure of Matthew's story, inaugurating Jesus' proclamation of the reign of God. However, this verse is only part of this whole scene (4:12-24) which introduces Jesus' public ministry. See the foregoing discussion of Matthew's structure, pp. 28-31.
5. See Ulrich Luz, *The Theology of the Gospel of Matthew* New Testament Theology (Cambridge: Cambridge University Press, 1993), 46-51.
6. Hans Dieter Betz traces the origin of the Sermon on the Mount to an early Jewish Christian collection of sayings of Jesus; see *The Sermon on the Mount* Hermeneia (Minneapolis: Fortress, 1995), 7-9. Other studies of the Sermon are: Robert Guelich, *The Sermon on the Mount* (Dallas: Word, 1982); Jan Lambrecht, *The Sermon on the Mount* GNS 14 (Wilmington: Michael Glazier, 1985); Georg Strecker, *The Sermon on the Mount: An Exegetical Commentary* (Nashville: Abingdon, 1988). A survey of recent literature on the Sermon is found in Warren Carter, *What Are They Saying About the Sermon on the Mount?* (New York: Paulist, 1994).
7. See, e.g., Prov 3:13; 28:14. On the Beatitudes, see Dennis Hamm, *The Beatitudes in Context* (Collegeville, Minn.: Liturgical Press, 1990).
8. On this see Luz, *Theology of the Gospel of Matthew*, 42-45.
9. On this important text in Matthew, see John Piper, *"Love Your Enemies": Jesus' Love Command in the Synoptic Gospels and the Early Christian Paraenesis* SNTS 38 (Cambridge: Cambridge University Press, 1979); William Klassen, *Love of Enemies* OBT (Philadelphia: Fortress, 1984); Willard M. Swartley, ed., *The Love of Enemy and Non-retaliation in the New Testament* (Louisville: Westminster/John Knox, 1992); Lisa Sowle Cahill, *Love Your Enemies: Discipleship, Pacifism, and Just War Theory* (Minneapolis: Fortress, 1994), esp. 15-38.
10. On the relationship of the Lord's Prayer to Matthew's theology, see Mark Kiley, "The Lord's Prayer and Matthean Theology," in James Charlesworth, ed., *The Lord's Prayer and Other Prayer Texts from the Greco-Roman Era* (Valley Forge, Pa.: Trinity Press International, 1994), 15-27; see also Oscar Cullmann, *Prayer in the New Testament* OBT (Minneapolis: Fortress, 1995), esp. 37-68.
11. See the extensive discussion in Betz, *Sermon on the Mount*, esp. 370-72. Although the Lord's Prayer has similarities to several ancient

Jewish prayers such as the Kaddish or the Shemoneh Esreh, it has its own distinctive theology.

12. This becomes a strong theme in the eschatological discourse of chaps. 24–25; see the discussion of these texts to come, pp. 160-64.

13. "Ethics by example" is a phrase used by Luz, *Theology of the Gospel of Matthew*, 54: "This technique of 'ethics by example' means that the individual commandments in the Sermon on the Mount have a fundamental validity. They far transcend themselves, governing all walks of existence and serving as a guide for life in its entirety." In an excellent essay on interpreting the sermon, Lisa Sowle Cahill speaks of the commands of the sermon as "focal instances"; see "The Ethical Implications of the Sermon on the Mount," *Interpretation* 41 (1987): 144-56.

14. See foregoing, Part 1, pp. 59-61.

15. Held himself did not want to make his divisions of these chapters too rigid: "It is obvious that they [i.e., the three themes of christology, discipleship, and faith] may not and cannot be taken in any mutually exclusive sense, for they not only overlap in actual content but they occur in each single story overlapping each other in some way or other. The themes mentioned thus simply indicate the prevailing interest in the retelling of a miracle story." Hans Joachim Held, "Matthew as Interpreter of the Miracle Stories," in *Tradition and Interpretation in Matthew* (Philadelphia: Westminster, 1963), 169.

16. On this important issue in Matthew, see Part 1, pp. 45-52.

17. In the journey section of the gospel (16:13–20:34), the Matthean Jesus will link discipleship to the motifs of suffering, renouncement of possessions, and giving one's life for the sake of the gospel.

18. A classic analysis of this story, one of the first essays demonstrating the method of redaction criticism, is that of Günther Bornkamm, "The Stilling of the Storm," in *Tradition and Interpretation in Matthew* (Philadelphia: Westminster, 1963), 52-57.

19. See Part 1, p. 64.

20. At the conclusion of the story, the crowds glorify God, who had given such authority to "human beings"; it is not certain whether in making the term "human beings" plural, Matthew also refers to the power given to the community (see 18:18).

21. In Mark's story the tax collector is named "Levi" (Mark 2:15); on the possible connection to the authorship of the gospel by Matthew, see Part 1, pp. 79-81.

22. On the mission discourse, see Donald Senior and Carroll Stuhlmueller, *The Biblical Foundations for Mission* (Maryknoll, N.Y.: Orbis, 1983), 233-54; Dorothy Jean Weaver, *Matthew's Missionary Discourse: A Literary Critical Analysis* JSNTSup 38 (Sheffield: JSOT, 1990).

23. See the discussion in Part 1, pp. 45-52.

24. On this see David B. Howell, *Matthew's Inclusive Story: A Study in the Narrative Rhetoric of the First Gospel* JSNTSup 42 (Sheffield: Sheffield Academic Press, 1990), esp. 205-48; and Weaver, *Matthew's Missionary Discourse*, 152-53.

25. This is the point made by Amy-Jill Levine, *The Social and Ethnic Dimensions of Matthean Salvation History. "Go Nowhere Among the Gentiles . . ." (Matt 10:5*b) (Lewiston, N.Y.: Edwin Mellen, 1988); see above, Part 1, pp. 50-51.

10. RESPONDING TO JESUS: REJECTION AND UNDERSTANDING (11:1–16:12)

1. On the issue of "wisdom" motifs in Matthew, see Part 1, p. 59.
2. See Part 1, pp. 54-57.
3. See Part 1, p. 64.
4. The contrast is strong with Mark's gospel where the disciples are repeatedly portrayed as not understanding. In Matt 16:12, for example, Matthew adds to the Marcan parallel the fact that finally the disciples do understand about Jesus' teaching concerning the leaven of the Pharisees and Sadducees; in Mark's version the disciples remain uncomprehending (see Mark 8:14-21).
5. See the foregoing discussion of Matthew's portrayal of the disciples, pp. 65-66.
6. See Donald Senior and Carroll Stuhlmueller, *The Biblical Foundations for Mission* (Maryknoll, N.Y.: Orbis, 1983), 217-20.
7. On Matthew's portrayal of Peter, see Part 1, pp. 67-70.
8. See, e.g., 8:3; 12:13.
9. The New Revised Standard Version translates the verb *proskuneō* as "worship." Matthew often uses the verb in connection with the title "Lord" *(kurios):* See, e.g., 8:2; 15:25; and the two instances in this story (14:30, 33)—all of these passages are unique to Matthew.
10. See Part 1, pp. 45-52.

11. THE JOURNEY TO JERUSALEM (16:13–20:34)

1. As noted in our discussion of the structure, Kingsbury and others consider 16:21 with its temporal note—"From that time on . . ."—as an important structural turning point in the gospel. However, it seems preferable to consider the entire scene at Caesarea Philippi (16:13-28), not just this single verse, as the transition intended by Matthew. See the foregoing discussion, pp. 28-31.
2. In Mark's gospel no human being confesses Jesus as "Son of God" until the centurion at the cross in 15:39. Therefore, Peter's confession of Jesus solely as "the Christ" in Mark 8:29 may be seen as insufficient, one element in the overall incomprehension of the disciples in Mark. Also in Mark's story Jesus does not bless Peter but immediately begins to speak of the suffering that awaits the *Son of Man*, seeming to shift attention away from Peter's acclamation of him as Messiah; on this see Donald Senior, *The Passion of Jesus in the Gospel of Mark* Passion Series 2 (Collegeville, Minn.: Liturgical Press, 1984), 31-35.
3. This is the first of three instances of the term *ekklêsia* meaning "assembly" or "church" in Matthew (see also 18:17). The extension of

this word is difficult to determine; here it seems to refer to the entire community of those who will follow Jesus. See the discussion of chapter 18 to come, pp. 143-45.

4. See the extensive discussion in W. D. Davies and Dale C. Allison, Jr., *The Gospel According to Saint Matthew* 3 vols. (Edinburgh: T & T Clark, 1988), vol. 2, 635-41.

5. See Part 1, pp. 67-70.

6. This is not an exclusively Roman Catholic viewpoint, however. See the conclusions of Davies and Allison, *Gospel According to Saint Matthew*, vol. 2: "Peter was not simply a representative disciple for Matthew, and he was not just the first disciple to be called. He was the pre-eminent apostle, which meant he held a significance and authority the other disciples did not hold. His role in salvation-history was pivotal, and probably his authority continued to make itself felt in the living traditions of Matthew's community" (651-52).

7. Ten of the thirty uses of the title in Matthew occur in this section alone; on this title in Matthew, see Part 1, pp. 55-57.

8. The disciples are warned not to use the title "Rabbi" in Matt 23:9, and only Judas addresses Jesus in that way (see 26:25, 49).

9. A point made in William G. Thompson's study of the community discourse, *Matthew's Advice to a Divided Community. Mt. 17,22–18,35* AnBib 44 (Rome: Biblical Institute Press, 1970).

10. See the Rule of the Community 5:24–6:1 in James H. Charlesworth, ed., *The Dead Sea Scrolls*, vol. 1, *Rules of the Community and Related Documents* (Louisville: Westminster John Knox Press, 1994), 25-27.

11. On this text, see Raymond F. Collins, *Divorce in the New Testament* (Collegeville, Minn.: Liturgical Press, 1992), 104-45.

12. A parallel but not identical case would be Paul's directives in 1 Cor 7:15, the so-called Pauline privilege, which seems to allow dissolution of a marriage "for the sake of peace" in the case of a Christian married to a non-Christian. But it is not clear that Paul believes the Christian so separated is now free to marry; see Collins, *Divorce in the New Testament*, 63-64.

13. This does not mean, however, that the interpreter of the text would be unable to deal pastorally with issues of marriage and divorce. See our foregoing discussion on the interpretation of the Sermon on the Mount, pp. 108-10.

14. See the comments of Ulrich Luz, *The Theology of the Gospel of Matthew* New Testament Theology (Cambridge: Cambridge University Press, 1995), 110-12.

15. See Daniel J. Harrington, *The Gospel of Matthew* Sacra Pagina (Collegeville, Minn.: Liturgical Press, 1991), 276. He refers to such Jewish sectarian groups as the Qumran community and the Therapeutae as examples. John the Baptist, Jesus himself, and Paul are examples in the New Testament.

16. See above, p. 110. Harrington's comment on this section of Matthew is pertinent: "The issues of marriage and divorce, celibacy, and the status of children remain controversial today. Sometimes the debated

aspects distract attention from the more basic teachings of Jesus on these matters. The ideal of marriage as a lifelong commitment in which two people become one remains a magnificent (if often elusive) ideal. The ideal of a celibate life consecrated to the kingdom of heaven is a striking challenge to the values of modern Western societies. The respect for children and their ability to symbolize the proper approach to God's kingdom seems particularly important in view of recent revelations about child abuse" (*Gospel of Matthew*, 276).

17. See particularly the community discourse of chapter 18, where Jesus teaches the community leaders precisely these values; see pp. 143-45.

18. Cf. Matt 20:29-34 and Mark 10:46-52. Matthew's story is reminiscent of an earlier cure of blind men in 9:27-31. Mark has framed his journey narrative with two stories about healing blindness (Mark 8:22-26 and 10:46-52), probably intended as a "comment" on the struggle of the disciples so much in evidence in the journey narrative itself. Matthew, however, does not retain this framework; the earlier story is incorporated in the collection of miracles in 9:27-31. Yet the symbolic dimension of the healing of blindness is still evident in the placement of Matthew's story in 20:29-34, coming as it does at the conclusion of the journey narrative and in the aftermath of the Matthean disciples' struggle with the challenge of Jesus' teaching.

12. IN THE HOLY CITY: CONFLICT, DEATH, RESURRECTION (21:1–28:15)

1. Mark employs the parable of fig tree as a "frame" around Temple cleansing, interpreting Jesus' action as a condemnation of the temple. Jesus curses the fig tree for not bearing fruit as he and the disciples are on the way to the temple the day following his triumphal entry (see Mark 11:12-14), and the next day after the temple cleansing they see that the tree has withered (11:20-21). On this point, see J. Donahue, *Are You the Christ? The Trial Narrative in the Gospel of Mark* SBLDS 10 (Missoula: Scholars Press, 1973), 42-43, and Donald Senior, *The Passion of Jesus in the Gospel of Mark* Passion Series 2 (Collegeville, Minn.: Liturgical Press, 1984), 24-28.

2. On this title, see Part 1, p. 56. On Jesus' role as a humble and "servant" King in Matthew's gospel, see David R. Bauer, "The Kingship of Jesus in the Matthean Infancy Narrative," *CBQ* 57 (1995): 306-23.

3. This ethical emphasis itself is part of traditional Jewish teaching, namely that obedience to the Torah defines the essence of what it means to be a true Israelite; on this point, see Jacob Neusner, "Was Rabbinic Judaism Really 'Ethnic'?" *CBQ* 57 (1995): 281-305.

4. On interpretation of the law in Matthew's gospel, see Part 1, pp. 39-44.

5. Matthew's typical transitional phrase indicating the conclusion of a discourse and the return to narrative comes in 26:1, identifying 24–25 as the fifth and last of the discourses of the gospel (note: "When Jesus had finished *all* these sayings . . .").

6. It is difficult to know exactly what Matthew means by this exhortation to "do whatever they [i.e., the scribes and Pharisees] teach you and follow it," because they "sit on Moses' seat" (23:2-3), in a context in which his gospel bitterly attacks the leaders. Presumably this is as a concession to the fact that the leaders hold positions of authority within the community of Israel and their position is worthy of respect. Yet, at the same time, Matthew appears to reject much of their teaching and their integrity as teachers. For a presentation of the various ways this text has been interpreted, see Mark Alan Powell, "Do and Keep What Moses Says (Matthew 23:2-7)," *JBL* 114 (1995): 419-35.

7. See the foregoing discussion of the community discourse, pp. 143-45. Note that Matthew's term for a community member is "brother" and "sister" in keeping with the instruction of 23:8-12: see, e.g., Matt 5:22, 23, 24, 47; 7:3, 4, 5; 10:21; 18:15, 21, 35; 28:10.

8. For biblical precedents see the "woes" of prophets such as Amos (5:18-20; 6:1-7) or Isaiah (chap. 5; also 10:1-3; 28:1-4; 29:1-4, 15; 30:1-13; 31:1-4).

9. On the question of Jewish persecution of early Christian missionaries, see Douglas R. A. Hare, *The Theme of Jewish Persecution of Christians in the Gospel According to St. Matthew* SNTSMS 6 (Cambridge: Cambridge University Press, 1967).

10. Matthew's view of the place of Israel in salvation history subsequent to the death and resurrection of Jesus is much debated. For some authors, Matthew no longer foresees any mission to Israel as such (obviously individual Jewish converts would still be welcomed); now the community must turn its mission activity to the Gentiles (as seems to be the viewpoint of 21:43). Others, however, while conceding that the failure of the mission to Israel becomes the occasion for the community to turn to the Gentiles, believe on the basis of 23:39 that Matthew may still foresee a time when Israel as a corporate entity would accept Jesus as the Messiah and resume its place within salvation history, similar to Paul's view in Romans 9–11. It is possible that Matthew's gospel itself may not have been entirely clear about this point, which is not surprising in view of the painful paradox the failure of the mission to Israel posed for his community.

11. On this see Anthony J. Saldarini, *Pharisees, Scribes, and Sadducees in Palestinian Society: A Sociological Approach* (Wilmington: Michael Glazier, 1988), esp. 277-97. While emphasizing that historical sources for reconstructing the history of the Pharisees are meager, Saldarini identifies the Pharisees as a reform movement seeking to revivify Judaism through strict adherence to the norms of the covenant. Their particular emphasis on tithing and ritual purity in the cause of Jewish identity and reform probably set them apart from Jesus and his followers.

12. For correlation between this section of the discourse and the book of Daniel, see Daniel J. Harrington, *The Gospel of Matthew* Sacra Pagina (Collegeville, Minn.: Liturgical Press, 1991), 338-41.

13. See Part 1, pp. 55-57.
14. See Karl Donfried, "The Allegory of the Ten Virgins (Matt. 25:1-13) as a Summary of Matthean Theology," *JBL* 93 (1974): 415-28. However the evidence for interpreting the oil as a symbol of good deeds is rather thin and has to be inferred from the context in Matthew. Other commentators prefer to interpret the parable simply as a warning about being prepared; see, e.g., Donald Hagner, *Matthew 14–28* WBC 33b (Dallas: Word Books, 1995), 725-30.
15. On the history of the interpretation of this parable, see S. W. Gray, *The Least of My Brothers: Matthew 25:31-46: A History of Interpretation* SBLDS 114 (Atlanta: Scholars Press, 1989).
16. See Harrington, *Gospel of Matthew,* 346-47.
17. On Matthew's passion narrative, see Donald Senior, *The Passion of Jesus in the Gospel of Matthew* Passion Series 1 (Collegeville, Minn.: Liturgical Press, 1985); John T. Carroll and Joel B. Green, *The Death of Jesus in Early Christianity* (Peabody, Mass.: Hendrickson, 1995), 39-59. An encyclopedic treatment of the passion narratives in general is that of Raymond E. Brown, *The Death of the Messiah: From Gethsemane to the Grave.* 2 vols. (New York: Doubleday, 1994).
18. On this particular fulfillment text, see Part 1, pp. 34-36.
19. The words of the Psalm also appear in Wisdom 2:18, where mockers attack the trust of the suffering "Just One" of Israel.
20. The format of Psalm 22 may have had some influence on Matthew's presentation of this scene. This lament psalm begins with the anguish of the psalmist, who cries out to God in a moment of torment and seeming abandonment but ends on a note of triumph, as the psalmist experiences God's vindication. That vindication is felt even in Sheol and inspires the praise of the nations (see Ps 22:27-31). The movement from anguished trust to overwhelming vindication in the Psalm parallels the movement of the crucifixion scene, especially in Matthew's gospel; see further, Senior, *The Passion of Jesus in the Gospel of Matthew,* 126-50.
21. Note that she gains this insight in a "dream," a sign of divine revelation in Matthew; see 1:20; 2:12, 13, 19.
22. If there is some ambiguity about the response of the women in Mark's account because they departed in silence after receiving the angel's message and "said nothing to anyone" (Mark 16:8), that is not the case in Matthew. After their encounter with both the angel and the risen Christ himself, Matthew notes that the women "were on their way" to the apostles in 28:11, and the presence of the "eleven" at the mountain in Galilee confirms they got the women's message.
23. See Donald Senior, "The Death of Jesus and the Birth of a New World: Matthew's Theology of History in the Passion Narrative," *CurTM* 19 (1992): 416-23.
24. Although the word *kairos* can mean ordinary time, Matthew and other New Testament writers often use this term to refer to the end time, as in 8:29; 13:30; 16:3; 21:34, 41; 24:45.
25. Earthquakes, the opening of the graves, and other such cosmic por-

tents were some of the typical events associated with the end of the world in Jewish apocalyptic literature: e.g., earthquakes, see Judg 5:4; 2 Sam 22:8; Ps 68:8; 104:32; Joel 3:14-17; splitting of the rocks, 1 Kgs 19:11; Ps 114:7-8; also 4 Ezra 9:2-3; *2 Apoc. Bar.* 32:1; *1 Enoch* 1:3-9. Dan 12:1-2 and Ezek 37:11-14 both mention the opening of the graves and the resurrection of the just.

26. See the thorough discussion in Brown, *Death of the Messiah,* vol. 1, 830-39.

13. FINALE (28:16-20)

1. See discussion of structure, Part 1, p. 32.
2. A survey of various opinions is found in Benjamin Hubbard, *The Matthean Redaction of a Primitive Apostolic Commissioning: An Exegesis of Matthew 28:16-20* SBLDS 19 (Missoula, Mont.: Scholars Press, 1974).
3. See the discussion of Matthean christology, Part 1, pp. 53-61.
4. The precise translation of Matthew's phrase, *hoi de edistasan* (28:17) is difficult. It could mean "but some hesitated" or even "but they [that is, *all* of the disciples] hesitated."
5. See the debate between Douglas Hare and Daniel Harrington ("'Make Disciples of All the Gentiles' [Mt 28:19]," *CBQ* 37 [1975]: 359-69), who believe that in using the term *ethnoi* in 28:29 Matthew means "Gentiles" only, and John Meier ("Nations or Gentiles in Matthew 28:19," *CBQ* 39 [1977]: 94-102), who argues for a more inclusive translation of "nations." Ulrich Luz, while conceding that the word *ethnoi* could mean either "Gentiles" or "nations," believes that the context of Matthew's gospel prepares the reader for a shift from a mission restricted to Israel to one turned to the Gentiles. Thus the context, not the word itself, argues in favor of a more restricted sense to the word (see *The Theology of the Gospel of Matthew* New Testament Theology [Cambridge: Cambridge University Press, 1993], 139-40).

SELECTED BIBLIOGRAPHY

PART ONE: MODERN BIBLICAL SCHOLARSHIP AND THE INTERPRETATION OF MATTHEW'S GOSPEL

Barth, Gerhard. "Matthew's Understanding of the Law." In G. Bornkamm, G. Barth, and H. J. Held, eds., *Tradition and Interpretation in Matthew,* 58-164. Philadelphia: Westminster, 1963.

Bauer, David R. *The Structure of Matthew's Gospel.* JSNTSup 31. Sheffield: Almond Press, 1989.

Brown, Raymond E., and John P. Meier. *Antioch and Rome: New Testament Cradles of Catholic Christianity.* New York: Paulist, 1983.

Carter, Warren. *What Are They Saying About the Sermon on the Mount?* New York: Paulist, 1994.

France, R. T. *Matthew: Evangelist and Teacher.* Grand Rapids: Zondervan, 1989.

Howell, David B. *Matthew's Inclusive Story: A Study in the Narrative Rhetoric of the First Gospel.* JSNTSup 42. Sheffield: Sheffield Academic Press, 1990.

Kingsbury, Jack Dean. *Matthew: Structure, Christology, Kingdom.* Philadelphia: Fortress, 1975.

———. *Matthew As Story.* Rev. ed. Philadelphia: Fortress, 1988.

Levine, Amy Jill. *The Social and Ethnic Dimensions of Matthean Salvation History.* "Go Nowhere Among the Gentiles . . ." (Matt 10:5b). Studies in the Bible and Early Christianity 14. Lewiston, N.Y.: Edwin Mellen, 1988.

Luz, Ulrich. "The Disciples in the Gospel According to Matthew." In G. Stanton, ed., *The Interpretation of Matthew,* 2nd ed., 115-48. Edinburgh: T & T Clark, 1995.

———. *Matthew in History.* Minneapolis: Fortress, 1994.

Meier, John. *The Vision of Matthew: Christ, Church, and Morality in the First Gospel.* Theological Inquiries. New York: Paulist, 1978.

Neirynck, Frans. "Synoptic Problem." In *The New Jerome Biblical Commentary,* 587-95. Englewood Cliffs, N.J.: Prentice Hall, 1990.

Overman, J. Andrew. *Matthew's Gospel and Formative Judaism: The Social World of the Matthean Community.* Minneapolis: Augsburg Fortress, 1990.

Saldarini, Anthony J. *Matthew's Christian-Jewish Community.* Chicago: University of Chicago, 1994.

Senior, Donald. *What Are They Saying About Matthew?* Rev. ed. New York: Paulist, 1996.

———, and Carroll Stuhlmueller. *The Biblical Foundations for Mission.* Maryknoll, N.Y.: Orbis, 1983.

———. *The Passion of Jesus in the Gospel of Matthew.* Passion Series 1. Collegeville, Minn.: Liturgical Press, 1985.

Stanton, Graham. *A Gospel for a New People: Studies in Matthew.* Edinburgh: T & T Clark, 1992, 346-63.

Stendahl, Krister. *The School of St. Matthew and Its Use of the Old Testament.* Philadelphia: Fortress, 1968.

Wainwright, Elaine Mary. "The Gospel of Matthew." In Elisabeth Schüssler Fiorenza, ed., *Searching the Scriptures: A Feminist Commentary,* 2:635-77. New York: Crossroad, 1994.

Wilkins, Michael J. *Discipleship in the Ancient World and Matthew's Gospel.* Grand Rapids: Baker Books, 1995.

PART TWO: READING MATTHEW

Boring, M. Eugene. "The Gospel of Matthew." *The New Interpreter's Bible,* Vol. 8. Nashville: Abingdon, 1995.

Davies, W. D., and Dale C. Allison, Jr. *The Gospel According to Saint Matthew*. International Critical Commentary series. 3 vols. Edinburgh: T & T Clark, 1988.

Garland, David E. *Reading Matthew: A Literary and Theological Commentary on the First Gospel*. New York: Crossroad, 1993.
Gundry, Robert H. *Matthew: A Commentary on His Handbook for a Mixed Church Under Persecution*. 2nd ed. Grand Rapids: Eerdmans, 1994.

Hagner, Donald A. *Matthew 1–13*. Word Biblical Commentary. Waco: Word, 1993.
———. *Matthew 14–28*. Word Biblical Commentary. Waco: Word, 1995.
Harc, Douglas R. A. *Matthew*. Interpretation series. Louisville: Westminster/John Knox, 1993.
Harrington, Daniel J. *The Gospel of Matthew*. Sacra Pagina. Collegeville, Minn.: Liturgical Press, 1991.

Luz, Ulrich. *Matthew 1–7*. Minneapolis: Augsburg Fortress, 1989. (N.b.: The remaining two volumes of Luz's commentary are being translated from the German and should be available to English readers in the near future.)
———. *The Theology of the Gospel of Matthew*. New Testament Theology. Cambridge: Cambridge University Press, 1993.

Meier, John. *Matthew*. New Testament Message 3. Wilmington, Del.: Glazier, 1981.

Powell, Mark Allan. *God With Us: A Pastoral Theology of Matthew's Gospel*. Minneapolis: Fortress, 1995.

Stock, Augustine. *The Method and Message of Matthew*. Collegeville, Minn.: Liturgical Press, 1994.

INDEX